Martians and Misplaced Clues

Martians and Misplaced Clues:

The Life and Work of Fredric Brown

Jack Seabrook

Bowling Green State University Popular Press
Bowling Green, OH 43403

Grateful thanks to Linn Brown for permission to quote from Elizabeth Brown's unpublished autobiography, *Oh, for the Life of an Author's Wife*, and from his own letters to the author.

Portions of several chapters of this book appear in slightly revised form in the Fall 1993 issue of The Armchair Detective and are used here with permission.

To Lorrie

Acknowledgements

In writing this book, I had a great deal of help.

It began as an annotated bibliography done while I was a graduate student at Rutgers University in Newark, New Jersey, and I thank Dr. Heyward Ehrlich for his aid and inspiration in those early stages. The work then turned into my Master's Thesis, and I received considerable help from my advisor, Dr. H. Bruce Franklin, as well as Professor John A. Williams, Dr. Henry A. Christian, and Dr. Virginia Tiger. The collections of Fredric Brown stories that Dennis McMillan published from 1984-1991 were an important source (I couldn't have done without them), and Dennis himself became a friend as well. Inspiration was also forthcoming from the late Harry Altshuler, Fredric Brown's agent and lifelong friend, who tirelessly answered questions by mail and sent me material until his death. It was his insistence that I expand the Thesis to book length that made me believe it was really possible. His daughter Jean was also a great help.

In preparing the book I became friends with Linn Brown, Fredric Brown's son, whose fascinating letters supplied many important details about the man. I also received welcome help from Walt Sheldon, Brown's old friend and fellow writer, as well as from the wonderful mystery writer Edward Hoch.

Library staffs from coast to coast were also tremendously helpful, and my family offered constant support. Finally, to my friends Alex Verstegen and Gabriel Cubillo, whose encouragement from overseas helped me complete the book, I owe a debt of thanks.

Of course, none of this could have been done without my wife, Lorrie, who was and is the inspiration for everything I do well and nothing I do badly.

Contents

Chapter One
A Brief Biography

Cincinnati lies in the southwestern corner of Ohio, near the eastern border of Indiana and the northern border of Kentucky. The Midwest begins here, more or less, and even today the city's population is well under a million. The Ohio River runs through it, and, in 1906, it was home to a large German-American community, many of whose members lived in an area called "Vine-Street-Over-the-Rhine," so named because it was across the river from the main part of town and because its streets were filled with remembrances of old Germany (Brown, *The Office* [1987] 95).

Into this environment was born Fredric William Brown on October 29, 1906, two scant days before Halloween. His parents, S. Karl Lewis and Emma Amelia (nee Graham), were working people; his father, a newspaperman. Fred was the only child. The family lived through the early years of the century; Fred was a boy of ten when the United States entered the Great War.

In the spring of 1920, when Fred was 14, his mother took ill and died. He later recalled running through the streets of Cincinnati praying that she'd live, but to no avail. He credited the failure of these prayers with the solidification of his lifelong atheism, although he may have had some influence in that direction from his father, who Fred said was an atheist as well. Fred spent the night with his family's Presbyterian minister—his parents had joined a church for his sake and made him attend from the ages of nine to 14, which he later called "the most mixed-up period of my life" (Brown, "It's Only Everything" 25-26).

Brown began working that summer, in between school years, at the Potter Shoe Company. His father, Karl, died the next year, in 1921, leaving Brown alone. His later writing suggests that he lived with the family of a friend in Cincinnati until he completed high school in June 1922; apparently, he had an uncle in Oxford, Ohio, who acted as his guardian and "doled out" support from the proceeds of an insurance policy that Karl Brown had had (*The Office* [1987] 28).

Fred managed to finish high school, graduating from Hughes High in June 1922. His yearbook listed him as one of the smallest boys in his class, and the photograph printed there shows a young, elfin lad with a big smile. In high school he was already known for his writing, which he apparently submitted for some sort of publication but which has not survived. He also seems to have been active in various business clubs, demonstrating an interest in practical matters as well (Brown, *The Pickled Punks* 177).

Several weeks after being graduated, Fred secured his first permanent job, as an office boy at a machine tool jobbing firm. He remained there until 1924, writing little but daydreaming and reading as much as possible. This two-year period is covered in Brown's 1958 novel, *The Office*. The novel does a wonderful job of evoking the time and the place, but Brown is reticent about supplying details of his own life; except for a fascinating tidbit here and there, his role in the novel is that of an observer. But what a series of observations!

After the office closed in 1924 (Brown was only 17 years old by this time and had been out of high school two years already), the young man presumably found one job or another to keep body and soul together. In 1927 he spent a semester at Hanover College in Hanover, Indiana, enrolling on January 3 and studying English, history, and the Bible. He followed this with a semester at the University of Cincinnati, beginning in August 1927, but it seems that money ran out and he had no inclination to continue (Baird, "Chronology" 16).

At some point in the latter years of the Roaring Twenties, Brown began corresponding with Helen Ruth Brown, a woman who may have been his distant cousin. Little is known about this courtship, but it is known that Brown had only seen a snapshot of Helen when he proposed to her by mail (L. Brown, Intro. to *Nightmare in Darkness* 7). They were married in 1929.

It was a rough year to begin a marriage. Brown was only 23 years old, but had already been on his own for more years than most young men of his age. Their first son, James Ross, was born the next year; their second, Linn Lewis, was born in 1932. Brown seems to have worked wherever he could in the Great Depression years. He later wrote that, before 1936, he worked only in offices.

The Browns had moved to Milwaukee by 1930, and they would remain there throughout the decade. Milwaukee was a working-class city, on the southeast edge of Wisconsin, sharing a shoreline of Lake Michigan with Chicago. Milwaukee is much further north than Brown's old home of Cincinnati, and the winters are cold and harsh. Brown, small and frail to begin with, must have struggled with the unfriendly climate as he tried to find and keep jobs to support his family during these troubled years. At one point, broke and jobless, he boarded a train as a hobo and rode free all the way to Los Angeles, looking for work. Finding none, he returned to his family in Milwaukee without a dime in his pocket (E. Brown, *Oh for the Life* 17).

In an article in a 1949 issue of the *Unicorn Mystery Book Club News*, it is said that Brown worked as a stenographer, an insurance salesman, a bookkeeper, a stock clerk, a dishwasher, a busboy, and a detective; sadly, no more details on these early jobs ever appeared ("The Bloody Moonlight" 6).

There was a bright spot, however, in his writing. Brown had written on and off since his early teenage years in high school. He does not seem to have been very productive until the early thirties, though, since nothing before that has survived. At some point in the early 30s he took a series of his own poems, set them in type, and printed several copies on a printing press where he worked. Happily, two copies survived, and they are probably the earliest examples of his writing.

In the early 1930s, a group of writers living in Milwaukee joined together to form the Allied Authors, who had their meetings at the Milwaukee Press Club. Other members of the Authors included William Campbell Gault, Brown's longtime friend, and Larry Sternig, who later became an agent. Apparently, they were mostly young and inexperienced, with small or no sales to their credit. This good company may have spurred Brown on because, in 1936, he began writing humorous short stories for a number of trade magazines. In September of that year he also debuted as a regular columnist for *The American Printer*, an industry magazine that was published in New York. Brown wrote a column every month for the next ten years, by which time he was well established as a writer of popular fiction and could abandon all peripheral work.

A logbook of earnings beginning in 1936 has survived, and shows that Brown worked for the Fowle Printing Co. in Milwaukee that year as a proofreader. He also received money from the federal Works Progress Administration, though whether he did any writing for them is unknown.

In 1937, Brown quit his job at Fowle and began working as a proofreader for the Milwaukee *Journal*, where he would continue to work intermittently until 1945. He also worked for the Cuneo Printing Co. in 1937, and his trade magazine sales skyrocketed, giving him a small but important supplemental income. According to his logbook, Brown was selling his writing through two agents: Otis Adelbert Kline, who had written his share of adventure fiction years before, and A.L. Fierst. Brown was apparently proofreading pulp magazine copy (presumably at Fowle Printing Co.) in 1936-37, and, as he later said, he read so much of it that he decided he could do a better job of writing it himself (Brown, *The Water Walker* dust jacket).

His first detective tale, "Monday's an Off Night," was written by June 7, 1937, and sold, through Otis Kline, to Winford Publications on April 13, 1938. Brown continued to write extensively for the trade magazines while experimenting with the occasional detective story. Some sold, some didn't—but this was the direction in which Brown wanted his writing to go, probably because it was a booming market that offered plenty of opportunity for a beginning author.

Brown published one detective story, "The Moon for a Nickel," in 1938, and four more in 1939. During these years he was still writing extensively for the trades, locking himself in a back room of his 27th Street apartment at night to work while Helen fended for herself with James and Linn, by now boys of eight and six years of age. According to Linn, the marriage was not a happy one, and he later wrote that Fred did not recognize him as a person until he was old enough to have a drink (Letter to the author, 1 Jan. 1991).

In 1939, Brown met Harry Altshuler, who was to be his agent for the next 23 years or so. Altshuler was also a young man, working for Shade Publications in Philadelphia, PA. Fred told him that he was unhappy with Kline and Fierst, his agents up to that time, partly because they were charging fees for reading his manuscripts. Fred thought he should try gearing his writing toward the "spicy" pulps—with an emphasis on sex—and sent several stories to Altshuler, who rejected them out of hand and advised Brown to channel his energies in another direction (Altshuler, "The Early Career" 23).

Soon, Altshuler agreed to take one of Brown's stories, and he claimed that he never rejected another, though Brown's logbook shows otherwise.

By 1940, Brown's trade magazine writing was dwindling as his pulp output grew. He wrote and sold a number of stories that year; 1941 was even more productive. By the end of 1941, Brown was writing almost exclusively for the pulps, with the bulk of the stories written in the detective and mystery vein and a few westerns, science fiction tales, and "straight" stories thrown in for good measure. During the early 1940s the Browns moved to Albuquerque, New Mexico, in an attempt to help Fred's allergies, which had hit him hard in the northern city of Milwaukee. His son Linn recalls him being taken from the apartment on 27th Street in Milwaukee on a stretcher with Oxygen—clearly, his health was always a problem.

Little is known about the years Brown spent in Albuquerque. Linn recalls that it was two or three years, and that Fred worked at a desk job for the Santa Fe railroad while they were there. Judging from his published output during these years, Brown must have been writing furiously at night.

On December 7, 1941, the United States was drawn into World War Two. Fredric Brown tried to enlist, but he was rejected due to his terrible health. The family moved back to Milwaukee, again on North 27th Street, and Brown made a contribution to the war effort by working in a defense job at a foundry. In the meantime, his writing continued to sell, and his reputation as a master pulpsmith grew. By 1944 he was working on his first novel, *The Fabulous Clipjoint*, set in the gritty tenements of Chicago. Brown's second wife later wrote that he had spent some time in the near-north side of Chicago, talking to the denizens of the slums and researching his book. She also wrote (as did Brown) that he spent two weeks with a friend who was a carnival mentalist, soaking up the atmosphere and writing down the colorful slang used by the carneys (*Oh, for the Life* 17). Both experiences were essential parts of *The Fabulous Clipjoint*, and Brown poured his heart into it.

In 1945 and 1946, Harry Altshuler tried to sell the novel. He approached 12 publishers and they all turned it down. Some claimed Brown couldn't write, others seemed to think the novel too naturalistic or perhaps too realistic—the prevailing mysteries of the time were of a different sort.

During this period of uncertainty, Brown's writing skills grew by leaps and bounds. He wrote fewer stories, but their quality was outstanding. Serial rights on *The Fabulous Clipjoint* were sold to *Mystery Book Magazine*, where it appeared in a shortened version under the title "Dead Man's Indemnity" in the April 1946 issue. Nick Wreden, an editor at Dutton, also bought the novel around that time.

The year 1947 was a year of great change for Fredric Brown. His first novel was published to great acclaim, he published three brilliant short mystery stories, and he wrote his second novel, *The Dead Ringer*.

According to Harry Altshuler, Brown had written *The Fabulous Clipjoint* as a one-shot deal; he hadn't intended to continue with the characters in a series ("The Early Career" 24). But Brown signed a contract with Dutton for eight novels and he needed an idea for a follow-up; what better than to continue the saga of Ed and Am Hunter, the nephew and uncle team of amateur detectives who had been so successful in the first book? Combining elements from several old stories and framing them in a new and exciting tale, Brown produced *The Dead Ringer*. Serial rights were sold and the novel was published almost verbatim in the spring 1948 issue of *Mystery Book Magazine*. Dutton bought the book and published it soon after.

At this point, with his marriage a shambles and his wife's health beginning to decline steadily, Brown moved out; first, to an apartment across the hall from his family, and, finally, to a room at the Antlers Hotel. As his son Linn later noted, Brown could finally afford a divorce (Intro. to *Nightmare in Darkness* 7). He met a woman named Elizabeth Charlier at a party; they fell in love and were married in New York City on October 11, 1948 (Brown's divorce had come through in 1947 or early 1948).

Fred and Beth Brown's life together was somewhat nomadic and purposely bohemian—quite the opposite of the life Brown had lived up to that point. He left his wife and sons in Milwaukee—Jim was 18 in 1948, Linn was 16—and, while he paid alimony and child support and helped put the boys through college, he was never again a family man, tied to a town by responsibilities and the need to make a decent living.

Beth Brown had been raised in the countryside of Wisconsin; she had grown up and moved to the big city of Milwaukee, where she worked as a secretary for 20 years before her life was rearranged by meeting frustrated bohemian Fredric Brown. During their courtship,

Brown received an offer from Leo Margulies, powerful pulp publisher in New York City, to come to New York and act as editor for $7500 a year—a good salary in those days. Brown jumped at the chance and moved to New York, but he quickly learned that the salary was actually $75 a week—he had mistaken Margulies's offer of "75"! (Klass ix). Undaunted, Brown quit the job and decided to try his hand at surviving as a full-time writer of fiction. He called Beth in Milwaukee and proposed marriage; she joined him in New York and they were married at Grace Methodist Church, with Harry Altshuler and writer Veronica Parker Johns as witnesses.

After a honeymoon trip through New England to Cape Cod, during which Fred impressed Beth with his drinking ability and somewhat quirky behavior, they settled in a three-room, third-floor walkup in a Puerto Rican slum on Manhattan Avenue near New York's Central Park.

Brown's literary star continued to rise when he learned that he had been awarded the Edgar Allen Poe award for the best first novel of 1947 by the Mystery Writers of America. The Brown's attended the awards banquet in New York, and Fred was the star attraction. But happiness in New York was too expensive to keep—the apartment was overrun with roaches and the winter terribly cold. Very early in 1949, the Brown's traveled to the Midwest to see old family and friends, living for a short time in an apartment at Chicago's Dearborn Plaza. After a few weeks of bitter cold they gave in. Brown recalled his earlier years in Albuquerque and suggested they try moving there. Already growing accustomed to frequent changes of scene, Beth acquiesced.

Before they made it to Albuquerque, they decided to visit Taos, which had long been an artists's colony—D.H. Lawrence had lived there, and his widow was still a member of town society. Fred and Beth quickly found an apartment in the Governor Bent House, which had been the site of the murder of New Mexico's first governor on January 18, 1847, by angry Indians. The apartment was big and cheap, and Taos was a bohemian paradise for the newly married couple. Fred met and befriended Mack Reynolds, an aspiring science fiction writer, and rekindled his friendship with Walt Sheldon, whom he had met in Philadelphia through Harry Altshuler in the late 1930s (Sheldon, Letter to the author, 7 Jan. 1991).

While in Taos, Fred continued to write steadily, writing several novels and the occasional short story in between. He and Beth grew accustomed to the somewhat remote life there, enjoying the freedom of smalltown life and absorbing the unique scenery and mix of Mexicans and whites. Radio and television began buying Fred's stories in greater numbers, and the fledgling video medium aired a few programs based on his works in these early years.

The Browns spent almost three years in Taos, from early 1949 to early 1952, taking many vacations in between writing novels and growing accustomed to life in the Southwest. By the beginning of 1952, however, the travel bug had bitten Fred again, and he decided to move to California, probably to be near the center of motion picture and television production. They moved to Venice, buying a small house with a goldfish pond and a large yard. Beth spent much of her time working in the yard, while Fred continued to write novels, stories, and the occasional teleplay. Late in 1953 the Browns moved to nearby El Segundo, but by 1954 the southern California climate proved too much for Fred. His lifelong problems with allergies and asthma were getting worse, and he arranged to go to the Mayo Clinic in Rochester, Minnesota, for testing. He stayed there for six weeks and underwent a large series of tests; at the end, he was diagnosed a "classic atopic," which basically means that he had a congenital problem with allergies. In her autobiography, Beth concluded that Fred physically had to take things easier than the average man, although she admitted that he had always been an expert prevaricator. Upon returning to El Segundo, Brown took the advice of his doctors and moved in June 1954 to Tucson, Arizona, known for its dry, clear climate and long a haven for those with breathing problems.

As Beth described it, Tucson in 1954 was a young but growing city, sprawling but far from crowded. It didn't take long for the Browns to make friends with the writers in the area; as usual, Fred joined the local writer's group and attended meetings.

Throughout the rest of the 1950s, Fred and Beth lived in Tucson, with Fred writing novels at a slower pace than before and probably surviving on royalties from paperback and television sales. He wrote quite a few "short-shorts"—stories a page or two in length that could be used as fillers in magazines—and became known as a master of that form. He also completed *The Office*, the somewhat autobiographical novel that he had begun in 1945. By 1960, his writing output had dwindled to about one novel a year and only a handful of short stories.

In fact, from that year on he published only four more novels in his lifetime, the last in 1963.

As his literary output dwindled and his health continued to decline, Fred once again set his sights on Hollywood, first commuting to Los Angeles to write scripts for the *Alfred Hitchcock Presents* television series in 1960. In 1961, he moved to Van Nuys, California, next door to Los Angeles, and signed with the Scott Meredith Company and the Ashley Steiner Agency, leaving Harry Altshuler, who had been his agent and close friend since 1939. Little is known about Fred's actual output during the two years he lived in Hollywood; he signed with the Goldstone-Tobias Literary Agency in 1963 to write screenplays, but by June he and Beth had moved back to Tucson, where they would remain until his death.

By the end of 1963, Fred's health had declined to the point where he could barely write. He published a short-short in 1964 ("Why, Benny, Why?) and then his last story ("Eine Kleine Nachtmusik") in 1965, but even that was a collaboration with another writer, Carl Onspaugh. Brown wrote several other brief pieces in this period but did not publish them. He also wrote the first portion of a science fiction novel, *Brother Monster*, which he was unable to complete. He finally shipped the incomplete manuscript to Harry Altshuler in 1971, asking him if he'd like to finish the book. The unfinished manuscript was finally published in a limited edition in 1986.

Fred also worked on a screenplay tentatively titled "Pygmalion 2113" for Roger Vadim, the French director and husband of actress Jane Fonda. Though some writing may have been done, the project was apparently abandoned. In one letter written around this time, Fred admitted that he had not written a story in a long time (*Happy Ending* 163-65).

Brown's last years saw him declining steadily. His son Linn recalls that Fred was drinking heavily whenever he visited him in Tucson during this period, and tells of spur of the moment rides to Nogales, on the Mexican border, to buy gallons of Mexican brandy. He also recalls that Fred did no work during these times (Letter to the author, 23 June 1991).

Meanwhile, Brown's novels were not being reprinted, and his hundreds of stories were rotting away in the fragile pages of long-forgotten pulp magazines. In 1968, *Daymares*, a paperback collection of some of his short stories, was published, but received only a few unfriendly reviews. *Mitkey Astromouse*, a children's book version of Brown's 1942 story, "The Star Mouse," was adapted by Ann Sperber and published in Germany. Published in America in 1971, it received generally good reviews but had little to do with Fred himself.

In the summer of 1970, Fred's first wife, Helen, died (Altshuler, Letter to the author, 13 Sept. 1988). After Fred had left in 1948, she managed to keep the rest of the family together while James and Linn finished high school and went on to college and the military. Like her ex-husband, she developed a drinking problem, and her health began to deteriorate. She moved to Portland, Oregon, to be with her brother and family in her last years, ending up in a nursing home where she died from heart trouble.

Fred survived slightly longer. By 1970 and 1971 his health was terrible and he was going blind. On Saturday, March 11, 1972, he finally died. He left a note for his family: "No flowers, no funeral, no fuss" (L. Brown, Intro. to *Nightmare in Darkness* 8) The family had a small private funeral, however, and the body was cremated.

In the years after Fredric Brown's death, his widow, Beth, became the guardian and chief promoter of his writings. *Paradox Lost*, a collection of previously published short stories Fred had worked on before his death, was published in 1973 to generally favorable reviews. *The Best of Fredric Brown*, an outstanding collection of short stories with an interesting introduction by Brown's friend and fellow writer Robert Bloch, was published in 1976, and Brown's work again found itself in the public eye. Since that time, many of his novels have been reprinted in both English and French, more short-story collections have surfaced, and 20 limited edition volumes have been published, bringing nearly all of Brown's long-lost pulp stories to light and publishing for the first time much of the previously-unpublished material that has so far been found.

Beth Brown guided this resurgence of interest until her death on April 30, 1986. She had lived out her years in Tucson, with Harry Altshuler moving in to help care for her at the end (McMillan, Letter to the author, 10 Jan. 1988). After Beth's death, Harry was left with Fred's files, and he promoted his old friend's work actively until his own death on June 2, 1990.

The Brown family has now dwindled to two: his sons James and Linn. Neither has children; James turned 60 in 1990 and Linn reached that mark in 1992. As Linn puts it, "the family has reached a dead end." Still, he considers himself the family historian and librarian, and took possession of his father's papers and files at Harry Altshuler's death.

James lives in San Francisco; Linn, in Kansas City, Missouri. They and a considerable body of writing are all that remain of Fredric Brown's long and colorful life and career.

* * *

The details of a man's life are strange things. Whether they are easy to amass or not, the total picture is probably false. Fredric Brown was reticent about publicizing his private life, and the result is this rather brief chapter. What matters most about a writer is his work; after he is dead, that is all that he leaves to those who never met him. That is why the rest of this book is devoted to discussing Fred Brown's real legacy, his stories and novels, in the hope that some understanding of the man may be gained by what he set down on paper.

Chapter Two
Writing for Rent

In the depths of the Great Depression, money was hard to come by for Fredric Brown, the working husband and father of two boys. He was working in offices, apparently moving from job to job, never staying at anything for a very long time. It's not surprising, then, that Brown would have been looking for ways to parlay his longtime interest in writing into extra cash by writing short articles, humorous stories, and even a regular monthly column for various magazines directed to specific industries or trades—trade magazines.

Brown's earliest writing seems to have been done while he was a student at Hughes High School in Cincinnati. According to the brief written material that appears beneath the photo of the young "Brownie" in the yearbook, Brown is one of the school's "litterateurs," and "his stories and poems have received notice in many of the exchanges" (*The Pickled Punks* 177). Just what these stories and poems were must be left to the imagination, for none of them have survived. It is also tempting to wonder what "exchanges" are referred to—the yearbook writer does not say that any of Brown's writing was published, only that it received notice.

In *The Office*, Brown's memoir of his first years out of high school, he writes that he had a growing realization that it would take time to become a writer. His one story submission in the past year, he notes, was thrice rejected, and he says that he wrote a few but only submitted one ([1987] 185). According to the novel, writing "stories" was the young Brown's goal ([1958] 33); he liked H.G. Wells, Jules Verne, Sax Rohmer, Edgar Rice Burroughs, and Henrik Ibsen, whom he was doggedly reading but not comprehending. He names Wells as his "favorite author" ([1958] 73) and states that he hasn't finished any writing since his work for the high school magazine.

13

By his own admission, Brown wrote little in the years following high school. The earliest work of his that has been found is his poetry, a short volume of which is dated 1932. Since Brown continued to write poetry throughout his career, this aspect of his work deserves a separate discussion (see chapter five).

As the Great Depression dragged on and Brown struggled to support his family, it must have become apparent that, if he wanted to make a living as a writer, poetry and "stories" were not the best way to start. He soon discovered the benefits of "writing for rent," which he did by writing humorous short pieces and advice columns for a series of trade magazines.

The nonfiction Brown wrote in this period falls into two categories. The first, and most brief, is that of miscellaneous articles and puzzles. Brown wrote an article for *The Feed Bag*, published in the May 1937 issue, detailing a file card system to help feed dealers keep track of their clients and make following up easier. The article quotes "a Michigan feed dealer whose modesty makes him insist upon keeping his name a secret"—clearly a device to make a fictitious system sound real. Brown also wrote several puzzles for children, some in story form ("Paper, Stone, and Scissors" and "Rainy Afternoon Shadows") and some in crossword puzzle form ("Trickword Puzzles"). It is unknown where these were published because Brown kept clippings in his files but didn't note the source.

The second category of Brown's early nonfiction writing is made up of his work for *The American Printer,* a monthly magazine published in New York City for persons in the printing industry. Brown was introduced to the magazine's readers in the March 1937 issue as the author of the "Proofreader's Page," a monthly, full-page column in which he would answer any and all questions submitted by proofreaders. The column features a small photograph of Brown, looking very serious in round glasses, suit, and tie, and the editor's introduction names Brown as "chief proofreader for the Fowle Printing Co., one of Milwaukee's largest plants, and a man with a long and varied experience in job, book and magazine proofreading." This may have been an exaggeration—Brown was only thirty years old at the time! His first column is a general discussion of the role of a proofreader, and Brown's prose is careful and correct, demonstrating erudition and knowledge beyond his years.

The column continued to appear every month, with Brown answering hundreds of questions. His wide reading is evident in May 1937, where he demonstrates a knowledge of Greek and Latin, and in December 1937 he mentions Rudyard Kipling's "Recessional," a title he would later use for a short-short of his own. April 1938 finds mention of John Milton, and in April 1939 he mentions Lord Dunsany and James Thurber.

The January 1940 column replaces the stern photo of Brown with a rather uninspiring drawing of a pencil, but this was replaced by a simple line drawing of Brown's profile in 1941. The old photo returns in 1942, and in the May column of that year Brown—by now a writer with many stories published—admits, "I used to write humor departments for several trade magazines."

Nineteen forty-three begins with a new photo of Brown, looking somewhat like actor Wally Cox and sporting a small mustache. The monthly column is once pre-empted by a special article, "The Proofroom in Wartime," in which Brown advises proofreaders on how to cope with the manpower shortage caused by the military draft. Other great writers are mentioned in passing this year (J.M. Barrie in April, Bulwer-Lytton in May, Fowler in June), and the Bible also rates a note, as it again does in the March 1944 column.

By September 1944, Brown is an old-timer with the magazine, noting (in a response to a question about placement of apostrophes) that "from its first appearance in March, 1937, through the December, 1943, issue it was 'The Proofreaders' Page.' With the first issue of 1944, it became and remained 'The Proofreader's Page.' " Brown admits that he didn't notice the change at first, and even states that, "back in 1937, I flipped a coin to see which form I'd use, so little did it matter."

In July 1945 Brown refers to *Black Mask*, although only in a discussion of the use of illustrated initials to begin a story. Samuel Taylor Coleridge is mentioned in January 1946, and Brown's final column appears in November of that year, bringing to an end ten and a half years of a regular monthly page and paycheck: until 1946, Brown earned $10 a column; the last 11 months he earned $12.50 each. This writing shows Brown's extensive knowledge of grammar and proofreading techniques. His name and photograph usually appear on the column, and he is not the reclusive, publicity-shy writer he would later become. When he began the column, he had just begun sending humorous short stories to trade magazines; when he finished, he was a novelist with a top reputation in the mystery field. At age 30 he set himself up as an authority; by age 40, he had proven it.

When he gave up the column in November 1946, Brown had finished writing his second novel and was on the verge of leaving his wife and children to begin life anew as a rather transient freelance novelist. He would never again work a regular job, and he would never again write a column like this one. *The American Printer* provided a forum for one side of Brown's writing while he was developing the other side. In 1946, he put it all behind him.

Brown's trade magazine work in the late 1930s had another aspect, one which led gradually to the type of writing for which he would eventually become famous. This was his fiction, in the form of a large number of very short humorous stories with characters and situations directed toward the particular trade magazine to which they were sold. Records are incomplete, but it appears that Brown began selling stories to these magazines in 1936, the same year he began his column in *The American Printer*.

The earliest stories may have been the V.O.N. Munchdriller series, which appeared in a magazine called *The Driller* and were aimed at those who drilled wells. The one-page stories all feature a primitive cartoon illustration and no byline, so it is only their discovery in Brown's files (and their style) that lets the reader know they are the work of Fredric Brown. Of the ten stories that have survived, only one is dated: "Munchdriller's Vacuum Vengeance...," which bears the date of September 1936. It follows the style of the series, opening with the "editor's" brief note that

We are exceedingly glad to report that we have just received another letter from V.O.N. Munchdriller, an eminent correspondent from Talltale, Ark.

The rest of the story is in the form of a letter from Munchdriller, in which he relates the story of how he overcame a seemingly insurmountable problem in well-drilling. Here, he uses vacuum tubes to stop a well from producing oil until a chiseler pays what he owes for a drilling job. In other stories, Munchdriller uses his pet chipmunk, Ozzie, to outsmart a witch, harnesses a thunderbolt to drill through a stratum of copper, stops a forest fire by pouring seltzer in a well and creating fizz, and drills the first horizontal well. There are ten stories in all (to my knowledge) and they occasionally follow one another in sequence. They are entertaining "tall-tales" that succeed in making a very dry subject interesting and diverting to the readers of the trade magazine. Brown seems to have given up on V.O.N. Munchdriller by mid-1937, because the character is not mentioned in the logbook of writing that begins June 1, 1937.

Brown's next series character was William Z. Williams, who appeared in *Excavating Engineer*, a magazine directed at those working in its title profession. These are the most entertaining stories Brown wrote for the trades, and thus the funniest stories he wrote before breaking into the pulps. Each story is about four pages long, detailing the adventures of William Z. Williams, salesman of power shovels for the D. Itch Digger Company. The stories consist of letters, telegrams, phone calls, and news articles; the correspondence is usually between Williams and D. Itch, president of the company. Williams knows little about shovels but has plenty of enthusiasm and imagination, usually getting into a complicated situation that ends with him making a big sale to a person grateful for his help.

Brown begins to develop his "raconteur" style in these stories; he often has Williams make a remark about an event he has not yet explained, then Itch grows frustrated until Williams explains in full, usually in a subsequent letter. This creates suspense and heightens the humor in these funny stories.

Williams's first appearance, in "Business is Booming" (November 1936), finds him selling shovels to movie mogul Mr. Gigantrix, who's filming "The Epic of Suez." "We've Tried Everything!" (February 1937) details the making of the film; "But You Never Know" (April 1937) continues the story, as Williams digs a ditch for irrigation, accidentally floods it, and finally sells the whole mess to Japanese tourists for use as a rice field! Later stories find Williams in the midst of a Central American revolution, promoting a shovel derby, and digging out a pit of quicksand to save the town of Elysian Fields, Indiana. Twelve stories have survived, with publication dates from November 1936 to March 1942, but it appears that Brown probably wrote them all by 1938, because the last mention of Williams in his logbook is dated June 15, 1938. The Williams stories are very good, and all but one were reprinted in *The Gibbering Night* (1990).

Brown also wrote a series of short "filler" pieces for the *Ford Dealer Service Bulletin*, which was undoubtedly sent out by the Ford Motor Company to dealers selling Ford cars. These pieces feature Willie Skid (a punning name), a car serviceman, and they are all about 30-40 words long. Here's a typical example from July 1937:

> A monologue, says Suzanne, is a conversation between a man who's just bought a new Ford V-8, and anybody who will listen to him.
>
> *(The Pickled Punks* 195)

Seventy-five of these Willie Skid pieces have been reprinted in *The Pickled Punks*, and Brown's logbook shows that they were written on various occasions in 1937 and 1938. Short pieces like these are useful to layout editors of magazines because they can be used to fill empty holes on pages, and Brown's early aptitude at writing funny short-shorts would later develop into the many short detective and science fiction pieces he published in numerous magazines in the 1950s and early 1960s.

One of Brown's most lucrative early creations was Colonel Kluck. The Colonel seems to have appeared first in *The Michigan Well Driller* in 1937. The Colonel Kluck columns are not signed by Brown; rather, they are a series of fictional questions and answers on various drilling problems, such as this undated one:

Dear Colonel Kluck:

A brewery in my town has requested me to drill a well for them, but they make an unusual stipulation—they insist that the well must yield charged water. Shall I accept the job?

ANSWER: Insist on cash or nothing. This business of charging is extremely dangerous. Look at what it got the Light Brigade!

In the *Michigan Well Driller* columns, the Colonel is said to be "a retired driller," and six columns have survived, though Brown's logbook suggests that seven or more were written by October 1937.

Colonel Cluck (note the change in spelling) also appeared in *The Independent Salesman*, another trade magazine, from 1937-39. In these, the Colonel is a renowned salesman, who has invented countless numbers of bizarre items to solve unusual problems. The questions and answers are directed to salesmen and repeat many of the jokes and puns that appear in the *Michigan Well Driller* columns. Brown sold Colonel Cluck to the *Independent Salesman* at the same time he sold it to the *Michigan Well Driller*; presumably, they had discrete audiences. While the *Driller* stopped buying columns in October 1937, the *Salesman* continued to publish the Colonel until May 1939, which seems to have been the last column. The Colonel's last question and answer?

Dear Colonel Cluck:
Should a salesman marry young and settle down?
Enamoured

Dear Enamoured:
If one is financially sound, it's always a good idea to marry and settle down. Otherwise he should stay single and settle up.
Colonel Cluck

Brown also wrote another brief series for the *Independent Salesman*—"Dear Boss...(Letters of a Traveling Salesman to His Wife)." Brown's logbook suggests that he also sold six or seven of these columns to a magazine called *How to Sell* in 1937 and 1938, but the only example he saved was published in the March 1937 *Independent Salesman.* It is in the form of a letter from Ray, a traveling salesman, who tells his wife about meeting a young necktie salesman in a bar and giving him much-needed confidence by convincing him to sell a tie to the bartender. The letter home is a clever device, and the bar a soon to be familiar meeting place for Brown's characters. In fact, another salesman named Ray would have an important meeting in a bar in the 1959 novel, *Knock Three-One-Two.*

Fredric Brown sold quite a few stories and short pieces in the late 1930s to an agricultural trade magazine, *Feedstuffs*. The first series was called "Barnyard Bill," and Brown's logbook reflects that he sold some of these in June and September 1937 (earlier sales are also implied). These are similar to the "Willie Skid" fillers; each is about a paragraph long, but here they concern farm happenings, as this one demonstrates:

Olaf, our hired man, stuck his head into the barn this morning to ask if he could borrow the pig pen to write a letter to his aunt. I told him to send her a barbed wire instead.

(*The Pickled Punks* 190)

Thirty-one of these short pieces have survived, and they give further evidence of Brown's early ability to write humorous short pieces on themes that are attractive to a particular audience of readers.

The majority of Brown's work for *Feedstuffs* (and, in fact, the longest series he wrote for any trade magazine) was in the series of stories concerning the feed dealership of Feedum and Weep. The stories appeared in 1937 and 1938 (and maybe 1936), and nineteen have been found so far. Brown received about $6.00 for each story. The stories concern Ernie Scofield, the assistant at the feed store run by Barnabas Weep and his partner, Mr. Feedum. In each story, the dealer learns about an unusual occurrence involving a client. Ernie then finds a way to visit the client, usually under the auspices of making a delivery, and stays until he solves the puzzle, reporting back to his boss by phone. The boss tends to grow angrier with each minute Ernie delays, but Ernie's detective skills usually earn the dealer a big order from the client, soothing the boss's ruffled feathers.

Although the stories are repetitive when read all at a gulp, they are funny and creative, showing a number of themes that would recur in Brown's later stories. In "Ernie, Minister of Peace and Goodness, or the Case of the Multiplying Eggs," Mr. Jenkins converts to Lutheranism and secretly replaces eggs he had stolen before. The hens thus lay too many eggs, leading to a mystery for Ernie to solve. "The Case of the Haunted Haystack" involves a circus passing through town and an elephant being used to steal a haystack. "The Case of the Apocryphal Ark" also includes religious and circus themes: Harry Schwartz tells people he's building an apocryphal ark, and they misunderstand and think he's referring to the Apocalypse. It is left to Ernie to straighten matters out and explain that Harry is simply building a sandwich stand so he can rejoin a carnival.

Religious themes recur in "You Can't Get Broadway's Goat, or The Case of the Kidnapped Kid," when Deacon Broadway's goat is stolen and replaced by a carved wooden goat; this reminds Ernie of the "golden calf" in the Bible. Finally, "The Case of the Conjurer's Cat" has the same plot as Brown's later story, "Footprints on the Ceiling"; in both, people are baffled by cat footprints on the ceiling of a room being remodeled.

While not as funny or original as the William Z. Williams stories, the Feedum and Weep stories are entertaining, and they serve as a good introduction to many of the ideas that would inform Brown's later fiction.

The last series Brown wrote for a trade magazine featured young salesman Homer Magnus and appeared in *The Inventor*, presumably a magazine aimed at aspiring Thomas Edisons. "Cause and Defect" (March 1940) tells the story of young Magnus visiting L.B. Sanger, president of Golem Manufacturing Co., to pitch his new triangular sardine can. Sanger has a hangover and kicks the hyperactive salesman out. "The Case of the Rattled Robber" (May 1940) finds Magnus working at Mr. Wilburworth's filling station. He invents a device to foil a robbery and uses it when holdup men come to the station. Unfortunately, the invention does as much harm as good. These two stories are all that have survived of Homer Magnus, and they are decidedly minor—light, humorous stories aimed at a specific group of readers.

Although not written for a trade magazine *per se*, the Young Doctor Young series belongs in this chapter because it is something of an anomaly in Brown's career. Two stories appeared in *The Layman's Magazine*, a religious publication of the Episcopal Church. The first, "Miracle on Vine Street" (January 1941), introduces Roger L. Young, D.D., "known to his parishioners as the young Doctor Young" (*The Water Walker* 37), and his wife Martha. He solves the mystery of cat footprints on the ceiling of a recently-wallpapered nursery (recycling a Feedum and Weep plot device), but counsels his wife that the real miracle is the baby about to be born, not the mysterious footprints. The second story, "The Sematic Crocodile," appeared in February 1941 and found Dr. Young unraveling the inexplicable sighting of a crocodile by little Tommy Clayton, the sheriff's son. The crocodile turns out to be a device used by a local thief to frighten the boy away from his hideout.

The hero/detective of these two stories is a priest, seemingly a very unusual choice for Fredric Brown, who made it known that he was (at best) an agnostic. In these early years Brown was clearly a "writer for hire," writing stories for a wide variety of audiences and specialty magazines, with characters and situations tailored to appeal to particular groups of readers.

Brown's greatest success in the years from 1936 to 1940 was in the trade magazines, where he published extensively. But, as early as 1936, he was setting his sights elsewhere and writing stories which would later become the backbone of his career. These were written for one of the most popular fiction markets of the time, the detective pulps.

Chapter Three
Early Mystery Stories

In 1936 and 1937, Fredric Brown was working as a proofreader for Fowle Printing Co. in Milwaukee, and some of the galleys he read were for pulp magazines. While he had had some success with his writing for trade magazines, Brown also decided to branch out and write for what was probably the biggest fiction market at that time, the detective pulps. Dozens of these cheap, gaudy periodicals crowded the newsstands in the late 1930s; they sold for a dime or a quarter and featured stories filled with action, mystery, and sex. They appealed to the "average Joe," hit hard by the Depression, who could buy a pulp and lose his troubles in a world of clever investigators, beautiful women, and devious villains.

The pulps had various formats, but each issue was usually a mix of novels, novelettes, and short stories. They paid writers about a penny a word, and steadily gobbled up huge amounts of writing. Brown's first detective story seems to have been "Monday's an Off Night," written by June 7, 1937, and sold for the princely sum of $20 (.5 cent/word) in April 1938. Not exactly a gold mine, but it was a start. Published in *Detective Yarns'* February 1939 issue as "There Are Bloodstains in the Alley," it is a routine story of a police investigation into a murder, punctuated regularly by characters commenting "Monday is an off night" in ironic contrast to the violent action that occurs on the Monday in the story.

Brown then wrote a story titled "Rio Bound," which was sent to "Barnes" on June 9, 1937, and rejected December 3, 1937. That story appears to have remained unpublished and been lost; whether it was a mystery or not is uncertain.

The story that has been traditionally called Brown's first is "The Moon for a Nickel," completed by June 10, 1937, and published in the March 1938 *Detective Story*. Like Brown's other early detective stories, it is a simple and rather primitive tale of a downtrodden man who operates a telescope in a public park, sees a robbery, and, after being saved by the police, cleverly uses his telescope to make the money he needs for his wife's operation by charging 50 cents a head to view the scene of the crime. "The Moon for a Nickel" shows that, from the start, Brown was not content with writing formulaic detective stories; simple as it is, it avoids private detectives and eschews violence or murder in favor of a little character sketch and a clever twist. The writing style is straightforward, consisting of punchy, journalistic, third-person narration.

Brown next wrote "Old Judge Lynch," which was completed by July 12, 1937, and rejected at least twice over the next two years. It seems lost.

"The Cheese on Stilts" followed, on July 17, 1937. It features Carter Monk, a reporter who investigates a lawyer's murder, and it is as standard as Brown's stories ever got. It includes several murders, a beautiful secretary named Sugar, gangsters, a nightclub, and a conclusion in which the hero explains how the crime was committed. Monk works for the *Daily Blade* (a newspaper name Brown was to use often), and the action implies an urban setting. It was published in the January 1939 *Thrilling Detective*.

After "The Cheese on Stilts," Brown wrote three more stories in 1937: "Fairyland ABC Book" (done by July 22, 1937, and probably not a detective story, judging from the title), "Murder Wears Red" (completed by August 4, 1937), and "No Story" (finished by December 5, 1937). All were rejected by Brown's agents and all have been lost.

Brown's first year as a writer of detective stories was thus less than a smashing success. He wrote eight stories that may have fit this category, and sold a grand total of one—"The Moon for a Nickel"—for $25.50. It was not even published until the next year. Brown certainly knew that the detective pulp market was not yet going to provide the income he needed to support his family, but he persevered with this while continuing to write and sell large amounts of material to trade magazines.

The detective pulp market was somewhat kinder to Fredric Brown in 1938. "The Moon for a Nickel" appeared early in the year, and Brown's other two stories—"The Cheese on Stilts" and "Monday's an Off Night"—sold on February 24 (for $42.50) and April 13. Meanwhile, Brown continued to write, sending out 17 stories to agents and publishers, selling three in 1938 and one, after heavy revisions, in 1942. "Murder at 10:15" was submitted February 11, 1938, and revolves around Benny Boyle, a cop whose weight keeps him off the force until he proves his worth by saving the son of the chief of police. The story was published in the May 1939 issue of *Clues*.

"Wheels Across the Night" was submitted March 13, 1938, and published in *G-Men Detective*'s July 1941 issue. It is a very poor story about a motorcycle cop who solves a murder in a rural area. "Beware of the Dog" was submitted March 21, 1938, and returned late in 1939; it was submitted again in 1942 to Harry Altshuler and, after revisions, published as "Hound of Hell" in the February 1943 *Ten Detective Aces*.

Finally, "Blood of the Dragon" was mailed April 6, 1938, and published in the February 1939 *Variety Detective*. This story introduces "Deadpan" Dunn, a detective who would turn up again (with a different last name) in 1940's "Murder Draws a Crowd." "Deadpan" lost his face in a nitroglycerine accident years ago, and a plastic surgeon gave him a new one that left him unable to register expression. This story finds the hero tracking down counterfeiters by investigating a child's tale of a dragon roaming behind her house—the dragon is crafted to scare the child away from the criminals' lair, but the red and green printer's inks used to decorate it tip off the detective to its true nature. This gimmick was later recycled for the plot of "The Sematic Crocodile," one of Brown's "Young Doctor Young" stories (see chapter two).

Nineteen thirty-eight was thus a slightly better year than 1937 for Brown in regard to detective stories, but not by much. Thirteen rejections (all of which have been lost; see the bibliography for details) and a total of five sales—two of which had been written the year before. Still, by the end of 1938, Brown had only had one detective story published.

The portion of Brown's logbook for the period from January 1939 to May 1940 has not survived, and there is no way to tell how many stories were written and not sold during these 17 months. Judging from the remainder of the 1940 logbook, his output in this area did not increase greatly. However, by looking at the record of his published stories, it is clear that his 1940 published stories were written during this 17-month period.

Among these stories, "Murder Draws a Crowd" (*Detective Fiction Weekly* July 27, 1940) features newspapermen, a private detective, and plenty of violence, and "Footprints on the Ceiling" (*Ten Detective Aces* September 1940) has Carter Monk solving another unusual murder and explaining it to Sugar. Brown's first successful attempt at breaking the mold of the standard mystery is "Teacup Trouble" (*Detective Fiction Weekly* July 13, 1940), which uses delightfully slangy first-person narration in a comedy of crimes committed solely by a kleptomaniac. The story is told by Slip Wilson, a slightly dishonest character who meets Cadwaller Van Aylslea, a rich kleptomaniac. Unfortunately, Cad's kleptomania sometimes works in reverse, causing him to give back more than he stole. Cad then begins to think he's Napoleon (a condition shared by other, later Brown characters), and finally becomes convinced he's a teacup! At the end, Slip learns that Cad's brother is also crazy and, as a result, Slip vows to go straight. "Teacup Trouble" is a funny story that profits from its likeable characters. There is no detective and really no mystery; it is simply an entertaining tale in which petty crime serves as a backdrop.

Another unusual early story is "Town Wanted" (*Detective Fiction Weekly* September 7, 1940), which is the earliest detective story of Brown's that can be classified as a short-short, later one of his trademarks. In it, narrator Jimmy describes his meeting with the dishonest boss of a town and his plan to take control, which is met with no surprise by the boss. Jimmy is given a stake to set himself up in another town and tells the story from Miami, asking the reader if his own town may be ripe for corruption. More social commentary than mystery or crime story, the narrative tricks of "Town Wanted" foreshadow those of "Don't Look Behind You" (1948), in which the narrator plans to murder the reader after he finishes the story.

Besides Carter Monk, who appeared in three stories, and Deadpan, featured in two, Brown created two other series characters in this early period. The advantage of such characters, of course, is that they allow an author to forego exposition as details accumulate from story to story. The first such character is Carey Rix, a private detective who solves crimes in "The Strange Sisters Strange" (*Detective Fiction Weekly* December 28, 1940) and "Client Unknown" (*Phantom Detective* April 1941). Although amiable, Rix has no unique qualities, and these two stories are distinguished only by some eccentric characters and intriguing gimmicks in the way crimes are committed.

The other series character was insurance salesman extraordinaire Henry Smith, whose exploits began in "Life and Fire," published in March 1941.

Brown published five other stories in 1940: "Bloody Murder" (*Detective Fiction Weekly* January 10, 1940), a funny story in which bookkeeper Henry Minto dreams he's on a tropical island with the girl he loves. Thunder and lightning threaten; he awakens to bright light and a loud knocking at the door, only to be dragged to the police station and accused of murder. This sort of humorous, wish-fulfillment type of dream would recur in *Murder Can Be Fun*, Brown's third novel.

"The Prehistoric Clue" (*Ten Detective Aces* March 1940) tells of Barry West, night watchman at a museum, who gets involved with murder among archaeologists. Barry is a necrophobiac whose phobia is cured when he falls on a corpse in the dark—one of a number of psychologically-disturbed protagonists in Brown's pulp stories.

"The Little Green Men" (*The Masked Detective* Fall 1940) is a dull story about Carter Ronk (who, were it not for a misprint, would surely be Carter Monk, discussed earlier), and "Herbie Rides His Hunch" (*Detective Fiction Weekly* October 19, 1940) is a bit of Depression-era entertainment: fat Herbie Austin is a county relief worker who hauls free goods to poor families in a wagon. He accidentally catches some bank robbers, gets a reward, and is thus able to pay for his sick wife's medical care. This gimmick was also used, of course, in "The Moon for a Nickel." Brown's other published story in 1940 is "Trouble Valley" (*Western Short Story* November 1940), a conventional western with a hero named Don Marston. This story would be forgettable were it not for Brown's later story and novel, *Martians, Go Home*, in which the writer/hero Luke Devereaux at one point sits down to write a western and names his hero Don Marston!

The basic shape of Brown's most standard work was already clear by the end of 1939: unusual heroes, usually newspapermen or cops who are either dynamic (like Monk and Deadpan) or underappreciated (like Boyle), solve a crime (with some violence or murder along the way) and win the prize they seek. Brown outlined his ideas about writing detective fiction in a letter published in the October 1940 issue of *The Author and Journalist*. Condemning Superman, who had flown to fame just two years before, Brown says that the new tendency will be away from heroes who are invincible and toward the perfectly ordinary guy, who isn't a paragon of strength or courage, who, through no fault of his own, gets into a mess of trouble with criminals who are stronger than he, but who, through the courage of desperation, manages to pull a fast one and come out on top.

Brown thus took great strides as a writer of detective fiction in 1939 and 1940. The surviving portion of his logbook picks up in late May 1940, and notes seven stories in a row that were sent to Harry Altshuler and rejected, before the final three of the year were accepted and eventually sold. Brown published a total of nine detective stories (and one western) in 1940, exactly twice the total he had published in 1938 and 1939 together. From this point until the end of his career detective fiction would be the mainstay of his writing, and 1941 was the year he began to write and sell it on a constant basis.

Unfortunately, because of the break in Brown's logbook, another sixteen stories written in 1939 or early 1940 reached publication in 1941 but cannot be dated as far as writing. Brown's first science fiction story to be published, "Not Yet the End," appeared in the Winter 1941 issue of *Captain Future*, but his science fiction stories deserve a chapter of their own.

Among the early detective stories is "Life and Fire," the first appearance of another series character, one who demonstrates some of the eccentricities that set this author apart from his contemporaries in the detective fiction field. He is Henry Smith, agent/investigator for the Phalanx Life and Fire Insurance Company, who appears in the following stories:

"Life and Fire" (*Detective Fiction Weekly* March 22, 1941)
"The Incredible Bomber" (*G-Men Detective* March 1942)
"A Change for the Hearse" (*New Detective* March 1943)
"Death Insurance Payment" (*Ten Detective Aces* October 1943)
"The Bucket of Gems Case" (*Detective Story* August 1944)
"Whistler's Murder" (*Detective Story* December 1946)

A pattern is set in "Life and Fire," the first and best of the series. Smith visits a remote house in order to sell insurance and is taken hostage by members of a gang who are also holding millionaire Jerome Kessler in an upstairs room. Through a combination of luck and quick thinking, Smith saves himself and Kessler and outdoes the criminals. Were this the extent of the story, it would have little importance. However, Brown takes pains to make Smith seem as ordinary as possible, as is shown by a descriptive passage from "A Change for the Hearse":

> There was nothing very special about Mr. Smith...[he was] middle-aged, small and dapper. He wore gold-rimmed pince-nez spectacles on a black silk cord fastened to his lapel, and he wore a conservative business suit with pin stripes...

In "Life and Fire," Smith is confused by the gangsters' use of the slang term "sap" and is nearly killed because he does not even know that a gun's safety catch must be released for the gun to be fired. Smith's main characteristic is his selfless devotion to his job: all of his troubles are the result of his attempts to sell insurance or collect a premium, and when he solves a crime it is nearly always because he sees the solution as being beneficial to his company's interests.

In all but the last story, "Whistler's Murder," the denouement finds Smith selling insurance either to a grateful policeman or to someone whose name he has cleared of a crime. Although there is often violence around him, Smith rarely has to resort to physical activity; his powers of observation and deduction are usually enough for him to solve seemingly insoluble crimes. In this way, Smith may be Brown's most traditional detective: he uses the methods of Sherlock Holmes, but not for the public good or out of a sense of moral duty. Rather, Smith is the perfect corporate employee, doing everything on behalf of the insurance company for which he works. Taken in this light, the character could become annoying, but Brown's humor makes him instead a wonderful eccentric: he is the underdog destined to win, merely because he is a more careful observer than anyone around him, he is completely unflappable, and his motives are so direct. The final Smith story demonstrates the little man's superiority over "hard-boiled" private eyes—he is the only person able to solve a crime committed in broad moonlight right before the eyes of two well-paid operators from the city.

In May 1941, Brown published his first novelette, "Homicide Sanitarium" in *Thrilling Detective*. The story is a whodunit in which a private detective takes a job impersonating a lunatic in an asylum in order to flush out a murderer. The story is action-packed and entertaining, but it only breaks new ground for the author by its length. "Trouble Comes Double," published in the December 1941 *Popular Detective*, is another long piece, profiting from the use of several disguises and a fast-paced first-person narrative (as did "Homicide Sanitarium"). As Brown grew more experienced, he began to use the first-person style more and more to tell his stories; it eventually became his most effective method.

Other stories in 1941 vary in quality, but overall they show Brown finding his voice. He quickly discarded the idea of writing stories featuring private detectives and relied instead on average, working-class characters for his heroes. "You'll End Up Burning!" (*Ten Detective Aces* November 1941) stands out, both for the twists and turns of its plot and for its punchy, first-person narration. "Thirty Corpses Every Thursday" (*Detective Tales* December 1941) is also notable, mostly for its regional detail—it tells of a harrowing bus trip through the Southwest. Again, Brown's prose is functional and quick; he is writing at a high level for the pulps, but he has yet to reach the more lyrical style of his mid-forties work.

Finally, one of Brown's best early stories appeared in the August 2, 1941 *Detective Fiction Weekly*. It is "Little Boy Lost," a brief tale of a young man who wants to join a gang on a robbery and the grandmother who seems to live in the past and think of the young man as her little boy. The ending is nearly tragic: a policeman comes looking for the boy because his friends were captured while their confederate, who shot another policeman, escaped. The boy's mother is terrified until the grandmother reveals that she put sleeping pills in a drink she gave the boy, and that he has been asleep in his car across the street the whole time. "Little Boy Lost" is a moving story in which the characters are beautifully drawn and the third-person narration just omniscient enough to reveal the necessary thoughts and feelings of those involved. An urban tragedy with a classic twist, it is a nutshell sample of the type of realism and humanity that Brown would use so successfully in *The Fabulous Clipjoint*.

By the next year the country was at war, and Brown was writing stories at a terrific pace, publishing 40 in 1942 alone. Consequently, there are some duds, but there are also a number of stories that show his skill growing rapidly. In many stories published in 1942, Brown's prose becomes lyrical in passages, signalling a move away from the more journalistic style with which he began his career. One of his lesser efforts, "A Cat Walks" (*Detective Story* April 1942), at one point evokes his unpublished poetry:

There was a thin sliver of new moon playing hide and seek among high cumulus clouds, fast drifting, although down on the ground there didn't seem to be a breath of wind. (*Before She Kills* 152)

"Little Apple Hard to Peel" (written in February 1941 and published in February 1942) is one of Brown's most chilling tales, about a boy who is completely evil and what happens to him as he grows up. It features first-person narration and a detailed evocation of a small Midwestern town. John Appel, the antagonist, is without virtue, and the shock of his vengeful actions on the innocents of the town is powerful. Finally, when one of the characters is pushed beyond his limit of endurance and kills Appel, the result is only relief: no punishment is deserved or given. In her autobiography, Beth Brown recalled this story as one which violated a taboo but was so good that it sold. "The thing that mainly made it off-trail," she wrote, "was that a character, though a sympathetic one, was permitted to get away with a crime, without punishment" (*Oh, for the Life* 82). Although this taboo is now a thing of the past, the story remains shocking and powerful due to its crisp prose and striking imagery.

"Death in the Dark" (written as "The Black Dark" in September 1941 and published in the March 1942 *Dime Mystery*) is another taut story about a man conquering his fear of the dark and reaffirming his love for his wife. Here, Brown examines a psychological problem and thus hints at what would become a major concern in his later novels. In fact, several stories published in 1942 contain ideas that would later appear in Brown's novels. "Handbook for Homicide" (*Detective Tales* March 1942) includes an unusual book that gives the story's killer the ideas for his actions; this theme is echoed in *Compliments of a Fiend* (1950), in which one of Charles Fort's books is used by a kidnaper to his own advantage, and in *Night of the Jabberwock* (1950), in which the works of Lewis Carroll are used for various criminal purposes. The character of Sibi Barranya, a fortunetelling killer in "A Date to Die" (*Strange Detective Mysteries* July 1942), predates that of Ramah Singh, who serves the same function in *Compliments of a Fiend*.

Brown's most experimental novel, *Here Comes a Candle* (1950), is foreshadowed in several early stories. "Red is the Hue of Hell" (*Strange Detective Mysteries* July 1942) features a hero who must conquer his own pyromania in order to contribute to the American war effort (in the later novel, Joe Bailey is unable to overcome his obsessive psychological fear of candles and hatchets). "The New One" (*Unknown Worlds* October 1942) has a similar plot but also includes elements of fantasy. Dreams are used effectively (in a manner similar to that of *Here Comes a Candle* and parts of *Murder Can Be Fun*) in "Nothing Sinister" (*Mystery Magazine* September 1942), a story concerning an advertising man whose wife and friend are trying to kill him.

One of the strongest stories of this period is "A Little White Lye" (*Ten Detective Aces* September 1942), in which Brown first tries out the germ of plot he would later use so well in *The Far Cry* (1951) and begins to experiment with the narrative process. Briefly, the story concerns Dirk and Ginny, newlyweds who buy a house in which a man had previously murdered his wife and dissolved her body in a tub of lye. Ginny begins to suspect that Dirk is the murderer, fearing that his new identity is a ruse that will allow him to search the house for money hidden by the murdered woman. In the end, Ginny is wrong, but she must tell a white lie in order to avoid admitting the truth of her suspicions to her innocent husband. Although the story is told in the third person, it is occasionally broken by parenthetical passages which express Ginny's thoughts as interior monologues. The suspense is great, and the narrative pace and style serve to heighten the tension. Yet for all its good qualities, "A Little White Lye" is merely a story; when it is expanded and colored by personal experience in *The Far Cry*, it becomes one of Brown's finest moments.

There are other fine moments in Brown's 1942 work, and by the end of the year he was writing in a manner that set him apart from all but the best of his pulp contemporaries. "Get Out of Town" (*Thrilling Detective* September 1942) reads somewhat like early Raymond Chandler and features a scene that recalls Hemingway's *To Have and Have Not* in a story about courage, whether in fighting, denying old age, or plying one's art as one sees fit. "I'll See You at Midnight" (*Clues* November 1942) includes several passages in which the lead character recalls happier times with his estranged wife and concludes with their reuniting:

And then I quit trying to be funny and sat down on the edge of the bed and put my arms around her. I said, "Honey, I went around to find out and we can get the same apartment back that we had before. Thank God it doesn't take as long to get remarried as it does to get divorced, and everything will be the—"

The same? No, I knew it wouldn't, and from her eyes I could see that she felt that way about it, too. Not the same, but a thousand times better. You have to lose something first and then, miraculously and unexpectedly, get it back, before you can begin to understand how much better.

(*Thirty Corpses Every Thursday* 57)

In October 1942, Fredric Brown published his longest story yet, "The Santa Claus Murders," in *Detective Story*. He had completed it in April 1942, after working on and off for several months. The seed of the 1948 novel *Murder Can Be Fun*, this story concerns Bill Tracy, writer of the radio soap opera "Millie's Millions," who writes scripts for a new radio show called "Murder Can Be Fun" and is the prime suspect when the murders he plots on paper begin to occur in real life. Other highlights of this busy year include "Double Murder" (*Thrilling Detective* November 1942), which begins with a chapter written from the perspective of a psychotic killer and thus anticipates *Knock Three-One-Two* (1959); and "A Fine Night for Murder" (*Detective Tales* November 1942), which recalls "I'll See You at Midnight" in its portrait of an estranged couple reuniting and anticipates *Night of the Jabberwock* (1950) in the lamentation of a policeman that nothing ever happens in his town on Monday nights (a theme continued from "Monday's an Off Night," as well). All in all, 1942 was a major year in Fredric Brown's work; he wrote and published so many stories and explored such a variety of themes that he began finding new methods of expression in his prose, his plots became inventive enough to be mined for later novels, and his characters grew farther and farther away from the cardboard detectives and villains that dominated the detective pulps.

Brown's short story output from this point on is more manageable, as he began to rework several themes that reveal interesting facets of his concerns. Perhaps the most important theme is that of the influence of philosopher Charles Fort. "Charles Fort," explains one character in *Compliments of a Fiend*, "was a New York newspaperman who died about twenty years ago. He was either a screwball or a genius, and plenty of people think he was a genius; people like Ben Hecht and Tiffany Thayer, and Carl Sandburg and Sherwood Anderson. They organized a Fortean Society and published a periodical. I don't know whether it's still running or not."

"But what did he write about?" I asked.

"Damn near everything. He believed that *science*, especially astronomy and meteorology, was screwy, that it had gone off the beam somewhere and led us astray. He gathered facts—mostly in the form of news clippings from everywhere—of things that didn't fit in with the current opinions of the scientists and are therefore ignored or explained away. Rains of frogs, rains of fishes, mysterious appearances and disappearances, werewolves, spaceships, sea serpents, earthquakes and meteors, Martians and mermaids. It's damned fascinating stuff..." (70)

A collection of Fort's books was published in 1941, and it is possible that Brown read it, for "The Spherical Ghoul" (written in April 1942 and published in the January 1943 *Thrilling Mystery*) and "The Angelic Angleworm" (written in September 1941 and published in the February 1943 *Unknown Worlds*) are both clearly influenced by Fort's writing.

In "The Spherical Ghoul," Jerry Grant is a student working nights at the morgue while finishing studies for his Ph.D. and developing his thesis in "The Origin and Partial Justification of Superstitions." He reads the scholarly text, *The Golden Bough*, throughout the story, and is a completely different character than the young night attendants at morgues who solved crimes in earlier Brown stories ("Fugitive Impostor" and "Twice-Killed Corpse," for example). The crime in this story belongs in the classic mystery category of the locked room: how did a corpse in a glass case in the basement of a guarded funeral parlor get its face destroyed so thoroughly that it could not be identified? The solution to the mystery is ridiculous—an armadillo lowered through a small opening above the coffin did the job—but the methods Jerry uses to solve it are what matter.

"Death is a Noise," written in May 1942 and published in *Popular Detective* a month after "The Spherical Ghoul," demonstrates the truth of a claim Brown made in a 1949 article in the *Unicorn Mystery Book Club News*, discussing a trip to Los Angeles during the Great Depression:

"I traveled to Los Angeles and back, broke flatter than a tortilla, and, during six months in L.A., Tucson and Phoenix, got a beautiful Grapes-of-Wrath view of the underside of things which has probably influenced my writing ever since. I hitch-hiked out, but by the time I came back I was an expert "bo" and rode the redball freights, including the top of a reefer through a dust storm in Kansas that I'll never forget." ("Murder Can Be Fun!" 7)

In the story, George Scardale rides a train as a hobo, heading for a job driving a nitroglycerine truck through the mountains. He describes the beginning of his train ride:

The third of the string was an empty, with the side door open. I ran alongside and got in.

The back end of a box-car is the best place. You can sit facing forward with your back against the wall. I took a newspaper out of my pocket and unfolded it to sit on while I walked into the darkness of the back of the car. Walked slowly, feeling the way with my feet, so I wouldn't stumble over any bo who happened to be there.

I reached the back end without stepping on anyone, put down the paper and sat on it. I gave a contented grunt to be out of the wind, and shoved my hands into my pockets to get them warm again. (*Who Was That Blonde* 136)

By this point, Brown was capable of enriching his stories with details from his own experience, and his writing was mature enough to evoke successfully the world of the hobo.

Not all of Brown's 1942-43 work is dependent on characterization and atmosphere, however. "The Wicked Flea" (written in July 1942 and published in *Ten Detective Aces* in January 1943) turns on a biblical pun: "The wicked flee when no man pursueth." In a very funny short story, "The Sleuth from Mars" (*Detective Tales* February 1943; written in January 1942 as "Nitwit's Nightmare"), Terry Wilson dresses as a Martian for a costume ball and catches bank robbers while still dressed in his bizarre outfit. The fast pace and outlandish humor of this tale prefigure Brown's 1949 science fiction masterpiece, *What Mad Universe*. "Hound of Hell" (*Ten Detective Aces* February 1943) is a short tale which relies solely on a good plot set-up to deliver a vicious twist ending. It was originally written in 1938 as "Beware of the Dog" but seems to have undergone revision. "Death's Dark Angel" (*Thrilling Detective* May 1943), although relatively poor, includes a plot element that appears in a number of Brown's wartime stories: that of the hero's signing up to fight the war and thus thawing a love interest which had previously been cold. There are quite a few other stories in this period that deal with war themes; most are terribly dated and rather forced. Brown's work in this year is varied: he is striving toward longer, more personal and complex tales, yet in several places he continues to reuse old formulas and season his plots with the simplest contemporary issues.

An unusual element also found its way into Brown's fiction in 1942: that of the carnival, the strange world of freaks, vagrants, and people on the fringe that Brown would use so well in *The Dead Ringer* (1948) and *Madball* (1953). "The Freak Show Murders," written in July 1942 and published in the May 1943 *Mystery Magazine*, is an important early novelette that features many of the characters and events of *The Dead Ringer*, as well as a prototype of Ed Hunter, the young hero of that novel and six others.

"The Freak Show Murders" begins with the murder of Al Hryner, a carnival hanger-on, and then moves right into the romance between Pete Gaynor, the young narrator, and Stella Alleman, the "snake girl" whom he loves. They ride the Ferris wheel at night and Pete muses on the combination of beauty and ugliness that he sees when he looks down at the carnival in a passage similar to one found in *The Dead Ringer*:

It was funny, to be up on top of the world like we were when our car was way up there. Looking down on the midway full of toy tents and toy people walking around and knowing that you were seeing the mixing of two worlds down there. The carneys and the outsiders.

And there was an ugly side of each. Lies and gaffs and deceit and never give a sucker an even break, on the carney's part. But the marks, too. It was because the marks were what they were that the carneys had to be that way. It was larceny in their hearts that made them mob the gambling concessions, trying to get something for nothing...

....

Then the ferris wheel went round again and this time, up on top, I forgot all that and saw it as it should be seen. The beauty and pageantry, and brave bright pennants waving in the wind, the brave bright brass of the carney band and the red of their uniforms. The ripple of canvas and the ripple of laughter and the ripple of movement. (*The Freak Show Murders* 111-12)

Passages like this reveal Brown's poetic side. One of his strengths was his ability to see the good and the bad in the world and in his characters; by spinning a ferris wheel he could include both sides in his portrait without one precluding the other.

By the time he wrote "The Freak Show Murders" in mid-1942, Brown was clearly capable of writing a novel. But he waited, and instead wrote more stories, including two that continued the carnival theme. "Tell 'Em, Pagliaccio!" (*Detective Story* September 1943) includes a circus kidnapping, using the same method as that of an earlier story, "The Monkey Angle," in which a kidnapped child is hidden by drugging him, putting him in a monkey suit, and keeping him in a cage. "The Motive Goes Round and Round" (*Thrilling Detective* October 1943) is Brown's third carnival tale, and features a nicely written conclusion:

> He stood there for a moment, just looking at her, and then turned and walked, almost blindly, to take down a sidewall curtain of silk brocade to reveal a carousel of solid gold whose glittering menagerie was of jade and lapis lazuli steeds with rubies set for eyes. (*Mostly Murder* 70)

By 1944, when Brown began work on his first novel, his stories had grown quite personal and his prose was mature. His first story of the year, "The Djinn Murder" (written in October 1942), was published in the January issue of *Ellery Queen's Mystery Magazine*, a digest rather than a pulp, and probably the most respected magazine in the field at that time. The story is far-fetched and fun, with the crime solved by a psychology professor and incidental references to Maeterlinck's *Life of the White Ant* and the Seal of Solomon thrown in for good measure. Even "Murder in Miniature" (*Detective Story* January 1944), which is a more standard murder mystery, is distinguished by its hero, Walt Trenholm, who must overcome his necrophobia to solve the case and rejoin the war effort.

Brown's humor resonates in "The Ghost of Riley" (*Detective Tales* February 1944), in which a lazy policeman is revered as a hero when he seems to die saving a small group of girls from an assassin's bomb. Ironically, he must be paid off and sent away when the mayor learns that he is alive and not a hero at all. The treatment of small-town politics is clever and recalls "Town Wanted" in its demonstration of the ease with which corruption spreads. The story is a comedy, though, and as such is quite successful; Frank D. McSherry, Jr., has called it "perhaps the funniest story in the entire mystery field" (60).

There are some average stories in this year, as well, like "The Ghost Breakers" (*Thrilling Detective* July 1944) and "The Devil's Woodwinds" (*Dime Mystery* March 1944), but it is clear that, at its peak, Brown's 1943-44 work demonstrates that his apprenticeship is over. This is nowhere more evident than in "Murder While you Wait" (*Ellery Queen's Mystery Magazine* July 1944, but written in May 1943), in which plot is overshadowed by narrative technique; the story is narrated in the first person by Larkin, a private eye, who is revealed as the murderer at the conclusion by the seemingly naive fat boy he has hired as his assistant. The story uses various standard plot elements—war shortages, the private eye, the fat boy kept off the police payroll because of his weight—and combines them in a fresh and entertaining manner enriched by the twist ending where narrator is revealed as criminal.

Another marvelous 1944 tale is "The Jabberwocky Murders" (written in May 1943 and published in the Summer 1944 *Thrilling Mystery*), which, combined with "The Gibbering Night" (written in November 1943 and published in the July 1944 *Detective Tales*), would become *Night of the Jabberwock*, Brown's excellent 1950 novel. "The Jabberwocky Murders" is great fun, using Brown's substantial interest in Lewis Carroll's works to weave a tale of crime in small-town America. Other engaging stories include "To Slay a Man About a Dog" (*Detective Tales* September 1944), featuring Peter Kidd, a detective with horn-rimmed glasses who likes explaining the roots of words and can quote Alexander Pope's poetry at will; and "A Matter of Death" (*Thrilling Detective* November 1944), which tells the story of Jack Pratt, a young man who returns to Cincinnati after his father's death only to find himself disliked by old friends due to a false rumor that was spread while he was away. In these stories, Brown uses bits and pieces of his experiences, his reading, and his old plots to create a mix that is original and unique. By November 1944 he had completed *The Fabulous Clipjoint*, and his stories from then on must be discussed in that light.

The period from 1936 to 1944 was thus a period of training for Brown as a writer; he began with simple detective stories and progressed through a number of experiments in plot and narrative, working with formulas and personal experience until he was able to forge a style all his own.

How then are these early stories to be taken? There are many that can stand as classics of the mystery or suspense field, as well as several which would stand out in any genre. Many themes run through the work, and many ideas are raised which provide starting points for later novels. In his article, "The Structure of the Detective Story: Classical or Modern?" Timothy Steele makes several points that are helpful in studying the early detective fiction of Fredric Brown. Emphasizing the importance of plot and resolution in the mystery story, Steele writes:

Although much modern fiction represents a flight from prearrangement and order, the successful detective story inevitably offers a narrative which is clearly structured; and whereas much modern fiction exhibits an interest in the psychological elaboration of character at the expense of plot, detective fiction embodies, generally speaking, an elevation of plot over character. (556)

Brown's early efforts demonstrate such a clearly-structured narrative for the most part; it was not until he began writing novels that he began to experiment repeatedly with storytelling methods. His plots are often one of his greatest strengths, yet character is emphasized in many of the better early works, such as "A Little White Lye" and "The Freak Show Murders." Appearing in the pulps, these stories had little opportunity to grapple with intellectual issues—they were chiefly meant to be entertaining, and a fast pace was essential. Brown's fascination with language is not yet fully evident in these stories, either, but his treatment of serious emotional issues is often quite good: for instance, courage is addressed in "Get Out of Town," marital trust is dealt with in "A Little White Lye," and despair is examined in "The Numberless Shadows." Brown may have felt more comfortable dealing with intellectual issues in his science fiction stories; regarding matters of emotion, however, Brown's early detective stories are often very serious, and many deserve a closer look.

"Teacup Trouble" and "Town Wanted" are early examples of stories that break the detective fiction mold: there is more humor than crime in the first, and a clever narrative style lifts the second to the level of social commentary. The series of stories featuring insurance salesman Henry Smith demonstrates Brown's penchant for unusual heroes, and novelettes like "Homicide Sanitarium" and "The Santa Claus Murders" show the author beginning to stretch toward novel length. By 1942,

Brown was writing stories that he would later mine for elements to use in his novels, and such stories as "Death in the Dark" and "Red is the Hue of Hell" point toward the psychological concerns that would dominate his later work. "I'll See You at Midnight" is one of several stories that recall the author's poetry and treat marital relationships with insight.

Brown's ideas about philosophy begin to creep into his work with "The Spherical Ghoul," and elements of his personal experience (which again recall the poetry) are behind "Death is a Noise." In "The Freak Show Murders" and several other stories, he integrates his carnival experience into original plots that prefigure *The Dead Ringer* and, by 1944, he was being published in the top magazine in the field as well as writing quirky tales like "To Slay a Man About a Dog." Brown's ability to invent and control his fiction grew rapidly in this early period and, even though the stories were written for the popular pulp market, he often succeeds in transcending the simple concerns of the detective story with his unique style. Brown's style and variety are what set his early detective fiction apart from that of his pulp contemporaries; in the best of these early stories he is capable of deep emotion and highly-controlled prose, tools that were to serve him well as his work grew longer and more complex.

Chapter Four
The Hunters

I went in the living room and picked up a magazine. It was starting to rain outside, a slow steady drizzle.

It was a detective magazine. I started a story and it was about a rich man who was found dead in his hotel suite, with a noose of yellow silk rope around his neck, and he'd been poisoned. There were lots of suspects, all with motives. His secretary at whom he'd been making passes, a nephew who inherited, a racketeer who owed him money, the secretary's fiance. In the third chapter they'd just about pinned it on the racketeer and then *he's* murdered. There's a yellow silk cord around his neck and he's been strangled, but not with the silk cord.

I put down the book. Nuts, I thought, murder isn't like that.

Murder is like this.

(The Fabulous Clipjoint 41-42)

In his detective fiction prior to 1944, Fredric Brown most often deals with murder of one sort or another, always in the short story form. In 1944, when he wrote *The Fabulous Clipjoint*, he was finally able to address a larger subject, one only incidentally related to murder. In an article published in about 1952 in the *Unicorn Mystery Book Club News*, Brown's longtime agent and friend, Harry Altshuler, describes the genesis of the novel and writes that Brown had begun work on it in August 1944. He continues: "the book was finished by the end of 1944 …but the first 12 publishers I submitted it to resisted it firmly" ("About Fredric Brown" 16). The book was finally published in 1947 by Dutton, and won the Edgar for best first mystery novel of that year, an award presented in late 1948.

According to Brown's logbook, he sent 33,000 words of *The Fabulous Clipjoint* to Harry Altshuler on October 23, 1944, with a synopsis of the rest of the novel. The remaining 27,000 words were sent

November 19, 1944. As Altshuler related, the novel's road to publication was a rocky one. First serial rights were sold to *Mystery Book Magazine* on May 29, 1945, for $750, and a slightly edited version of the book was published in the April 1946 issue. The novel was finally sold to E.P. Dutton & Co. for $1250 on April 26, 1946, and the money was paid as a $250 bonus on March 2, 1946, a $500 advance on April 26, 1946, and $500 on publication on March 8, 1947.

Unlike many of Brown's short mysteries, *The Fabulous Clipjoint* is not topical. Although the country was at war when it was written, there is no mention of this in the novel, which is set in the slums of 1940s Chicago. Instead, the author's concern is with his characters, especially with that of the 19-year-old narrator, Ed Hunter. *The Fabulous Clipjoint* is Ed's rite of passage; at the beginning of the novel he is going nowhere as a printer's apprentice, still living at home with his family. By the end, he has left home and entered the adult world; the last scene finds him and his uncle riding out of Chicago on a boxcar, with Ed happily looking forward to the challenge of life. Ostensibly a mystery novel, *The Fabulous Clipjoint* actually sabotages that which it pretends to be: the central murder is barely a murder at all, the villains turn out to have had nothing to do with the crime, and detecting—the process of collecting clues and following leads—is in the end less important than the exploration of memory and the understanding of the past.

The story involves the attempt to solve the murder of Wally Hunter, a drunken, middle-aged printer found dead in an alley. His son Ed enlists the aid of his Uncle Ambrose—"Uncle Am"—and, after investigating a number of false leads, they discover that Wally had *wanted* to die and had led his friend Bunny Wilson into committing a murder that was really a substitute for the suicide Wally could never bring himself to commit. A large part of the novel is taken up by Ed and Am's investigation of Harry Reynolds, a gangster whose brother was convicted by a jury that Wally had once sat on. Yet Reynolds is a convenience, not a necessity: he never appears in the book, and the characters that Ed meets on the gangster's trail are important only in that they mark stages of the boy's growth, not because they are essential in understanding the crime.

Thus, *The Fabulous Clipjoint* is a novel of an adolescent's growth from boy to man, played out among Chicago's gritty, working-class characters. The formula for hysteria is evident from the first: Ed dreams an overtly sexual dream of his young stepsister, wakes up and walks past her room, where she lies topless, clearly tempting him. His stepmother is drunk from the night before, and he soon learns that his father has been found dead in an alley. In such a situation, what can Ed be but bitter? He thinks of Chicago as a disgusting place, where people are only interested in the sensational deaths of others. Quite understandably, he runs away on a train to Janesville, where his uncle's carnival awaits.

The carnival life, as presented in chapter two, represents an adult world of freedom which Ed is not yet able to comprehend but which is saner and more supportive than the environment he has left in Chicago. It is to the carnival that Ed returns at the end of the novel when he is ready to begin life as an adult.

As Ed returns to Chicago, the investigation begins in earnest. He and Am enlist the aid of Frank Bassett, a policeman (and another "specialist" whose speech Ed cannot understand, like that of the carnival performers), and begin to retrace the steps Ed's father took on the night he died. The next few chapters trace Ed's growth on two fronts, as he begins his investigation and as he tries to keep his family together and sober for his father's funeral.

Ed is already maturing as these events occur: he is responsible for building order out of the chaotic strands of his life and must resist his own fear and temptation to avoid being devoured by the world around him. Once Ed has passed these tests, the real concerns of the novel begin to unwind: he learns that his father, who had appeared to be little more than a "drunken bum," had had a romantic youth which included duelling in Mexico, bullfighting in Spain, and acting in vaudeville. Wally Hunter also wrote poetry in secret, and Ed thus learns that his murdered father had a character far deeper than he had realized. From this point on, solving the mystery becomes the key to tying together the various pieces of evidence. In chapter eleven, Ed and Am visit Gary, Indiana, and the scenes of Ed's boyhood, and it is here that Ed's memories flow to the front of his mind. His life becomes not merely the day-to-day existence it had been in Chicago, but rather a continuum of past, present, and future; he finally understands his past and is able to put his present in perspective, thus clearing the way for the future.

Ed's realization of his own past, triggered by the trip to Gary, is the highlight of *The Fabulous Clipjoint* and, one could argue, its climax as well. After Ed and Am return to Chicago, Ed can no longer feel comfortable in his home—"it seemed like I was going back there after having been away for years. It didn't seem like home or anything, though. It was just a familiar room" (166). Ed takes matters in his own hands and visits Claire Reymond, Harry Reynolds's mistress, in her fancy hotel room. There, Ed kills a gang member and sleeps with Claire before she leaves Chicago for good; no longer the boy of the novel's early chapters, he is in control of his life and acts in the world, not merely in the microcosm of his family. When, at the novel's end, the killer is revealed to have been Bunny Wilson, the crime is already meaningless. It is clear that Ed's father had wanted to die; he had been devoured by the environment that Ed spends the novel trying to escape and had become a hollow shell of a man whose romantic past was relegated to a cheap suitcase at the bottom of a locker.

Ed has resisted and is able to set out on his future life with some measure of control. Two parallel scenes demonstrate the change: in the first, Ed and Am look out of the window of Am's hotel room after Ed has just resisted his stepsister's drunken attempt at seduction:

> I went over and looked out. It was still foggy, gray. But you could see south to the squat, monstrous Merchandise Mart Building, and between the Wacker and it the ugly west near-north side. Mostly ugly old brick buildings hiding ugly lives.
> "It's a hell of a view," I told him. (66)

In the second scene, which occurs after the murder has been solved and just before Ed and Am leave Chicago, they look out of a window in the "very swanky cocktail bar" on the top floor of the Allerton Hotel:

> We took a table by a window on the south side, looking out toward the Loop. It was beautiful in the bright sunshine. The tall, narrow buildings were like fingers reaching toward the sky. (178)

Ed has passed through the fire and his perceptions have changed accordingly. On the surface his situation has changed but little: his father is dead, his mother and stepsister are examples of the traps that can kill a young man's spirit. But beneath the exterior, Ed has acquired a new sense of purpose, a freedom that allows unlimited potentialities for the future.

At the end of *The Fabulous Clipjoint*, the possibilities are infinite, and Ed and his uncle speed off, hoboes on a train, toward an uncertain but promising future. A spark of hope has been ignited in the young man, and it is clear that he will succeed in escaping the societal forces that destroyed his father. The novel is thus a mystery only in passing, and its success demonstrates that the promise shown by Fredric Brown's best work in the detective pulps—rather than the annoying exercises in convention that mark the worst of his early work—would be fulfilled in his work as a novelist. The novel has autobiographical elements—Brown had lived in Chicago, his father had died and left him in an uncle's care when Brown was a teenager, he had traveled with a carnival and was familiar with the world of slums, bars, and hoboes—and Ed's triumph over his environment corresponds to Brown's triumph over the short mysteries he had been writing for the pulps, where plot was central and characterization a bonus. He sabotages the traditional mystery in *The Fabulous Clipjoint* by putting all of the answers in the narrator's head and then downplaying the murder and the murderer in favor of examining the boy's initiation into the adult world. All of the conventions of the hardboiled mystery are here, and Brown even writes an occasional scene in a Chandleresque style: when Ed pretends to be a tough guy, his narration recalls the irony for which Philip Marlowe was noted: "We had one more drink around, and then the two muscle-boys went out. It was very chummy" (86). Yet this "tough-guy" prose is just play for Brown—he satirizes the smug narration of Chandler's private eye by putting it in the mouth of the frightened young Ed Hunter. Ron Goulart noted that Brown

could work in the bard-boiled tradition...yet he comes across as a somewhat gentle tough guy, a man not quite as detached and cynical as some of his contemporaries. There is a sensibility underlying [*The Fabulous Clipjoint*], an appreciation of the people who have to make their way on the mean streets and still manage to hold on to their honesty. (vii)

It is this "sensibility" that sets the novel and its author apart from the standard mystery.

Brown's triumph in writing *The Fabulous Clipjoint* was not immediately evident. The novel went from publisher to publisher; as Harry Altshuler later remarked, it "was not the kind of book popular at the time it was written, at least not with the editors" (Letter to the author, 10 Jan. 1990). The version published in *Mystery Book Magazine* is very heavily edited: chapters begin and end at different points, and some of the harsher passages are cut. For instance, Ed's lament about the horrors of life in Chicago (in chapter one of the novel) is left out, as is a section about Ed's father ending up in a potter's field. A good bit of grand jury testimony is left out of the magazine version, as well. We will never know why this version of the novel is so different from that which was finally published in book form. The central concerns of the novel are present in this early version, only the words differ here and there. Brown does not seem to have done any heavy revising for publication as a novel, leaving one to wonder if the copy editors of *Mystery Book Magazine* were given a free hand.

Eventually the novel was published, and it was a success. *The Saturday Review of Literature*'s reviewer wrote that it was "No masterpiece of detection, but people, especially Ed and Uncle Am, are capitally done." Isaac Anderson of The New York *Times* was not as kind, calling the motive "cockeyed" and the plot "screwy," but Will Cuppy wrote that it was a "pleasing little item," adding that "the author has something of his own." Anthony Boucher, writing in the San Francisco *Chronicle*, gave the most praise: "a singularly effective job of portraying people as they are and murder as it is—a sordidly compelling story." The novel's success peaked in 1948, when it was awarded the Edgar Allen Poe award for best first mystery novel of 1947 by the Mystery Writers of America.

When Fredric Brown wrote *The Fabulous Clipjoint* in 1944, he had no intention of continuing the story. Once the novel had been accepted, however, Dutton suggested that his next novel concern itself with the further adventures of Ed and Am Hunter. The idea was new to Brown but not unpleasant; he began work on *The Dead Ringer* in 1946, mailing the completed novel to Harry Altshuler on New Year's Eve. It sold quickly. First serial rights again went to *Mystery Book Magazine* on January 26, 1947, for $1500; Dutton accepted and paid a $500 advance on April 11, 1947. The remaining $500 of Brown's advance was paid on publication, on or about March 22, 1948.

The Dead Ringer marks a turning point in Brown's life and career. His son Linn has written that

When he sold his second novel, THE DEAD RINGER, and it became apparent that he could support himself (and us) by writing full time, he moved across the hall by renting an extra bedroom there, ostensibly so he could write but as I look back it was part of a withdrawal plan. (Letter to the author, 1 Jan. 1991)

Linn also wrote that Fred and Helen Brown divorced

not only for the usual incompatibility reasons, but because the check arrived for his second novel, *The Dead Ringer*. He could suddenly afford it. (Intro. to *Nightmare in Darkness* 7)

Brown's second novel thus came at a time of great change for him. Whereas *The Fabulous Clipjoint* was the culmination of his early writing career as a contributor to countless pulp magazines, *The Dead Ringer* marked the onset of his career as a novelist, and from this point on the novel became his main form of expression.

It first saw publication in the Spring 1948 issue of *Mystery Book Magazine* and, unlike the magazine version of *The Fabulous Clipjoint*, it is virtually identical to the novel published on March 22, 1948. The novel picks up where *The Fabulous Clipjoint* left off, and concerns a murder at a carnival. In her autobiography, Elizabeth Brown writes:

He already knew the carnival background. Years before, he'd had a friend who was a mentalist with a carnival. Fred had spent two weeks trotting along with him, learning the workings, getting to know the people intimately, and picking up all the carney slang he could and making a list of it. (*Oh, for the Life* 16-17)

As the novel opens, Ed and Am are already working for the Hobart carnival, running a ball game. On a rainy night, the show closes and Ed relaxes by playing his trombone. He sleeps, but is awakened by a shot. Ed and Am investigate and find a crowd around a dead, naked boy with a knife in his back. Ed confronts Rita, a new girl in the posing show, and takes her for a moonlight drive. They kiss, but she breaks away, telling Ed she wants to marry a rich man.

Brown sets the scene nicely in this first chapter, getting the first murder out of the way and initiating Ed's first real love interest. The mystery deepens as Ed learns the murdered boy was actually a midget. Ed's relationship with Rita also deepens, and he visits her in the trailer she shares with strongman Hoagy and his wife Marge. Ed also becomes friendly with Armin Weiss, the detective investigating the murder, and has a jam session at Weiss's home.

Ed's attitude toward the carnival is ambivalent, as was his attitude toward the city of Chicago in *The Fabulous Clipjoint*. When he sees a carney named Skeets making money by exhibiting the site of the midget's murder he knocks him down, but later, walking on the lot, he perceives the carney in a different way:

> There was a fine mist in the air; it made haloes around all the lights on the lot. It made the ferris wheel seem a mile tall. It muffled sounds and made everything seem unreal. Even more unreal, that is, than a carney usually seems.
>
> I stood there at the curb outside, looking at the big entrance gate, big and bright and gay like the gates of Paradise, that was set back forty feet or so from the street. Through it and around it I could see the tops and the midway; I could hear the screech of the Whip, the thump of a bass drum call to bally, and the thousand voices blending into one big voice, a voice of the crowd and the carney mixed, all one strange sound. It was as though I'd never seen a carney lot before, or heard that sound. (49-50)

Ed is still maturing; his experiences and observations gradually allow him to see past the facade of things and into their heart.

As the novel progresses, the mystery develops along with Ed's infatuation with Rita. Another girl is introduced: Estelle, who is as infatuated with Ed as he is with Rita, and who allows Ed to sleep with her even though she knows he's pretending she's Rita. Meanwhile, the dead midget's identity finally is learned—he's Lon Staffold, who wasn't working for the Hobart carney—and Hoagy and Marge's pet chimp Susie is drowned in the high-diver's pool. The next night, Ed is spooked when he sees what looks like Susie's face looking through a trailer window; he and Estelle dig up the chimp's grave that night and find her still there.

The novel's third murder occurs when Jigaboo, a dancing black boy, is killed. Ed and Am realize that the three victims were all about the same size, and Am, an ex-private detective, agrees to help Ed look into the case.

Ed and Am travel to Cincinnati to visit Lon Staffold's landlady, Flo Czerwinski, an old carney friend of Am's who lets them look through the midget's possessions. A *Billboard* ad leads Am to discover that

Hoagy is the killer—he kidnapped a wealthy man's son while the carney was in Louisville, then kept him drugged and in a chimp suit while waiting for the ransom. Lon Staffold wore the suit before the kidnaping so the change wasn't obvious; he and Susie were killed to cover up the crime, and Jigaboo was murdered for discovering the empty suit.

The novel ends curiously: detective Weiss allows Hoagy and Marge time to make their peace, which they do by driving their car at high speed into a concrete wall and killing themselves. Ed also learns that Rita knew about the murders because she shared Hoagy's trailer. Her dishonesty ruins the relationship for him:

Oh, we could have had fun, Rita and I, spending that blackmail money. Except that that money had come from the kidnaping of a little boy and had led, indirectly, to the death of another little boy—a very black little boy who could dance like mad. (223)

Ed has already expressed interest in becoming a detective, and when Skeets—whom Ed knocked down early in the novel—buys the carney, Ed and Am quit. They decide to go to Chicago to live, with a fun trip to Cincinnati to see Flo Czerwinski on the way.

The Dead Ringer is a colorful, exciting novel that rewards the careful reader. Brown expands the characters of Ed and Am Hunter by synthesizing bits of earlier stories to concoct a mystery plot that fits in well with the concurrent story of Ed's maturation and romantic involvement.

Brown's first circus story was "Big-Top Doom," published in the March 1941 *Ten Detective Aces* and having to do with King Death, a dangerous lion. His second was "The Freak Show Murders" which, like *The Dead Ringer*, begins with the murder of a carney and is narrated by a young man (though Pete Gaynor, at age 36, is much older than Ed Hunter) who is not a specialist with the carney—he's just a spieler. Many of the characters are similar to those in the novel, and the complicated plot involving money and deceit is a primitive version of the novel. In "Tell 'Em, Pagliaccio!" (*Detective Story* September 1943), two carneys kidnap a rich banker's son, foreshadowing the kidnaping in *The Dead Ringer*. An even closer parallel is found in "The Monkey Angle" (*Thrilling Detective* November 1942), in which newspaperman Carter Monk solves the case of a kidnapped boy when he discovers that the kidnapers kept him drugged and in a monkey suit, with the kidnapers pretending that the monkey is sick to divert suspicion. This plot device clearly served as a model for *The Dead Ringer*'s crime. Brown's two other early carnival stories—"The Motive Goes Round and Round" (*Thrilling Detective* October 1943) and "A Voice Behind Him" (*Mystery Book Magazine* January 1947) share *The Dead Ringer*'s background but do not contribute to its plot or characters.

The *Dead Ringer* received strong reviews. *The Saturday Review of Literature* said: "Bull's eye—if not for squeamish" and noted its "craftily contrived solution which has its surprises." Edward Dermot Doyle called it "one of the season's choicer items" and advised readers to "start this one at a reasonably early hour because it's one of those jobs that you'll have to finish in one sitting. You'll get no sleep if you don't." And the Chicago *Sun* stated that *The Dead Ringer* was "an able successor" to *The Fabulous Clipjoint.* Clearly, Brown's career as a novelist was on its way.

The Dead Ringer is a special novel in another way, too. The love affair between Ed and Rita is complicated by her desire for a rich man, but they seem destined to be together throughout the novel. At the conclusion, when Ed learns that Rita knew of the kidnaping and took money to keep quiet, her peripheral guilt looms large to him as a betrayal of his trust, and he leaves her. There is no violence, only a sense of loss. Compare this to *I, The Jury*, Mickey Spillane's wildly popular novel of the year before, in which detective/hero Mike Hammer falls deeply in love with a woman, only to learn that she is the killer he has sought throughout the book. Their confrontation is pure exploitation, and has justifiably become famous: Hammer holds a gun on Charlotte as she does a slow striptease in front of him, promising to trade sex for protection while actually reaching for a gun. Hammer shoots her dead at point-blank range.

Ed Hunter talks to Rita and walks out on her. Mike Hammer watches Charlotte strip and then kills her. Brown's characters and situations are subtler and more complex than Spillane's, yet both authors' heroes are haunted by these first deep loves in later novels.

In Brown's third Ed and Am Hunter novel, *The Bloody Moonlight*, published on March 11, 1949, the pair have moved to Chicago, accompanied by Estelle, who still hopes to win Ed's love and takes an apartment not far from his. Ed and Am both work for the Starlock

Detective Agency, having left the carnival eight months before. Ed is assigned to his first case: he is to travel to Tremont, in southern Illinois, and investigate Stephen Amory, an inventor who claims to be receiving radio signals from Mars and who wants his wealthy cousin, Justine Haberman, to finance further experiments. In Tremont, Ed falls in love with Molly, a librarian, not realizing that she is the wife of the town's ill-tempered sheriff. He also finds the body of a man whose throat has been torn out, alongside an empty country road in the moonlight.

Ed does not get along with Sheriff Kingman, who hates private detectives from Chicago. After openly theorizing about lycanthropy, Ed finds himself the number one suspect in the murder. When both Amory and his assistant are found dead next to the sleeping and bloody Ed Hunter, he is arrested, and it is only through a heroic escape that he is able to enlist the aid of Caroline Bemiss—editor of the town paper and an old carney friend of Uncle Am's—to clear his name and expose the real killer.

As in *The Fabulous Clipjoint*, Brown parodies the Raymond Chandler style in chapter one of *The Bloody Moonlight*: Ed visits the beautiful, rich Justine Haberman at her ornate mansion, wisecracks his way through the conversation, and unintentionally attracts the rich woman, whose husband is drunk and dissolute. Ed has another brief romance with a girl in Tremont named Molly, but this one ends when he learns that the girl is married. One of the most interesting characters in the novel is Caroline Bemiss, who seems far above the other inhabitants of Tremont in intellect and wit. Like Flo Czerwinski of *The Dead Ringer*, she is an ex-carney; also like Flo, she's a drinking buddy to Ed and a confidant as well.

In many of Brown's novels (and most of the early ones) he finds inspiration in an earlier story. *The Bloody Moonlight* is expanded from "Compliments of a Fiend," featured in the May 1945 *Thrilling Detective*. In the earlier story, the hero is young Tommy Lederer, who—though he does work for a private detective agency in Chicago—is returning to his hometown of Haverton on business. Tommy has been away from his hometown for seven years and become a war hero in the meantime. The basic plot is the same, but the story seems somehow richer for detailing Tommy's ties to the town. He knows the people with whom he deals, and the relationships are colored by shared and unshared pasts. The basic characters and plot are the same (Carolyn Bemiss is "Aunt Margaret" in the story), but "Compliments of a Fiend" ends with Tommy and Mary (who corresponds to the novel's Molly, though here she's the sheriff's *daughter*, not his wife) planning to wed. The novel is changed by the addition of series character Ed Hunter and by the other changes therefore made necessary; it is longer, and includes more about the radio signals from Mars, but the original story has a punch and a depth the novel seems to lack.

Brown also sold the serial rights to the novel, and a very slightly edited version was published in the November 1949 issue of *Two Detective Mystery Novels* magazine.

Fredric Brown's fourth Ed and Am Hunter novel, *Compliments of a Fiend*, is completely original; it is not based on any story, nor did the serial rights ever sell to a magazine. In fact, the first edition, published on April 3, 1950, was the only edition—Bantam apparently declined to issue it in paperback. Consequently, Brown made little money on the book, and it is one of his least read novels. He was clearly getting tired of the grind of writing an Ed and Am novel each year, and this is reflected in the book's quality.

As the novel opens, Am disappears, and Estelle (who's still chasing Ed) suggests that the Ambrose Collector got him. An interesting subplot develops with Estelle; she obviously loves Ed, and he sleeps with her twice, but she realizes he does not love her. By the end of the novel, she has decided to marry the owner of the restaurant where she works. Am turns out to have been kidnaped and locked in a closet by a man whose real (and dangerous) name he learned while leafing through a book of Charles Fort's work in his apartment. Charles Fort seems to have been the impetus for writing the novel, which is prefaced by a passage from his book, *Wild Talents*, hypothesizing that an Ambrose collector was responsible for the disappearances of writer Ambrose Bierce and millionaire Ambrose Small. It takes Ed several chapters to learn that Ambrose Collector is a Fortean reference; the rest of the novel goes back and forth between the procedural search for Uncle Am and discussions of Charles Fort. It's ironic that Am was kidnaped because he discovered a criminal's name inscribed on the flyleaf of Fort's *Book of the Damned*!

The novel is also peppered with Ed's reminiscences of events in earlier novels; he recalls his father's death, Rita, and the night he and Estelle spent in the woods in *The Dead Ringer*. Brown is mining the same vein as Mickey Spillane here, since Spillane's Mike Hammer spends several books wrestling with the memory of the lover he killed in *I, The Jury*. The difference between the two writers is that Brown's characters are more wistful, their emotions on a lower, subtler register than those of Spillane's near-psychotic detective.

Brown also gets a chance to plug his own work at the end of the novel, when Ed and Am have decided to open their own detective agency with the money Ed gets from Augie, Estelle's fiancee, for cracking a numbers scam at the same time he found Am:

The stars were coming out. I looked up at them and remembered a story I'd read once in a science fiction magazine; the story was called *Pi in the Sky*, and in it the stars had moved across the sky and formed words. I thought they ought to do that tonight. If there was anything in astrology, they ought to get moving and spell out *Hunter and Hunter*, right now.

But they didn't.

And then, after a moment—behind my eyes if not before them—they did. And everything was all right.

More than all right. I left the streets and walked across the building tops, and then across the sky. (255-56)

Reviews of *Compliments of a Fiend* were generally good, focusing on the continuing story of Ed's growing up rather than on the mystery plot itself. As *Kirkus Reviews*' anonymous reviewer noted, the solution "involves footwork and persistence rather than wits." Hence, a disappointing novel, for Fredric Brown is often best when at his wittiest.

The fifth Ed and Am Hunter novel, *Death Has Many Doors*, was written in mid-1950 while Brown was living in Taos, New Mexico, and published on April 5, 1951. Like *Compliments of a Fiend* it is not based on any prior story and was never sold to a magazine. It did see paperback reprinting, however, and is more interesting and kooky than the novel that preceded it. The doors of the story are Sally Doerr and her sister Dorothy. As the novel opens, the Hunter and Hunter Detective Agency is already open for business, which is slow on a hot summer day in Chicago. Sally Doerr arrives to hire the Hunters to protect her from Martians she fears are trying to kill her. Although they refuse the case, Ed follows the pretty redhead, has dinner with her, and ends up spending the night on her couch to protect her from any Martians that might appear.

Ed fails to do so as the novel turns into a locked-room mystery: during the night, Ed looks in on Sally and finds her dead in her bed; yet he was guarding the only entrance to the room other than a high window leading to an airshaft. The mystery deepens when Doc Graham states that the death was natural, resulting from the failure of a weak heart. Ed follows the case and learns more about Sally's fear of Martians; this begins to sound real when he receives a telephone call from Yat-Dun, who claims to be a Martian and hires Ed to investigate Sally's death.

Ed soon becomes involved with Sally's sister Dorothy, whom he must protect from her fears of her own death. After dinner, Ed and Dorothy dine out along Lake Michigan. She suggests a nude moonlight swim, and drowns before Ed can reach her. Further investigation takes Am to Colorado and Ed to Evanston, Illinois, where he meets Sally's ex-fiancee, who gives him information that leads to his solving the case. The final piece of the puzzle is provided by the obnoxious boy Dickie Stanton, who demonstrates how to turn on a lamp by touching the shade. In the end, the Doerr sisters' eccentric uncle, Ray Wernecke, who learned that Colorado land the girls had inherited had Uranium under it, is revealed as the murderer.

Death Has Many Doors is a novel chock full of incidents, characters, and ideas, and it represents the farthest step in Ed Hunter's growth process. The Hunters now have their own detective agency and are getting clients; Ed is a young adult businessman as well as an investigator. The novel is spiced up considerably by its science-fiction overtones: when she dies, Sally is reading *Life on Other Worlds* by H. Spencer Jones; Ray Wernecke tells Ed that he's had clairvoyant communication with Martians (a theme that would recur in Brown's short story, "Entity Trap"); Yat-Dun claims he's hiring the Hunters to keep Martians' reputation clear; and so on. There are also elements of psychology, when Ray admits having given Dorothy a post-hypnotic suggestion that caused her drowning. Ray at one point claims to have been "a mentalist with an act in vaudeville" (42), a profession with which the Hunters were quite familiar.

Still, *Death Has Many Doors* is probably more fun to write about than it is to read. The plot jerks along clumsily, grinding almost to a halt after Sally's death and reviving when her sister appears, only to provide another corpse. The most interesting aspect of the novel is one it shares with *The Fabulous Clipjoint* and *The Dead Ringer*, a technique I'll call the misplaced clue. In all three novels, Ed Hunter's investigation centers on the vicinity of the murders until a point late in the novel, where he must travel out of town or out of state to discover something from the past that provides the missing link needed to solve the puzzle. In *The Fabulous Clipjoint*, Ed's trip to Gary helps him solve his father's murder. In *The Dead Ringer*, the visit to Flo Czerwinski in Cincinnati provides the clue Ed and Am need to understand the series of murders that began with that of midget Lon Staffold. And in *Death Has Many Doors*, Am must go to Seco, Colorado, while Ed visits Sally Doerr's old hometown of Evanston, Illinois, and speaks to her old fiancee about her fears. This recurring plot device allows Brown to change the scene of events and expand the scope of the novels; the first two times, it works hauntingly well, but in *Death Has Many Doors* it is not as effective.

Lenore Glen Offord, reviewing the novel for the San Francisco *Chronicle*, remarked that it was "neatly worked out and easy to read, but somehow the author's heart does not seem to be in it." This must have been true, because, after publishing five Ed and Am Hunter novels in the five years from 1947 through 1951, he did not publish another until 1959, and when he finally did it was evident that he had given up on the series as a continuing portrait of a young man's growth and instead begun to rely on Ed and Am Hunter as trusty series characters who could be used in any private detective plot.

The Late Lamented was published on or about February 12, 1959, though first serial rights were sold to *The Saint Mystery Magazine* and it appeared shortly before book publication in a shortened version in the February 1959 issue. The short version has been edited with a chainsaw; chapter divisions are eliminated, as are important characters and entire plotlines. The result is a rather confusing and colorless mystery story.

In the novel, Ed and Am are given a job by their old employer, Ben Starlock. Jason Rogers was the City Treasurer of Freeland, and he was run over by a car. He's suspected of having embezzled $40,000, and they are to investigate his daughter, Wanda, to learn if she knows the whereabouts of the money. Handsome, young Ed decides to befriend Wanda to facilitate this investigation, but she is bright and uncovers his motives immediately. She believes her father was innocent, and helps Ed as he delves into the mystery. Through a series of conversations with those involved, Ed learns that the embezzlement was the work of two of

Rogers's assistants (one picked up where the other left off), and he exposes the second one, who dies violently at the hands of his partner.

The plot is nothing special, but *The Late Lamented* benefits from Brown's varied writing in the eight years since the prior Ed and Am Hunter novel. It is distinguished by interesting characters and clever allusions; in fact, the sidelights are more entertaining than the story. Ed still plays his trombone, but now he plays along with a Dave Brubeck record. He wants to play a jam session with Wanda, who plays piano, and takes the stage at the club where she works to blow a rousing rendition of "Laugh, Clown, Laugh." This is to please Leon Cavallo, the midget owner of the club and an old carney friend of Uncle Am's. Typical of Brown's playful sense of humor, the characters all remark about the irony of the opera-loving dwarf sharing the name of the famous Italian composer and librettist, Ruggerio Leoncavallo. Also typical of Brown's impish nature is the literal way he spells out the clue to the criminal's identity. Wanda tells Ed:

"Dad's assistant at that time was John Whittaker, and he died five months ago."

"Died how?" I cut in.

"A heart attack, right at the office. And Dad hired a man named Wilbur Schwarz—it's spelled S-c-h-w-a-r-z but it's pronounced the same as the more common t-z ending, Schwartz—for the job and he's held it since. So there were two assistant treasurers during the period in question—and both of them could hardly have hit on *exactly* the same system of embezzling—and used the same bank account for the checks." (85)

It takes Ed the better part of the novel to figure out that Blackie, a bouncer at the club where Wanda works (and a suspicious character), is actually Schwarz—the German word for "black." Brown gives the reader the clue early in the novel and even spells it out to make sure it's not overlooked! Such playfulness makes the novel entertaining, if light; the fact that Ed Hunter's character has stopped maturing is forgotten as the reader is swept along by a series of diverting incidents. The reviewers were all in agreement: Sergeant Cuff of the *Saturday Review of Literature* thought it "sharp and brisk." Anthony Boucher of the New York *Times* wrote that the Hunters were "as likable as ever" and added that "You'll find the spectacle of Ed falling in love even more agreeable than Ed and Am as detectives." Ed's courtship of Wanda in *The Late*

Lamented is pleasant, and she's a bright and interesting character. One finishes the novel hoping that she'll return next time, like Estelle in *The Dead Ringer*, but, sadly, she never reappeared.

Ed and Am's next appearance was in the third issue of *Ed McBain's Mystery Book*, which appeared in 1961. This digest-sized magazine featured "Before She Kills" as its cover story, advertising it as the detectives' first appearance in short-story form. Other than short versions of novels, that's correct.

Hunter and Hunter are hired by Oliver ("Ollie") R. Bookman, who fears his wife, Eve, is trying to kill him. Ollie tells them that he met Eve eight years ago when she was a stripper, but that after the wedding she grew frigid and refused to grant him a divorce. He later fell in love with Dorothy Stark and fathered a son by her. Ollie fears Eve will kill him to prevent him from leaving his money to his lover and son.

Ed pretends to be Ollie's brother and searches his apartment. After saving Ollie from a heart attack by administering some timely medication, Ed tells him he didn't appreciate being deceived by Ollie's attempt to kill himself and frame Eve for murder. Am, in the meantime, learned that Eve was still married to a John L. Littleton when she married Ollie, so Ollie is free. Months later, he sends Ed and Am a new Buick and news that he and Dorothy have wed.

This short story has images that recall Brown's earlier and better work. It opens with flies buzzing around the room; this sign of impending danger was used in *The Deep End* to great effect. Eve, the frigid but gorgeous blond stripper, recalls Yolanda Lang of *The Screaming Mimi*, yet Eve is neither evil nor insane and the comparison leads nowhere. Overall, it's an uneventful story that adds little to the Ed and Am series, even though it moves quickly and is fairly entertaining. The magazine probably wanted a cover story for its 1961 issue and offered Brown a good amount to write his first Ed and Am short piece. In any case, the detectives were not heard from again until the fall of 1963, near the end of Brown's career as a writer.

Ed and Am Hunter's last two appearances in print were in "The Missing Actor," a short story published in the November 1963 issue of *The Saint*, and in Brown's last published novel, *Mrs. Murphy's Underpants*, whose first and only edition also appeared in about November 1963. The slow process of book publishing suggests that the novel was written first.

As it opens, Ed has fallen down the stairs of his rooming house and broken a rib and his trombone. While Ed is convalescing, young Mike Dolan, son of gambling boss Vince Dolan, breaks into Ed's room to steal his gun, claiming that he heard two men outside his room planning to kill his father. Ed takes the boy home and learns that Dolan just hired Am that afternoon to trail his wife. Ed becomes involved with Angela, Dolan's pretty daughter. The novel meanders for several chapters as Ed and Am take on side jobs; then, Angela is injured by burglars who break into the Dolan home. After a very minor investigation Ed learns that the voices Mike heard were those of Angela and her boyfriend, but that Mike thought Angela's voice was that of his mother and said he heard two men in order to protect her. Angela is sent for counseling and all ends happily.

The mystery plot in *Mrs. Murphy's Underpants* is so weak that the real interest in the novel—and even its title—comes from incidents that have nothing to do with the Dolan investigation. Ed and Am play a word game throughout, in which each tries to top the other in coming up with rhyming words to fill in the blanks of the phrase, "Who put the—in Mrs. Murphy's—?" One subplot involves Molly Czerwinski, an old intimate of Ed's (and distant relative of Flo Czerwinski of *The Dead Ringer*?) who wants to hire him to track down her ex-husband. When Molly finally arrives at the office at the novel's end she reveals her married name to be Mrs. Molly Murphy, leading Ed to utter the suggestive line: " 'Who put the fire ants in Mrs. Murphy's underpants?' " (184). Hence, the novel's title.

Brown does manage a nice bit of closure in the novel by having Ed and Am receive a letter from Carey Stofft, a mentalist whose carnival will be in Gary next week and who invites them to stay a night or a week. Am also tells Ed that, in 1946, he toured Alaska with a carney; this date does not exactly jibe with the events of *The Fabulous Clipjoint*, but by 1963 Ed Hunter should really be in his mid-30s, so it's clear that Brown wasn't too concerned with consistency of dates in this series.

The novel is disappointing and filled with talk, but the story that followed it is a more fitting conclusion to the published career of Fredric Brown's most famous detectives.

"The Missing Actor" tells the story of Floyd Nielsen, a truck farmer about to retire to California who hires the Hunters to find his son, Albee. It seems that Albee owes money to a gambler and has disappeared. After conducting an investigation, Ed deduces that Floyd is actually Albee in disguise, and that the boy killed his father. Ed confronts Floyd/Albee with this knowledge and barely avoids strangulation; Am and the police arrive like the cavalry in an old Hollywood western and announce that, in reality, Floyd killed his son and is establishing an alibi! The story ends with an embarrassed Ed hesitant to tell his uncle that he thought son killed father.

What makes "The Missing Actor" so good is its brisk pace and tight narrative; it resembles a pocket version of an early Hunter novel. The mystery begins in Chicago and Ed investigates till he's blue in the face, but the key lies elsewhere—in this instance, on a truck farm in Kenosha, Wisconsin, where Am journeys and learns that Floyd Nielsen killed and buried his son. This misplaced clue expands and universalizes the story, adding rural antecedents to an urban tale. Another highlight of the story is the beatnik slang Brown uses to make it seem current (for 1963): Albee lives in "a padded pad"—an apartment with a bed and pads all over the floor for sitting. Albee's girl, Honey, is "Hershey-bar colored"; this is a clear sign that times have changed since *The Dead Ringer* featured a black character named Jigaboo. Ed mentions author Norman Mailer in a discussion of the meanings of "hip" and "beat," and Albee's friend Jerry Score is said to be "a touch on the swish side." The story is fun and very much of its time, and it's a good way to say goodbye to the characters of Ed and Am Hunter.

* * *

In seven novels and two stories that span almost 20 years (and the bulk of his career as a writer), Fredric Brown portrays the young manhood of Ed Hunter. Always narrated by Ed, the stories range from an unforgettable classic (*The Fabulous Clipjoint*) to a light entertainment (*Mrs. Murphy's Underpants*), with plenty of interesting characters and situations in between. The characters of Ed and Am Hunter develop from a barely acquainted uncle and nephew to a pair of skilled detectives running their own agency; the emphasis is always on Ed, who is perpetually learning and usually falling in love.

From 1944 on, these were Brown's only recurring characters, and as such they have a special place in his fiction. They were featured in his first novel, and he chose to write his last complete novel around them.

While his other, non-series detective books range widely from light comedy to tense thriller, the Ed and Am books are always special, always undeniably the work of Fredric Brown.

Chapter Five
Poetry

Midway through Fredric Brown's second novel, *The Dead Ringer*, Ed and Am Hunter have gone to Cincinnati to trace the background of Lon Staffold, a midget who had been murdered while traveling with the carnival in which they all worked. Before going on the road, Staffold had been staying at a boarding house run by Flo Czerwinski, an old acquaintance of Am's from a carnival years before. Little is known about Staffold, but Flo shows Am a trunk of his belongings, which Ed and Am then go through in search of some clue to his life that might help explain his murder.

In the trunk they find midget-sized clothing and, tucked away at the bottom, a typewriter and a pile of papers. Upon examination they discover poetry, written and saved by the small carnival performer, probably never meant to be read. Uncle Am turns literary critic for a moment: " 'I'd say this isn't great poetry—whatever that is—but that some of it is damn good poetry. It's better than I expected' " (186).To the casual reader, Am's assessment is correct—the fragments he found are not great poetry. They deserve attention, however, because they are one of the only instances of Fredric Brown's published verse, and they are similar in theme to much of the poetry he wrote privately throughout his career. Brown's poetry is not going to establish him as a major poet, but it is nonetheless noteworthy for its variety, its themes, and its place in relation to his later work; he evokes images of the Depression and of Midwestern life in many of his early poems, and the imagery is quite strong.

Newton Baird, in his bibliography, lists two collections of Brown's poetry that seem to have been put together by the author in the very early 1930s. *Fermented Ink: Ten Poems* has survived intact, and was published in the 1987 collection, *Brother Monster*. Baird quotes a letter from Brown's widow, Elizabeth, which sets the scene for the poetry's private publication:

...as a young man, Fred was working in a print shop as a typesetter or proofreader in the daytime, but he had the boss's permission to come in at night to set type for his own use if he melted the type back. ("An Annotated Bibliographical Checklist" 44)

There is no date on this collection. Baird also lists another collection, *Shadow Suite: Fifteen Poems*, which has a copyright date of 1932 but which is merely typed, not typeset. Many of these 15 poems are lost and, while Harry Altshuler wrote regarding the collection that he "never saw it or heard of it" (Letter to the author, 28 June 1988), several of the poems were found in Brown's files and published in 1990 in the collection, *The Water Walker*. I thus begin my discussion of the poems with *Fermented Ink*, which may be analyzed as a unified work, and continue with the remaining fragments of *Shadow Suite* and scattered surviving poems before discussing the uses of verse in his short stories and novels.

The first poem in *Fermented Ink*, "Ode to a Stuffed Owl," is slight, and it is written in a clipped, imagistic style in which the lines are never more than five syllables long. The poem notes all of the things a stuffed owl *cannot* do by making a series of assertions followed by the question, "Right?" which may be rhetorical or which may call into question the truth of the facts just stated with firm conviction. Stanza two continues the list of the stuffed owl's inabilities, and suggests the problems that might be associated with sex—a recurring theme in Brown's work. The poem concludes with a statement that raises the possibility of thought in the stuffed owl: although it shows no signs of outward life, the owl may lead an active life in dreams. Yet even this suggestion is tentative, as the final lines demonstrate: "But its dreams/May be many/(If any)."

"Ode to a Stuffed Owl" is a fitting beginning for *Fermented Ink* because it mocks classical poetry like Keats's odes in its title and because its subject, a stuffed owl, is described only by the things it is unable to do. It is trapped, somewhat like the speaker of the next poem in the collection.

In "Interlude," the speaker addresses Yvonne, someone he seems to have known in the past. He recalls an event, presumably something that happened between them, and describes time passing "with muffled wings," continuing the bird imagery of the previous poem. Blind to the passage of time, he has been distracted from natural occurrences, which were beyond his range of hearing, and his struggles through "fields," "corn," and "turbid torrents" have led to nothing but "A pallid dawn." The first stanza is thus a portrait of frustration and failed effort, in which the imagery is natural and suggests a farm (possibly Midwestern) landscape.

The mood changes immediately in the first line of the second stanza. Again, years are associated with birds, and the energy of the speaker's quest is here transferred to them, as they seem to mock him. He creeps toward the birds—perhaps the best he can do in his apparently drunken state—and they fly away, as one might expect after the disappointments detailed in the first stanza. The birds' return makes this event memorable to the speaker (it is a change from stanza one), but their "vulture-wings" seem ominous, suggesting that they return to devour a man already dead.

The final stanza removes the speaker from the natural world of the first stanza, and makes the drunken vision of the second more concrete and ordinary. He recalls a drunken song, and the "remembered ecstasy" shows his sincerity, which might otherwise be in question, since the song was sung by a group of drunken men on a street corner. Clearly, the speaker's memories of "you" are precious, and even a "maudlin" event can call to mind a valuable time in the past. The final image of the poem demonstrates the depths to which the speaker has fallen from his tenuous connection with the natural world in the first stanza: he must be taken home by that most ordinary of men, a linoleum salesman.

The title of the poem suggests that the event in stanza two is one that merely interrupts a larger series of events, and is perhaps an unusually memorable moment in the speaker's unhappy life. The title also suggests the connection that Brown sees between poetry and music, something that he explores in many of his poems. "Interlude" is Brown's first attempt to deal with drunkenness, failure, and the urban condition, and its speaker shares qualities with the main characters of several of Brown's stories and novels, like *Murder Can Be Fun* and *The Screaming Mimi*.

"Gifts," the next poem, describes a series of presents: some are exotic, foreign, or ancient, some possess natural beauty, and some are ordinary and urban. The last stanza qualifies the gifts by adding that the emotions underlying them are more valuable to the speaker than the gifts themselves, yet the concluding lines lend an ordinary quality to the process of giving. As in "Interlude," lofty ideas and emotions are grounded in reality, demonstrating both the speaker's cynicism and his understanding that the mundane events of everyday life affect even the most beautiful things.

Next in the collection is the haunting "Unheard Serenade." The regularity of the lines suggests that this is a traditional poem, and its meter is a rough iambic pentameter. The poem has a sexual feeling, and uses religious imagery; branches bending in "grave supplication" suggest prayer, and the "high wind" of the first line recalls God's biblical manifestation in the whirlwind. The heavens seem to be in a state of chaos, and the moon is "haloed like a martyr," hinting at prior violence.

The focus of the poem shifts at the end of the first stanza, as the reader realizes that the heavenly events described are merely background for the human drama occurring below. The pair in the poem may be lovers, and they are "leaning to the wind"—either facing their destiny or yearning toward their God. The "Unheard Serenade" of the title occurs in the second stanza: it is the words of the speaker, unheard by his companion in their moment of ecstasy. In the end, the lovers experience the power of natural elements (God?), which precludes any ability or necessity to use human speech.

The musical nature of the next poem is established by its title, "Melodie Moderne," and it is a sordid, unpleasantly modern music. The poem is a chant, composed of a series of brief lines and phrases that paint an imagistic portrait of a "secondfloor speak" and a man drawn there again and again. The speaker's condition is virtually subhuman (he "laps" his drink), and although the atmosphere is one filled with danger and sin, he seems to find nothing unusual about it. An attempt to leave the place of sin and inhumanity is made in the last stanza: the speaker gathers his grief to leave, and the repetition of "secondfloor speak" from the second line of the poem suggests closure. But the speaker, in the end, is trapped and must return. "Melodie Moderne" is a frightening picture of life in Depression-era America. Its musical elements add not joy but a dirge-like background to the dreary events, and it continues Brown's examination of the fallen, drunken man that began in "Interlude."

"Rhapsody" is a lovely poem, in which the Wordsworthian pledge of the first lines promises common language and the speaker evokes Christ's words when he says he will speak as a child:

I write to you of simplicity, simply,
In words with an earth-tang,
As a child unto a child. (*Brother Monster* 122)

The speaker knows that he must be "like a child" to enter Heaven, and the stanzas that follow describe common folk in language that betrays a deep love for mankind. This is perhaps Brown's most beautiful poem, and the final stanza recalls the last lines of Joyce's "The Dead":

I saw night fall, and the moon and stars gleam quietly
Upon the dreamless sleep of trees, and winding roads, and men.
(*Brother Monster* 122)

These lines possess a peaceful, serene quality and wrap the simple, clear images of the preceding verses in an appealing final warmth.

Brown next uses a very conventional poetic format in "Hauteur" to describe both a cat and the poet, and the lines have a playfulness that redeems their tendency toward the singsong. The second part of the poem is most important, for here the speaker questions the power of creation—he also demonstrates some hauteur of his own, as he boasts of his control over the fictional cat. "Hauteur" is a minor poem, a bit of light verse, an experiment in discipline for the poet, and a meditation on the author's creative powers; Brown will continue to experiment with the author's place in narrative in such later works as "Don't Look Behind You" and "The Yehudi Principle."

In "Romance," Brown uses an almost prosaic style to relate a tale of a romance that never was, one which occurred only in a brief meeting of eyes. The eyes are important: they are the striking characteristic of the otherwise ordinary man described in the first stanza. The eyes of the woman in the second stanza—"blue ice," which "seemed to melt" after she saw the man—are important, too: Brown describes character and emotion with a single physical detail. The final stanza shows the effect of the meeting upon the woman, and asks a question central to the poetry of this collection: was the man an ordinary man or an artist? The casual cruelty evoked by the description of the woman's husband suggests that she desires the stranger to be an artist. In the same way, many of the characters in Brown's poems seem ordinary, but approach a higher level of importance through the poet's selection of details and through the methods he uses to present their stories.

The "man with the broom" described in the next poem, "Midnight Sonata," receives his only individuality from the object he holds; the machines about him "slumber" and seem more human than he. The factory-like repetition of the first line demonstrates the dreariness of this existence, while the moon, which "melloglows" the skylight glass, suggests a serene, natural world beyond the machines that is in sharp contrast to the mundane, realistic interior of the factory. The last stanza offers no escape, and concludes this meditation on another trapped individual—the poem is bleak, urban, and powerful.

The last poem in the collection details a "Slow Awakening" to the world described in the preceding nine poems. The first stanza has an imagistic quality, since it is comprised of only two sparse sentences, the words of which portray a strong picture:

> Sways the gibbet, black shadow
> Against a brightening sky.
> Thru an oval noose of white hemp rope
> Slinks the frightened dawn. (*Brother Monster* 126)

The "frightened dawn" offers little hope that the new day will erase whatever happened at the hanging place the night before.

The second stanza begins curiously—"I have been thus"—and the "thus" may refer to any of the images in the first stanza. The speaker, introduced in this stanza, has "marvelled" at three things:

> the shrill laughter
> of white bedposts,
> The rhythmic slow white arch
> Of a woman's thigh,
> The death rattle of white milkbottles
> Upon a dirty cement doorstep. (*Brother Monster* 126)

These images are connected by the adjective "white" as well as by their unsettling evocations of sex and death. The final words of the poem complete the speaker's awakening to reality; the poem as a whole is a fitting conclusion to a series of poems in which images of night, loss, and chaos have been frequent.

In all, *Fermented Ink* is a well-balanced collection of ten poems which range from the playful to the deadly serious. Brown experiments with poetic methods, often choosing to use musical rhythms and images to shape his ideas. His recurring obsessions here are night, moonlight, drinking, loneliness, animals, music, and love. Often urban and industrial, his poems reflect a bleakness that was familiar to the poor, urban, and rural characters portrayed.

Whether Brown ever attempted to reach a broader audience by publishing *Fermented Ink* is unknown; it was printed privately and not published for the general public until more than 50 years after its writing.

Brown's other collection, *Shadow Suite*, appears lost. Baird lists it as a 1932 work, however, and it thus seems concurrent with *Fermented Ink*, yet he says it is merely typewritten, which suggests that by the time Brown completed *Shadow Suite*, he no longer had an opportunity to set his own work in type.

Although the collection is unavailable, typed copies of several of the poems listed therein were found in Brown's files. The poems in *Shadow Suite* are listed by Baird as follows: "Red Wine," "Harlem Lullaby," "Prelude to Oblivion," "Shadow Dance," "Reflections," "Unseemly Queries," "Epic," "The Idol," "Cargoes," "Immortality," "The Oyster and the Shark," "Hymn of Hatred," "The Battle of the Lamp Posts," "Kol Nidre," "Scene Macabre."

Shadow Suite begins with "Red Wine,"[1] a much different poem from those in *Fermented Ink*; it is loose in form and chaotic in content, and the romance of the first line is made ironic by the casual brutality of the second stanza. In the third, the person the speaker addresses seems to gain a power over the elements about her, and in the fourth, the speaker drinks again, evoking the imagery of blood on the lips of she to whom he speaks. The fifth stanza continues the assault: neither primitive beasts nor futuristic war machines shake the composure of the woman addressed, and in the next stanza her eyes behold a kind of hell with complete calm. The monster crouched outside the door in the next-to-last stanza is a deeply troubling image; however, the woman of the poem merely taps her foot, purses her lips, and blows smoke "toward the black doorway."

Brown begins to use new imagery in this poem, including that of dinosaurs and spaceships, that foreshadows concerns in his later work. This poem is about a woman, however, and succeeds in establishing her cool nonchalance in the face of threats all about her. Religious echoes also seem to creep in—the teeth that "pierce the/tender veil" recall the tearing of the temple curtain at the death of Christ, and Hell itself is held "in the miracle of your hand"—but these echoes are quite subtle and not the poem's main feature.

A strange poem, "Shadow Dance,"[2] continues the prosaic, loose style of "Red Wine." The second-person address gives the speaker a strangely detached quality, and the insistence that the two people described "have no faces" makes this a shadow dance rather than a meeting of two people. The candles reflect body movements; the garments "chatter" and "rustle laughingly," yet only the hands and the fingers of the people seem to communicate. The final switch to the third-person address ends the poem on an uncertain note: it is as if the speaker cares nothing for the promise of the shadows for the next day, he is only concerned with the events of "Tonight."

"Hymn of Hatred"[3] is a brutal poem, written in the same general arrangement of prose verses that Brown used in the previous two poems in *Shadow Suite*. It deepens the portrait of people unable to communicate, and turns the uncertainty of the relationship in "Shadow Dance" into a concrete hatred, the sort of hatred that seems to lurk beneath the words of the speaker in "Red Wine." The archaic phrasing of the poem's first line, "Come thou not near me," sets the mood of discomfort and recalls the language of less secular hymns; the violent visions that the speaker describes portray a cruelty that is given no basis yet is clearly unfulfilled; the wishes for harm all seem to occur only in the speaker's mind. The final line suggests that the speaker addresses a living ghost who "haunts" him, one he wishes would die and leave him alone.

These first three poems from *Shadow Dance* paint a bleak picture of a relationship and are notable because they are written in a far more prosaic style than those in *Fermented Ink*. The next poem that is available is quite different, and shows a humorous, storytelling side of Brown's writing that was to flourish in the later years of his career, when he became known as master of the short-short story.

In "The Battle of the Lamp Posts," Brown returns to a familiar poetic form and tells an amusing story in six carefully crafted stanzas. The hero's tale of his "battle" with the lamp posts—which ends with him holding one tightly—is revealed in the last stanza to be a story told to a judge, and the entire poem has a light tone, reminiscent of Ogden Nash or Lewis Carroll. It further explores the character of the drunk that

Brown began examining in *Fermented Ink*, yet eschews serious meditation for a much-appreciated funny story.

"Kol Nidre" is the last surviving poem that can be attributed to *Shadow Suite*, and in it Brown returns to the form and content of the first three poems of the collection previously discussed. However, although a seemingly powerful "you" is again discussed, the speaker is now "we," rather than "I," as in earlier poems. "You" sings a song that produces unusual reactions in those who hear it, and Brown describes these using images now familiar in his poetry: night, skies, a candle, a cigarette.

The title of the poem refers to the beginning of the Jewish prayer for the annulment of private vows chanted in the synagogue on the eve of Yom Kippur, which suggests that this poem signals a movement toward a break in the relationship that seems to dominate the existing poems of *Shadow Suite*. The environment of the poem is decidedly secular, though, and the poet was an avowed agnostic, so perhaps this is his ironic version of the beginning of a sacred ceremony. Listed as the next to last poem in the collection, "Kol Nidre" may—like "Slow Awakening" in *Fermented Ink*—begin to resolve the situation set out in the poems before it.

Aside from these two collections, Fredric Brown's poetry is scattered. Ten more poems, eight of which are undated, were found in a folder with the poems from *Shadow Suite*. These loose poems have been published in the 1990 collection, *Happy Ending*. I feel it will be useful to discuss these as well, as some are of considerable merit, before concluding this chapter with a look at the forms Brown's poetry took in his later short stories and novels.

Two of these remaining poems are written in a form quite close to that of the four "relationship" poems in *Shadow Suite*, and thus may also belong in that collection, although their titles are difficult to determine. One is romantic, the other strange; both have religious ideas, yet use them in far different ways.

Brown's poetry in the first poem, which begins, "Sing unto me a song, o beloved, with your lips," is erotic and sensual, as the poet asks his lover to sing the "song/of songs" to him without speaking, in a kiss. The vocabulary is similar to that of the Old Testament poet/author of The Song of Songs: "beloved," "curve of your/young breasts," "white arms," and "virgins" all evoke the Hebraic love song, and Brown's use of Egyptian and mythical images gives the poem an ancient, exotic feeling. The "screaming sky" image is continued from "Red Wine," but here it suggests passion, while in the earlier poem it was part of a description of chaos. This is a poem about lovers, written with unmistakable emotion. Its prosaic stanzas suggest that it belongs with the poems in *Shadow Suite*, and those poems are deepened by the association; they are mostly concerned with hatred of a lover and with coldness in relationships that has little to do with romance. This poem presents another side of Brown's attitude, and perhaps the entire collection traced a relationship from youthful passion to older disenchantment.

It is tempting to accept the last poem written in such a sequence as "Scene Macabre," which is listed as the final poem in the collection. This poem may be the one which begins, "There is a dearth of darkness in the room," and I will treat it as such.

If the previous poem depicted the passionate beginnings of a relationship, this poem surely shows a potentially horrible end. It picks up the feeling of a pseudo-religious ritual from "Kol Nidre" and ends with an image of death and horror. Here, there are no shadows, for they are crucified "upon a blazing cross." Light is "blasphemous"; the three men who sit and observe are disconcerting. The naked "girl-child" on the table may be alive or dead. As the last stanza indicates, "Nothing moves" in this poem: it is a moment frozen in time, and the poet purposely is unclear about whether a horrible event has just happened or is about to happen. The last line explains that the "dearth of darkness" is "the bene-/diction," which suggests that this is a closing "prayer" or perhaps a moment of momentous importance (like the moment of transubstantiation in a Roman Catholic mass), signalling an ending or a dismissal.

If this is the final poem in *Shadow Suite*, it sums up the often violent, usually confusing portraits of the relationship between the sexes that Brown evokes. In "Red Wine," "Hymn of Hatred," "Shadow Dance," and "Kol Nidre," he explores different sides of this relationship, a battle that neither woman nor man ever seems to win. To end with the image of the men standing over "the naked body/of a girl-child" is to suggest violence and lack of resolution; it is a frightening conclusion to an unsettling collection of poems.

The next poem of Brown's that can be placed with certainty is an untitled piece marked "Milwaukee, 1933." It does not follow the style of the poems in either of his earlier collections, but its imagery evokes some of the concerns of both. Brown may be writing in response to his earlier poems in these verses as he begins, "I am a liar." His dreams that "become dragons" and spew ineffective smoke and flames may refer to his poems of hatred, and he laments his "curse of meaningless" and says he writes with "pink ink"—he is not even strong enough to use a violent red. Yet the woman he addresses rattles in his soul, and, in an image that recalls "Slow Awakening," he disregards all rattling (except for two specific types) as "superfluous." The speaker was distracted from the woman's speech the day before by things crawling in the corners (how different from "Scene Macabre," in which even the shadowy corners were filled with light), and perhaps the poet is also the one "crying underneath an elm" who played "a strange little tune" (poem?) on his flute (it is well known that Brown played the flute). He ends the long first stanza with a question suggesting that the "pink ink" may have been stronger than he thought.

The brief second stanza does not bode well for the relationship that seemed so promising in stanza one: the night is "monstrous," and the silence it brings with it seems dangerous and filled with foreboding. The final sentence—"And morning, and again"—demonstrates the repetitive nature of these concerns in a relationship and recalls the trapped man of "Melodie Moderne" as well as the scene in "Slow Awakening."

In her autobiography, Beth Brown describes a trip that her husband made when he lost his job during the Great Depression:

And, too, circumstances had forced him into a different kind of experience. It was during the depression when he had a wife and two young children. He lost his job in Milwaukee, and though he was willing to do *any* kind of work, he could find nothing. He and his family buried their pride and went on relief. Then, with nothing but a bare hope of finding a job, he went to Los Angeles, hitchhiking, riding in and on freight cars, sleeping in transient camps, going hungry, washing dishes in restaurants. Finding his luck no better in Los Angeles, with only a dime in his pocket to ride across Chicago, he returned to Milwaukee in the same way. (*Oh, for the Life* 17)

There is a poem of Brown's dated "Los Angeles, 1934," that almost certainly was written during the trip Mrs. Brown describes. In "All things are strange things, seen but dimly," all is strange to the man of 28 years, born and raised in Midwestern cities and thrust into the "rhododendron-bordered paths" of the City of Angels. Even the sunlight there is dark. The trip west, so well evoked in Mrs. Brown's memoir, was a march of "tall whispering mountains" and "glaring sands"—in the western desert a cow's skeleton spoke through its silence. Yet the silence of the desert is no stranger than the silence of Los Angeles crowds, the poet notes, where he feels a "roaring solitude" like that described by Nathanael West in *The Day of the Locust*. The other sounds are strange as well, and the poet, alone in strange territory, cannot have dreams of his own: he can only dream "that there were dreams." Brown thus describes the emotions and alien feelings he encountered on his trip to the West Coast. Like other writers of the 1930s, he felt the economic pressures of the times; he chose to express his confusion in verse.

The remaining six poems found in Brown's files are undated, but one may bear examination as a poem of the Depression, where financiers were leaping from the tops of tall city buildings in despair over lost fortunes. The title of this poem, "Mens Sana," comes from the Latin phrase, *mens sana in corpore sano*, or "a sound mind in a sound body"; here it is shortened to "a sound mind." The subject of the poem is given a problem in the first stanza, figures out a way to solve it in the second, and carries out his plan in the third. Brown again refers to the contrast between darkness and light that was so important in "Scene Macabre," yet here he uses it to explain the idea that "sorrow is the absence of illusion." The third stanza makes the poem's subject God-like—the "affectionate amusement" with which he surveys his "creation" recalls the beginning of *Genesis*—and then demonstrates in an ironic final line that he is merely a solipsist. The irony of this poem foreshadows Brown's later work, especially his vignettes, which usually rely on a final twist for their comic effect.

Another of Brown's undated poems, "Mighty King Mene-Ptah," recalls "The Battle of the Lamp Posts" in its form and humor. Since it is dangerous to attempt to analyze humor, I will not try to explain what makes this poem funny; instead, it must stand as a clever bit of verse that demonstrates Brown's capacity for humor in poetry as well as prose. The stenographers who compare the great Egyptian king to someone named Eddie seem unaware of the stature of the monarch they mock, and the contrast between ancient practices and modern preoccupations works well as a subtle meditation on the ravages of time, as if "Ozymandias" had been rewritten by Ogden Nash. The last stanzas bring the two worlds together: the stenographers are "modeled/By the same sculptor" as the Egyptian maidens thrown into the Nile, and the poet asks Mene-Ptah what he would give to return in the modern world, even as someone so unimportant as "Eddie."

"Scaramouche Sings of Love and Strums His Lute," another undated poem, is unlike any other Brown wrote, and perhaps this is for the best. In almost surreal poetry, Brown writes of a lover's unsuccessful courtship. The contrast between the seemingly romantic Scaramouche, his awful lyrics, and the curious "stage directions" that culminate with a bucket of cold water descending toward the singer makes for a strange poem indeed. The musical instructions interspersed between the verses add to the absurdity and, in all, this poem seems to show little more than an experiment in form (it recalls French surrealist plays of the teens and 20s) and demonstrates the poet's continuing interest in music and its connections with verse.

Brown returns to the Old Testament for inspiration in the next poem, "Solomon, Solomon." The key to this poem is in its final line, "the light white ashes of redundancy?" The poet asks the ancient Hebrew king, whose lust was legendary, if the shadows of the maidens dancing before him were not demonstrations of the lack of importance of these many women to a man who has had so many in his lifetime. The imagery here is strong: "night" is described as "the jeweled Etheopian wanton," and the palace of Solomon is evoked as a place where maidens cast dancing shadows under "swinging lamps," all for the eyes of Solomon. And Solomon, like Mene-Ptah and the maidens that served them both, eventually was reduced to "light white ashes."

The last two "lost" poems of Fredric Brown share the theme of destruction; like his later science fiction, they demonstrate an ability to prophesy in an age of warfare, and each is concerned with the essential inconsequentiality of man.

"Finale" sabotages the reader's perceptions. It moves from images of mass destruction in its first lines through smaller and smaller changes to be wrought by destruction; in the second stanza, the poet states that all will end "In an instant; when I die." Brown's ironically solipsistic view is thus continued from "Mens Sana," but this time it is more clearly the poet who is creator/destroyer of the world.

In "After Armageddon," Silence is a spectre which "burns his brand" on the lips of the dead. Natural elements will cover the corpses and eventually the jungle will exist "where once our motors sped." The first stanza recalls Carl Sandburg's "Grass," in which the poet speaks of the grass that covers every man's tomb. The second stanza, however, takes the poem in a customarily ironic direction: time and its events become circular, and a "creature of the wild" again evolves into the poet who will write "A sonnet which shall prophesy the end." As in "Finale," the destruction in the poem's first stanza is undermined by the self-reflexive irony of the conclusion.

All in all, these 25 poems establish Fredric Brown as a poet who was serious about his work. His first collection, *Fermented Ink*, is at times immature but often surprises the reader with its powerful images, and the poet uses different forms to expand upon several common themes. His second collection, *Shadow Suite*, survives only in fragments, but these fragments suggest that it is often consistent in its unusual poetic form and that it seems to consist mainly of a very passionate examination of the different aspects of a relationship that disintegrates into near-horror. The remaining poems vary in style and success: they show a willingness to attempt a variety of poetic forms and demonstrate a developing irony, humor and self-examination.

In 1954, Brown published two of his own poems in *American Poetry Magazine*, and these are the only two instances of his poems being published professionally outside the confines of his own collections.

The first of these poems is "Prelude to Tracy." The subtitle is "Chicago, 1934," suggesting either that the poem was written 20 years before or is a mid-1950s recollection of that time and place. The poem is comprised of eight four-line stanzas and shares the themes and mood of Brown's earlier poems. The speaker sounds like a man addressing a friend, as he begins: "So come and walk with me into the streets,/And we shall talk of ladies' legs and Keats..."; the reference is both to sex and Romantic poetry, in an urban context. It's Autumn ("feel the dim October sun"), and the speaker looks toward Spring as deleting all that exists in Autumn, in contrast to the usual poetic practice of portraying Spring as a time of growth and renewal.

The speaker's fondness for urban scenes, darkness, and Autumn is expanded in subsequent stanzas as he and his friend head for a bar. As dusk falls, the speaker draws a word-picture of it: "Night shall enter dancing, slightly stewed,/A fan-dance on the roof-tops, wholly nude,/With but an airway beacon for a fan,..." In stanza four, the speaker and his friend leave the "cold" sidewalk and find themselves "Before a bar and safe within the fold." The last four stanzas portray the events in the bar, as "purple chipmunks...dance a tarantelle upon the bar" and the drinkers "speak with tongues of angels..." The poem ends with the speaker tilting his hat and pointing "in awe toward a chair and say[ing],/'Twas there upon that chair once Tracy sat'."

Who is Tracy? And how is the poem a prelude to her? We are never told directly, but she may be a lost love of the speaker's friend, and the speaker may be trying to rouse him from "autumn's dimness." The poem is cheerful and regular in meter, recalling "The Battle of the Lamp Posts" as well as Brown's other poems about drunkenness, night, the city, and lost love.

The next issue of *American Poetry Magazine* featured another poem by Brown, "Hands." Unlike "Prelude to Tracy," "Hands" is written in free verse and is only eight lines long. The poem portrays an unknown man wholly through descriptions of his hands and speculation on their actions. The hands are "quiet-folded," but this is a deception, since they "seem to writhe...In contemplated contact with a naked flame/Or naked flesh." The fingers are both "captor-captive" and they "tell/Ten white impassioned lies." The poem thus delves into the question of appearance versus reality, as the seemingly quiet hands actually writhe in contemplation of passionate action. "Hands" recalls Brown's poems of love and violence from *Shadow Suite*, like "Shadow Dance" and "Scene Macabre." Taken together, these two poems represent a good selection of Brown's poetic range; it is curious that he published only these and appears never to have published any others.

A short piece Brown published in the May 1955 issue of *The Magazine of Fantasy and Science Fiction*, "Imagine," also belongs in the category of poetry, even though it's really in prose. It is subtitled "A Proem," a type of work defined as a preface or prelude, and it is simply a litany of fantastic things with a marvelous sense of wonder. The reader is asked to imagine a series of old legends and beliefs, then to imagine the future, and finally to imagine the hardest thing of all—the miracle of man, the universe, the earth. "Imagine!" it ends, in a tone at once commanding and wondering. The proem shares little with Brown's other poetry and much with his science fiction writing, which is more optimistic and forward-looking in scope.

Another short work of Brown's that belongs in the poetic category is the odd story, "The House," which appeared in the August 1960 *Fantastic*. In it, an unnamed man enters a house and walks through a hallway and various rooms before finding himself in total darkness. He lights candles until they're almost gone, then claws at the doors till his fingers bleed. The story is filled with symbolism: the man leaves a long road and idyllic fields to enter the house, the rooms of which each include bizarre items; the final room is the "east bedroom of his father's house near Wilmington, the room in which he had been born." The dates of items he finds seem to work backwards, until he finds he has only half an hour's worth of candle left before being enveloped by darkness, and he screams. The dark symbolism and troubling imagery recall Brown's poetry, but the story's purpose is obscure; is the house the man's mind, or the end of his life? The man's final screams may be due to the fear of the unknown darkness about to engulf him, or to a fear of the unknown from which we all are born, but it is unclear—the story is so obscure that it is bizarre.

The last examples of Brown's poetry in print appeared in four consecutive issues of *Rogue*, a men's magazine, from April through July 1963. Each issue includes one page of "Instant Novellas," telling "an entire story in four lines or less" and accompanying an old-fashioned cartoon. An example:

In a dream, Robert talked with his father but suddenly remembered: "Dad," he gasped, "you're dead!" "Be glad this is only a dream, son," his father snorted, "or I'd have to say, 'So are you!' " (May 1963: 35)

All 16 of these brief pieces mix irony, humor, and contemporary references, and Brown (or his editor) claims that this is an old French form of poetry. If this is true, it demonstrates Brown's variety as a poet, but it seems more likely that it's simply a gimmick.

* * *

In 1938, Brown began selling short stories to the so-called "pulp" magazines. From this point on, his poetic inclinations can be detected from time to time in his fiction, sometimes in quite revealing ways.

Compare these lines from "Wheels Across the Night" (*G-Men Detective* July 1941):

> The moon was out brightly now. He found it easy to see his way through the corn that was tall enough to screen him from the house.... he thought he saw something move in the tall wheat. (*Whispering Death* 84, 87)

to these from "Interlude":

> Nights under a strange moon
> I have walked and stumbled
> Across fresh plowed fields, climbed fences,
> Ripped a swath through tall corn (*Brother Monster* 118)

It may be unconscious, but Brown's poetic side occasionally shows through in the oddest places. For instance, " 'You'll Die Before Dawn'," published in the July 1942 *Mystery Magazine*, is one of many stories in which Brown's protagonist must prove himself worthy to remain on the police force while his superiors threaten his expulsion due, in this case, to his great weight. As Big Ben, the hero, heads down a dark street one night, he is described as "leaning into the wind" (*Brother Monster* 132). In a very subtle way, the mystery writer here may allude to his poem of ten years before, "Unheard Serenade," in which the lovers are spied "leaning to the wind." In both cases, the characters approach their destiny.

At one point in Brown's long story, "Madman's Holiday" (*Detective Story* July 1943), Hank Renmers, the hero, is in a sanitarium for a rest cure from stress built up in his job working with high explosives. As he walks across the grounds, he hears an inmate making a speech on a stump:

> —and the birds of Armageddon shall fly the
> shrieking skies and their droppings upon the
> quacking face of earth shall be fire and
> destruction and holocaust— (*Madman's Holiday* 41)

This echoes Brown's poem "Red Wine":

> Outside and overhead across a
> screaming sky sweep
> silhouettes of the pterodactyls
> that slew you yesterday... (*Happy Ending* 196)

as well as recalling the "red screaming sky" of "Sing unto me a song..."
and the title of "After Armageddon."

Not all of Brown's use of poetry is self-reflexive, though. In "The
Jabberwocky Murders" (*Thrilling Mystery* Summer 1944), Doc Bagden
thinks of Lewis Carroll's verse, "Father William" as he looks in a mirror,
and each of the story's seven chapters is prefaced by a four-line quote
from "Jabberwocky."

In "To Slay a Man About a Dog" (*Detective Tales* September
1944), the dog of the title wears a tag around its neck that reads: "I am
the dog/Of a murdered man,/Escape his fate, Sir,/If you can" (*The
Shaggy Dog* 15). The detective-hero of the tale, Peter Kidd, delights in
demonstrations of his erudition, and explains that the poem spoofs
Alexander Pope's famous dog-tag verse: "I am the dog/Of the king at
Kew./Pray tell me, Sir,/Whose dog are you?" Brown is thus conscious of
the poetic tradition, and his ability to weave it into popular detective
stories suggests that the roots of his interests in poetry are deep.

One of Brown's more unusual stories is "Four Letter Word"
(*Adventure* April 1948), one of his few attempts at fiction *outside*
the sub-genres of crime and science-fiction. The story is told as an
anecdote by an unnamed reporter who interviews Rupert Gardin, the
dean of American literary critics, and asks him what he thinks is the
greatest poem ever written. In response, Gardin tells the story of
Carl Marney, a shipwrecked heir who spends ten years alone on a
desert island trying to write the greatest poem of all time and who
finally distills it into a four-letter word which is, of course,
unprintable. The story ends with the reporter's comment that his
naivete ended when his editor pointed out that he had played the
fool. This delightful story lacks any element of crime or science
fiction. Rather, it is a portrait of the writing process gone mad,
dealing with a literary critic's practical joke. Surely Brown, who had
kept his poems private up to this point, could sympathize with the
poet trapped on an island, slowly going mad while he writes and
revises for years and years.

And so Brown, in *The Dead Ringer*, has his detectives uncover that sheaf of poems written by the dead carnival midget. The poems have lain hidden in a trunk, unseen, and they add immeasurably to the character of the little man. The first poem reads:

> The sere leaves of despair flutter down
> And heap about my feet and the roots of trees;
> A cool voice stirs them and they whisper
> With soft lutevoices like the never-weres
> In dreams under a pale dawn. (186-87)

Young Ed Hunter does not understand the poem; to him, " 'it's just words'." Uncle Am tells him " 'Don't be so damned literal, Ed...someday you'll run into a flock of 'never-weres';...' " Ed then reads another poem, "Cover my coffin slowly":

> Cover my coffin slowly
> That I may hear the thud of every striking clod
> With ears now dead to every other sound.
> And quiet shall I lie, nor dream.
>
> Soon, then, shall come the rains
> And make of earth one vast mud pie
> Wherein I shall be one of many raisins. So. (187)

Ed does not like this poem either: "There was something about it that made something inside me squirm, and maybe that was what the poem was supposed to do" (188).

The dead midget's poetry in *The Dead Ringer* is not very good, but then it is not meant to be. It shares something with Brown's two early collections—"The sere leaves of despair" is an image that could have come straight from *Fermented Ink*—but it is Brown's attempt to write poetry as his character might. This episode is unusual and significant: Brown's training in the short-story form taught him the need for quick, powerful ways to deepen the character of a figure who may not play a prominent role. Sometimes it is a physical detail, sometimes a taste for music. In *The Dead Ringer*, the discovery of Lon Staffold's poetry broadens the reader's understanding of a previously one-dimensional character. From an annoying, fearful midget in a carnival he becomes a tormented, morbid poet, with a rich, hidden past and an unrevealed talent.

Brown uses the same device in his first novel, *The Fabulous Clipjoint*, in which Ed and Am join forces to investigate the death of Ed's father. The father is first presented as a drunk, but as the novel progresses his character is filled in until he becomes a near-tragic hero. At one point, Ed and Am go through a small suitcase of his and discover souvenirs of his youth, including poetry in Spanish that he wrote while traveling. The fact that a man who was not thought to have led a very meaningful life could have written poetry and kept it hidden is again a method of deepening character and here, even more than in *The Dead Ringer*, the detail adds a passionately romantic side to Ed's father that the boy never suspected.

Other stories and novels used verse in different ways. In "Last Curtain" (*New Detective* July 1949), has-been actor Sir Charles Hanover Gresham recites passages from *Hamlet, The Rubaiyat of Omar Khayyam*, and *Macbeth* in an audition for a part and is killed because the speech he recites about blackmail is all too true! *The Rubaiyat* is again quoted at the conclusion of Brown's 1949 novel, *The Screaming Mimi*, when drunken newsman Bill Sweeney must keep talking to keep a lunatic at bay, and resorts to quoting every piece of writing he can remember, from "The Gettysburg Address" to "Hickory Dickory Dock." In 1950, Brown's *Night of the Jabberwock* combined "The Jabberwocky Murders" with another 1944 story, "The Gibbering Night," to make a delightful novel. As in the earlier story, some chapters begin with lines from Lewis Carroll's "Jabberwocky"; however, the novel runs to fifteen chapters, and Brown begins some of them with lines from other Carroll poems, including several from *Alice in Wonderland*.

A nursery rhyme found its way into the title and center of another 1950 novel, *Here Comes a Candle*, which concerns the psychological damage done to young Joe Bailey by the verse "Here Comes a Candle to Light You to Bed, Here Comes a Chopper to Chop off Your Head" and a series of tragic events. Joe ends the novel by reenacting the rhyme (literally) with his fiance on the night before their wedding.

Poems and rhymes continued to find their way into Brown's novels and stories in the 1950s. *Hamlet* is quoted in *The Deep End*, when newsman Sam Evans thinks that handsome Obie Westphal "may smile and be a villain" (102), and Sam later dreams that he sees Obie with a wolf's head saying "Turn again, Dick Whittington," from the traditional English verse. In "Witness in the Dark" (*New Detective* June 1953), detective George Hearn and his wife Marge argue about the correct wording and literary source of "When all candles be out, all cats be gray" (*The Freak Show Murders* 80) which is from chapter five of Thomas Heywood's early seventeenth-century *Proverbes*.

The carnival novel *Madball* and its short version "The Pickled Punks" include a number of poetic references: mentalist Doc Magus quotes *Julius Caesar* and heeds the advice of Cassius: "Then, with your will, go on" (11); he later quotes *Hamlet* ("It is a consummation most devoutly to be wished for" [130]) and puns on a line from *MacBeth*, saying "Is this a tenner I see before me?" (135). Magus also tells the idiot boy Sammy about *Alice in Wonderland* and discusses its author, and Brown quotes Wordsworth when he writes, "Sammy wandered lonely as a cloud" (129).

Other notable poetic references include Brown's allusion to Gertrude Stein's "A rose is a rose is a rose" at the beginning of *The Wench is Dead*: "A fuzz is a fuzz is a fuzz when you waken from a wino jag" (11). The novel's title is from Christopher Marlowe's *The Jew of Malta*, and the quotation ends Brown's novel: "yes, but that was in another country and besides, the wench is dead" (190). Brown's story of a mad artist, "The Little Lamb" (*Manhunt* August 1953), includes an obscene twist on William Blake's "Little lamb who made thee," as well as quoting from T.S. Eliot's "The Love Song of J. Alfred Prufrock" and having the main character complain that "Eliot...saw too deeply" (*And the Gods Laughed* 391-92).

In the unfinished novel version of *The Case of the Dancing Sandwiches*, Brown briefly recalls the subject of his own earlier poem, "Solomon, Solomon," when he has detective Peter Cole quote the biblical Solomon's "How beautiful are thy feet with shoes" and call it a "ridiculous mistranslation; obviously it should have been *How beautiful are thy sandaled feet...*" (70). Brown again used this biblical quotation in *The Office*, when office manager Geoffrey Willoughby plays Cyrano de Bergerac and writes a love letter to pretty office worker Stella Klosterman on behalf of shy bookkeeper Marty Raines, quoting Solomon's beautiful love poetry at length.

Brown again has a character quoting poetry in *His Name Was Death* (1954): as Darius Conn grows nervous about the possibility of his assistant's going to the police, he recalls his father saying "What a tangled web we weave, when first we practice to deceive" (120), a well-known line from *Marmion*, a little-known poem by Sir Walter Scott.

John Keats, the Romantic poet Brown had mentioned in "Prelude to Tracy," is quoted in the sixth Ed and Am Hunter novel, *The Late Lamented* (1959), as Ed Hunter thinks "I stood upon a peak in Darien, with a wild surmise." The famous final verse of Keats's "On First Looking into Chapman's Homer" reads as follows:

> Or like stout Cortez when with eagle eyes
> He stared at the Pacific, and all his men
> Look'd at each other with a wild surmise,
> Silent, upon a peak in Darien.

Ed then remarks, "Uncle Am, I've got a wild surmise."

Later in his writing career, Brown began quoting more modern poets. In the undistinguished *One for the Road* (1958), newsman Bob Spitzer chats with his girlfriend Doris about the murder of Amy Waggoner, a town souse. Bob says that their increasingly convoluted speculations are "Wheels within wheels," referring to Ezekiel's biblical vision, then Doris suggests they use the name "Vasserot" for their hypothetical killer. The name, as she points out, is from line one of "The End of the World," a twentieth-century sonnet by Archibald Macleish:

> Quite unexpectedly as Vasserot
> The aimless ambidextrian was lighting
> A match between his great and second toe...

The quotation demonstrates both the characters' and the author's familiarity with modern poetry, and subtly fits in with Brown's continuing interest in carnival oddballs.

Halfway through *The Mind Thing* (1961), Doc Staunton quotes "a nonsense poem by Edward Lear," saying "The Owl and the Pussycat went to sea, in a beautiful pea green boat." And *The Lenient Beast*, Brown's 1956 novel of a mercy killer, sports a portion of a contemporary poem by Lawrence P. Spingarn as its epigraph.

Brown's next-to-last novel, *The Murderers*, finds him again including original poetry in the midst of a story about adultery and murder among members of the beat generation and their associates in Hollywood. Willy Griff narrates—he's a 27-year-old film actor who plots with the wife of a seat-cover magnate to kill him. Early in the book Willy buys a "paperback copy of a book of American ballads" and Brown quotes the misanthropic classic "Sam Hall":

Oh, my name it is Sam Hall, it is Sam Hall,
Yes, my name it is Sam Hall, it is Sam Hall,
Yes, my name it is Sam Hall, and I hate you one and all,
Yes, I hate you one and all, God damn your eyes.

Soon after, Willy attends a beatnik party, at which poet Smoky Conover reads his newest work, entitled "Pattern":

Oh, the warp and the woof
And the woofer and the tweeter
And the warp
warp
warp
woof woof woof WOW woof woof woof
warp
warp
warp
And the woofer   tweeter
woofer   tweeter
woofer tweeter
WOW
tweeter woofer
tweeter   woofer
tweeter   woofer
Oh, the tweeter and the woofer and the woof and the warp
And the warp and the woof and the woofer and the tweeter. (29)

This is at once a good example of bad beat poetry and a satire on the entire movement. It's also a pretty good pictograph that made me laugh while typing it! Like the midget's poetry in *The Dead Ringer*, it demonstrates aspects of the character and his milieu better than a page of straight narrative ever could. The beat elements continue through the novel; Willy later chats with Essie, "a beatchick" in black leotard who discusses "Ginsberg and the other beat poets" and asks Willy if he reads "the *Evergreen Review*" (39). Finally, after Willy is involved in the killing of a wino, he is reminded of a poem by Kenneth Patchen, "The Murder of Two Men By a Young Kid Wearing Lemon Colored Gloves." According to Willy, this poem consists of the word "Wait," repeated with various inflections over a jazz accompaniment, until finally "Now!" is spoken over a blare of instruments (73). Reference to this poem reflects on the scene in the novel and helps set the mood; it also recalls Brown's own "Scaramouche Sings of Love and Strums His Lute," which included both verses and stage directions.

* * *

Brown's use of poetry in his work thus falls into three categories: original poems, poems supposedly written by characters in his novels, and quotations from poems by other writers. Other than the two published in *American Poetry Magazine*, he never seems to have tried to circulate his own poetry, and for him it was a serious, personal expression. Yet the poet can be seen behind the writer in a number of short stories, and poetry plays a small but important role in several novels. Harry Altshuler wrote that "almost to the end Fred kept on with his poetry" (Letter to the author 24 Aug. 1988) and poetry seems to have been the one constant in a long and varied career. From *Fermented Ink* to the later poems of Armageddon, Brown explored his obsessions and developed his ability to create terse images and leaven them with humor and horror.

Brown's use of other poets' work enriches many of his novels and stories, and often adds an extra level to characters of a literary or scholarly bent. Some, like Doc Magus in *Madball*, quote poetry at will and make puns in their thoughts and speech based on quotations that are sometimes rather obscure. Others, like Willy Griff in *The Murderers*, are immersed in a world where poetry is often used as a daily reference. Brown's most frequent detective, Ed Hunter, begins his career with little interest in poetry (*The Dead Ringer*) but is able to quote and pun off of Keats in a novel appearing only 11 years later (*The Late Lamented*).

All in all, Brown's writing is heavily influenced by his reading in poetry, and he seems to have been serious about writing it, as well. An awareness of Brown's interest in poetry is not essential to enjoyment of his work, but it helps the reader gain an understanding of his overall intentions as a writer. Brown had a poetic side but was never pretentious; it is left to the careful reader to uncover it.

Chapter Six
Late Mystery Stories

After he completed *The Fabulous Clipjoint* in late 1944, Fredric Brown's writing career moved steadily in the direction of the novel, the form in which he would do the majority of his post-war writing. His marriage was ending; in 1947 he would divorce his first wife and in 1948 marry his second. His lifestyle was also changing—he went from family man to wandering author in these years.

The fiction market was changing, too. Detective pulps, the backbone of the popular fiction market since the 1930s, were beginning to die out; within a few years they would be replaced by digests and paperbacks. Consequently, the number of magazines was dwindling at the same time Brown was beginning to write novels and no longer needed to write story after story to survive.

The result of these changes was that Brown's short mystery output, which had been so great before 1944, slowed until it stopped completely in 1957. This is not to say that Brown didn't write short stories after 1944, he did; however, they were mostly science fiction or short-shorts, two types of fiction he had only touched on before 1945. Brown also wrote a number of stories that were later expanded to novel length; these will be discussed with the novels. The other 22 mystery stories Brown wrote between 1945 and 1957 are often distinguished by their uniqueness, and deserve discussion as a separate group.

Brown's first mystery story after *The Fabulous Clipjoint* was "Madman's Concerto," which was completed and mailed to Harry Altshuler on July 26, 1945. The 18,500-word story sold for $280 on March 18, 1946, and was published in the July 1946 *New Detective* as "The Song of the Dead." Echoes of the recently-ended war abound in this long tale of a pianist's flight from imagined madness, as Jan Baran lives through a frightening plot of concealment concocted by fugitive Nazi war criminal Reinhold Neumann.

The story begins as Jan returns home after a normal day to find his dog Blackie lying dead and poisoned in a corner of the kitchen. His neighbors insist that Jan played a strange song on the piano the night before and that Blackie howled, but he cannot remember this and fears his sanity is slipping from him. When Blackie returns the next day and Jan finds his bathrobe in the grave where he had buried the dog, his worries increase. Other odd events cause Jan to consider suicide and get very drunk. He finally learns that the doctor who came to see Blackie was actually Neumann, the Nazi, who had planned to assume Jan's identity to avoid capture and prosecution for war crimes. The story ends happily as Jan sells a score to Hollywood and resumes his courtship of his pretty neighbor.

Brown's stories about Nazis and espionage during the second world war were never his best, and "The Song of the Dead" is not much better. It's too long, and the mystery is farfetched—would a Nazi war criminal go to such extremes to assume the identity of a composer? The love interest falls flat due to a lack of character development on the part of Amanda Haley, Jan's neighbor, and the coincidences make the solution rather obvious. It seems Brown's heart just wasn't in this one.

As is often the case, though, what happens on the sidelines is more intriguing than what happens in the main part of this weak story. For instance, witness Jan's recollection of the London Blitz:

I had lived through the rape of a city, and it had begun as simply—with a faint drone, as of bees, in the sky. (*Madman's Holiday* 86)

Jan later remarks that he's an American citizen, "Belgian by Birth," who found himself a pianist with the London Philharmonic when the war broke out in 1939. Like Fredric Brown he tried to enlist but was rejected; unlike Brown, he spent a year in a hospital after being close to a bombing and came out "pretty much of a neurotic wreck" (88). This story is the only one in which Brown deals with the effects of the second world war on civilians after the war; it ties in with his wartime tales about young men working to help the war effort in various ways and growing involved with mysterious enemies.

The musical aspects of the story are also handled nicely. Various classical music pieces are mentioned, and one of the story's highlights occurs when Jan improvises a madman's concerto:

And for a while I sat there watching and listening while my hands played. Anything, I didn't care, just so Dave didn't talk.

I played the kind of notes that should come from bloody keys. I sent discord crashing after dissonance like the shrieks of the damned and changed, without modulation, into a soft padding up and down the keys that might have been the footsteps of a black dog, a thing that was monstrous because it had never been. Then again dissonant sounds and—well, it wasn't music, maybe. Then again maybe it was.

The music a madman would make, upon a blood-smeared keyboard. (109)

The story as a whole is interesting but flawed; Brown seems to be forcing the issue at times and the mystery just isn't interesting enough to justify the length.

Brown's next short mystery was "A Voice Behind Him," sent to Harry Altshuler on March 9, 1946, and sold for $125 on March 25, 1946. Published in the January 1947 *Mystery Book Magazine*, it is a short but extremely effective little tale with a carnival background. It begins with this anecdote, both chilling and ironically funny:

There is a lovely little horror story about the peasant who started through the haunted wood—the wood that was, people said, inhabited by devils who took any mortal who came their way. But the peasant thought, as he walked slowly along:

I am a good man and have done no wrong. If devils can harm me, then there isn't any justice.

A voice behind him said, "There isn't." (111)

The story that follows concerns Tony Grosz, The Great Raimondi, Human Cannonball with the Dunn and Weber Combined Shows carnival. Grosz sits in a bar thinking about the bitter fight he and his wife had that morning, knowing he must leave her. He leaves her a curt note, does his act one last time, then walks past his silent wife toward the train tracks intending to catch a freight. He sees her shadow behind him and recalls her words of that morning—"You leave me and I'll kill you!"—then sees her shadow's arm rise as if to stab him. He turns and stabs her instead, killing her, then heads for the tracks. He hears no train whistle, and realizes that he still has wax in his ears from his cannonball act and could not hear his wife's pleadings—she had no knife, but was imploring him not to go. Realizing his error, he steps onto the train tracks, his back to the onrushing train, to await his own death.

"A Voice Behind Him" is taut and powerful, told by the narrator as a cautionary tale to an applicant for the now-vacant job as The Great Raimondi. The opening anecdote raises the story to the level of myth or fairy tale and it is short enough (in contrast with "The Song of the Dead") to sustain a high level of tension throughout.

Brown's next short mystery, "Don't Look Behind You," is justifiably one of his most famous. It was published in the May 1947 issue of *Ellery Queen's Mystery Magazine* and is a landmark of narrative experimentation. The story begins with a direct address to the reader:

Just sit back and relax, now. Try to enjoy this; it's going to be the last story you ever read, or nearly the last. (*Carnival of Crime* 120)

The speaker is Justin Dean, a printer, but the reader doesn't know it yet, since he tells the first part of the story in the third person, as if it's about someone else. Dean is a meek employee of the Atlas Printing & Engraving Company in Springfield, Ohio, who is approached by Harley Prentice to print counterfeit five and ten dollar bills. Dean moves to New York, where the plan works for awhile, until Harley calls from Albany and tells him to dump the plates and burn the remaining bills.

Harley is murdered, and Dean is interrogated by the police and, though they "didn't use clubs or rubber hoses" (124), their harassment causes him apparently to go insane. He is put in a hospital, where he stays until he convinces his doctors that he should be released. Unfortunately, Dean now believes that Harley is alive, and allows himself to be tricked by friends of Harley's, who drive him as far south as the Carolinas and torture him to make him reveal the location of the plates. Finally, they abandon him deep in a swamp. He awakes completely insane and converses with a vision of Harley, who leads him safely out of the swamp. He kills a farm woman, then a man, and goes on the road, killing anyone who stands in his way and taking instructions from "Harley." His goal: to find and kill the men who tortured him. But in the meantime, for fun, he tells the reader about a bet he made with Harley that he could tell a man he was going to kill him with a knife, tell him why and when, and succeed. The intended victim is the reader—this story has been specially bound in this copy of the book to alert the reader, and it ends on this chilling note:

Go on, just a few seconds or minutes, thinking this is just another story. Don't look behind you. Don't believe this—*until you feel the knife.* (132)

"Don't Look Behind You" is one of Brown's most brilliant stories. Its narrative style is highly unusual and complex, fitting neatly into the world of crime and psychopathy that infuses the tale. The narrator threatens the reader from the start, and tells us about Justin Dean, making sure we understand how dangerous he is before revealing that he is actually Dean himself. This direct address to the reader has appeared in Brown's stories before, but this is the first time the reader is directly involved in the narrative. The idea that Dean is a printer and has specially prepared the reader's edition of the book is unnerving; Brown (through his narrator) is so insistent about it that the reader is compelled to wonder—if even for a moment—whether it might be true.

Dean drifts into insanity midway through the story, though he never realizes it and, since he's the narrator, it is left to the reader to infer. Dean is smart enough to realize that he must be careful around other people, especially in regard to his vision of Harley, and this is a complex bit of psychology that rounds out the character and points in a direction Brown would often take in his later work. Dean is also rather autobiographical: he is 35 and Brown was about 40; he also, like Brown, "had to wear thick glasses because he'd worn out his eyes doing fine printing and engraving" (120). In addition, Dean mentions that he's "writing this directly on a linotype, late at night in the shop where I'm working days" (131). He says his boss gave him permission, as long as he'd melt the type metal back after he was done. This sounds suspiciously like Fredric Brown, who printed his book of poetry, *Fermented Ink*, under the same arrangements while working at a print shop in the early 1930s.

"Don't Look Behind You" finds Brown at the top of his form, and it is a perfect short story because it would not succeed in any other form, such as the novel. It has often been mentioned fondly by writers in their discussions of Brown, and is a favorite for reprinting.

Brown's next short mystery, "Miss Darkness," is much gentler but also quite effective. It was sent to Harry Altshuler on February 11, 1947, and sold for $100 on June 19, 1947, to be published in the 1947 issue of *Avon Detective Mysteries* (#3). Here, a straight, third-person narration is used, and rather than emphasizing any one character, Brown creates an ensemble by focusing on the various residents of a boarding house.

The story begins as Mary Westerman rents a room in Mrs. Prandell's rooming house. The nosy tenants grow suspicious of her because her room is always dark and nickname her "Miss Darkness." Soon they begin to suspect her of having driven the getaway car in a bank robbery that occurred the day she moved in. One day police Captain Thorber arrives, looking for Melissa Carey, the bank teller who was the only witness to the robbery. Co-boarder Walter Barry realizes Carey is Miss Darkness and disarms Thorber, who's actually one of the bank robbers. Mary, it turns out, was broke and too proud to borrow money for a light bulb!

"Miss Darkness" is a light, gentle mystery, much different in tone from "Don't Look Behind You" but still quite good. The story has a mysteriously warm feeling to it, and the happy ending is gratifying.

Fredric Brown's first short mystery in 1948 was "I'll Cut Your Throat Again, Kathleen," which was actually completed and sent to Harry Altshuler on January 21, 1947, and sold on February 21, 1947, for $140. It was published in the Winter 1948 *Mystery Book Magazine*, and probably appeared at the very start of 1948, making it one of his first stories to be published that year. It is brilliantly done.

As the story opens, narrator Johnny Marlin is an inmate in a sanitarium, having slit his wife's throat and his own wrists and then lost his memory. He manages to win a discharge, and eventually returns home to meet his wife, who survived. As they dance, he regains his memory: her brother slit her throat and she cut Johnny's wrists in order to end his career as a top jazz saxophonist and have him as her "kept man." Johnny flies into a rage and slits her throat—for good this time.

Johnny narrates this tale in a manner tough and sure. He's a top jazzman who's lost his livelihood, and Brown conveys the tactile sensation of useless fingers on a saxophone player nicely: "for playing sax and clarinet they were about as good as hands of bananas" (*Carnival of Crime* 146). Comparison is also made between the blue mirror in back of the bar where Johnny stops on his way home and sees his reflection as not "a bad-looking guy" (155). and the clear mirror in his own apartment, which causes him to reflect that "There wasn't any reason in that mirror why anyone should love me the way my wife must" (159). Johnny's mind is the focus of "I'll Cut Your Throat Again, Kathleen," and jazz is used in a number of ways to propel the story along: his devotion to his career precipitated Kathy's act, he is haunted by his lost talent, he is frustrated by music he hears on a jukebox, and a classic blues song ("St. James Infirmary") triggers his recall. The words of that song spur him on to kill his wife, yet the words are in his mind only—the recording that plays is an instrumental.

Johnny Marlin is a well developed character, whose life and thoughts we know from his conversations with others. His final argument with his wife is painful—perhaps Brown's own broken marriage, which he would flee not long after this story was published, gave added energy to this portrait of a doomed relationship. In any case, "I'll Cut Your Throat Again, Kathleen" is one of his best suspense stories.

"The Four Blind Men" (*Adventure* September 1948) is set in and around the Harbin-Wilson Circus. It is narrated by a man named Fred, who begins by telling Cap Gurney, a policeman, the old story about the four blind men trying to guess what an elephant was like by touching its various parts. Later, when Gurney is called to investigate the shooting death of Investigator Sopronowicz, he solves the case by recalling Fred's tale. It seems that three shots were heard, but that only one killed the man. By recalling the anecdote, Gurney realizes that the ringmaster had been charged by an elephant, fired twice in the air in an attempt to scare it off, and fired the third into his own head, thinking that a better death than being trampled underfoot. Fred reminds Gurney that the elephant wasn't the point of his story, to which Gurney replies: "But just the same, it *was* an elephant."

This brief tale of violent death with a circus background recalls "A Voice Behind Him" in the way it claims to use an old tale (or fragment of a tale) as a jumping off point. The story is a fairly straight mystery other than this, but its circus background makes it interesting in light of Brown's considerable interest in carney life.

Brown's next short mystery is a tour de force that synthesizes themes he had been working with for several years. "The Laughing Butcher" was completed and sent to Harry Altshuler on July 27, 1947; it sold for $50 in less than a week, on August 1, 1947, and was published in the Fall 1948 issue of *Mystery Book Magazine*. The story is told in a frame, as are many of Brown's stories in this period. The narrator is

Bill, a Chicago policeman. As he, his wife, and her brother play cribbage, he sees a story in the *Sun* about "the funeral of a dwarf downstate, in Corbyville" (*Carnival of Crime* 164), and recalls his honeymoon of five years before when he and his wife stopped in Corbyville and met Len Wilson and his beautiful wife, Dorothy. They learned that the town was peopled by ex-circus employees and, while Kathy played chess with Joe Laska, a dwarf who owned a luncheonette in town, Bill witnessed a confrontation between Gerhard Kramer, a massive butcher who pretended to dabble in black magic and lusted after Dorothy, and Len, who had a weak heart. Joe believed that Gerhard was trying to excite Len so that he'd die of a heart attack and leave Dorothy unprotected.

Bill remembers the rest of his honeymoon fondly—he and Kathy drove down to New Orleans, then passed through Metropolis on the way back, where they bought a paper and read about the "Corbyville Horror." It seems Len was found dead in the middle of a snow-covered field, with two sets of footprints leading to the body but none going back. The townspeople decided his death was due to Gerhard's black magic and lynched the butcher.

On the drive back to Chicago Bill solved the case: Len ran into the field with Joe, the dwarf, on his back, causing his own death of a stress-induced heart attack and throwing suspicion on Gerhard. Joe then put on Len's shoes and walked out backwards!

Many of the elements of Fredric Brown's best work mesh in "The Laughing Butcher," and the flashback and framing story dovetail nicely at the end to reveal the mystery's solution. The technique of having a character tell the story to a friend works well (as it did in "A Voice Behind Him") by allowing Brown to comment on the events without using an interfering authorial voice. The concept of Corbyville—a town made up entirely of ex-circus employees—lets Brown use the characters and quirks of the circus in a setting with more breathing room; it also provides a way for Bill and Kathy to become involved with the typically close-knit circus folk. The dwarf, Joe, recalls Lon Staffold in *The Dead Ringer*, but is more sympathetic. The Chicago setting recalls *The Fabulous Clipjoint*, and the placement of Corbyville in southern Ohio prefigures the setting of *The Bloody Moonlight*. Bill's description of Corbyville at first sight is both lyrical and ominous:

I pointed to the view through the windshield and down the hill into the valley, bright green and muddy brown from the recent rains. And with a little village at the bottom of it—three score or so of houses huddled together like frightened sheep. (166-67)

Bill's wife, Kathy, is an interesting character. She plays chess, has a master's degree, and gave up teaching to marry Bill, a policeman. She is beaten by a "knight's gambit" when she plays Joe, and Bill compares this strategy of sacrifice to Len's self-sacrifice; both moves are made in order to protect someone else. The scene between Len and Gerhard in front of the butcher shop is described in pantomime, because Bill watches it from the luncheonette across the street. It's quite effective, casting a spell of silence over the proceedings that remains unbroken until Bill, Kathy, and Joe run over to break the tension.

Finally, although this story was written in 1947, the central events would have occurred five years earlier, in 1942, when a big, laughing German butcher named Gerhard Kramer would have been an easy villain and a target for lynching in a nation that had just declared war on Germany.

In all, "The Laughing Butcher" is a brilliant story, showing Brown at the height of his powers as a writer of short mysteries. A different type of story, "If Looks Could Kill," followed next, in the October 1948 *Detective Tales*. This is a short, darkly humorous tale about Jim Greeley, a practical joke salesman whose jokes finally backfire on him. Brown tells the story with third-person narration to avoid imparting any sympathy to Greeley, and it is really a series of incidents strung together to lead to the final, gruesome twist. Titled "The Joke" in its reprintings, the story is powerful and ironic, a worthy addition to Brown's late 1940s short mystery work.

Another short tale, "Cry Silence," appeared in the fall of 1948, in the November 1948 *Black Mask*. Brown once again begins by having his narrator refer to an old story; this time, it's "that old silly argument about sound. If a tree falls deep in the forest where there is no one to hear, is its fall silent?" (*Carnival of Crime* 191). The narrator is not really involved in the central action of this story, as he was in "The Laughing Butcher." Here, he describes an evening when he sat in a railroad station and the station agent told him about Bill Meyers, a large man who sat quietly in the station as if deaf. The narrator learned that Bill killed his wife and her lover by locking them in his smokehouse and then claiming deafness and thus ignorance of their screams as they burned alive. Although he was cleared of the crime, the agent believed he was guilty, and accused him loudly and at length, hoping the constant railing would cause Bill to hang himself. Shaken, the narrator boarded his train and the story ends.

In "Cry Silence," the crime of murder is less important than the ethical question subtly raised: is the agent's vengeance justified? is it working? is Bill really deaf? and, if not, why does he pretend to be and why does he keep coming back for more abuse? The narrator, standing in for the author, offers very little in the way of value judgments, leaving it up to the reader to ponder this interesting situation.

Published in the November 1948 *Detective Tales*, Brown's next mystery story, "Red-Hot and Hunted," seems more like a story he would have written about five years before; perhaps he held on to it and published it in 1948, or perhaps it was sold earlier and not published until this date. In any case, the story follows Wayne Dixon, an actor, who tells Adrian Carr, a producer, that he's just killed his wife. Much is made of the suspicion that Wayne's allegation is part of an elaborate audition for a role in a new play, but a complicated and rather silly plot shows that his wife killed herself in error while trying to kill Wayne! The theatrical background is nicely done and the story has a good New York City feeling to it, but it is hardly up to the quality of the majority of Brown's late 1940s work.

Brown's first short mystery published in 1949 is the cleverly-titled "This Way Out" (*Dime Mystery* February 1949). The story follows Detective-Sergeant Weston's investigation of the death by razor of businessman John Carey, who killed himself in a hotel room three months after the death of his wife and son. Weston concludes that Carey's death was a suicide after interviewing his partner, Dave Greene.

As in "Don't Look Behind You," Brown experiments with narrative technique here—he tells the story by both the straight narration of Weston's investigation and the re-creation of Carey's mental state following his family's death. Through these thoughts, the reader learns that Carey had been tortured by voices telling him to kill himself. Greene then tells Weston two important facts: that he stood to receive a large insurance payment after Carey's death, and that he once had a ventriloquist act in vaudeville. By piecing together these bits of information, the reader may conclude that Greene drove Carey to suicide; however, Greene will never be convicted because no one in the world of the story will ever know about the voices that showed Carey the "way out." The morality of this story is ambiguous and chilling—the reader is powerless to right a terrible wrong that is placed before him.

On a lighter note, Brown followed "This Way Out" with "Murder and Matilda," published in the summer 1949 *Mystery Book Magazine*. Narrated by Sheriff Andy, it concerns a cover-up and identity switch by the Pearce brothers in order to collect on an insurance policy. Andy's deputy is a woman, Matilda Jones, and it is she who plays a big part in solving the mystery. The story is slight but entertaining, clearly tossed off by Brown in between bigger things.

In July 1949, Brown published "Last Curtain" in *New Detective*; this was later adapted for television's *Alfred Hitchcock Presents*, starring Claude Rains. The story is short and wonderful. Sir Charles Hanover Gresham, an aged actor, sits drunk in a bar reading *Stagecraft*, a thinly-veiled version of *Billboard*. He sees an announcement for a new play, *The Perfect Crime*, by Wayne Campbell, a playwright he has been blackmailing for years. Gresham calls on Wayne to insist he be given a part in the new play, only to be told he must audition for Nick Corianos, the gambling boss backing the show. Gresham recites the play's blackmailer's speech for Nick, who pulls a gun as Gresham realizes he's been tricked into speaking the truth. Before Nick kills him he asks permission to recite a speech from *Macbeth*. He does so and then dies!

"Last Curtain" progresses inexorably toward its ironic conclusion, and Gresham (a knighted actor) is a tragic hero whose desire to play *Macbeth* (a play actors traditionally fear due to the bad ends of many who have performed it) is fulfilled at his dying hour, as he falls victim to a plot of revenge. Shakespearean quotes fly fast and loose, and both actor and playwright recite them to demonstrate their good breeding. Brown mixes classic literature and modern crime situations to great effect, and his ability to use works of Shakespeare and other poets helps lift stories like this one above standard mystery fare.

A tough short story followed the next month in the August 1949 *Dime Mystery*: "Each Night He Died." Brown uses a framing device to comment ironically on the story of Dana Kiessling, whose thoughts tell the reader of his fear of the electric chair he faces for the murder of his selfish brother. Dana lies in his cell, face down on his cot and sobbing, not hearing the guards outside. In the story's frame they reveal that he's in an insane asylum and not on death row, and that he went mad before his trial ever began. He believes that he was sentenced to death and has been reliving the night before execution for six years.

"Each Night He Died" is essentially a mood piece with a twist; Brown's writing concentrates on the details of execution and on Dana's all-consuming fear. Albert Camus's *The Stranger* is directly recalled at one point in Kiessling's thoughts, and it is possible that Brown, an atheist/agnostic, was thinking of French existentialist philosophy when he wrote these two passages:

And after pain, the eternal night of death. He was afraid of that, too; he didn't want to die. He was afraid to die.

The fear of that never-ending *nothingness* gripped him so hard that he bit the pillow between his teeth to keep from crying out. He'd always been afraid of dying. (*Carnival of Crime* 198)

He wrenched his mind back to George. Why did they, people, make such a horrible thing of killing one's own brother? Why did they think it worse than killing a stranger? (200)

The story of Dana Kiesling is tough, relentless, and no fun. Brown would not publish many more short stories like it.

"The Cat from Siam" (*Popular Detective* September 1949) is long and undistinguished; it reads like a story he would have written for the pulps in about 1942 and has little to recommend it. "The House of Fear" (*New Detective* September 1949) is better but still light—an entertaining, brief mystery involving a bank teller and his clever wife who get involved with an embezzler.

From the time he completed *The Fabulous Clipjoint* and the end of the decade, Fredric Brown wrote and published only 16 short mystery stories that were not connected with novels. This represented a major change in the form in which he did his work; 16 stories had been the average output of a few months' time in busy years like 1941 and 1942. By 1950, however, Brown had lost interest in writing short mysteries almost entirely, and published only six such stories that were not related to novels in the rest of his career, with none at all appearing after 1957.

The two 1950 stories are not bad. "Death and Nine Lives" (*Black Book Detective* Spring 1950) is similar to "The House of Fear" in that its narrator is an investigator on the trail of an embezzler and murderer named Calvin E. Vernal. The story is short and entertaining, gaining great benefit from Jerry Jackson's witty narration. He chats with his cat Taffy and interprets her looks as various responses. There's lots of action and fun here; it's about the last of Brown's mystery stories to be written in classic pulp style.

"The Nose of Don Aristide" (*Two Detective Mystery Novels* Summer 1950) is straight comedy with a mystery theme—its hero is a famous French detective whose sensitive nose and brilliant methods of detection are widely respected, even though he fails utterly in solving the crime at hand. The story is narrated by a French policeman who tells it to an American detective applying for a job on the Rio de Aires police force. The narrator recalls the great Don Aristide, who worked on a single case for them. The case involved a quarter-inch piece of microfilm hidden somewhere at the studios of the Panamera Moving Picture Company; the police knew that Senora de Rodriguez was a spy, and Don Aristide visited her and had her provide him with a disguise, including shaving his mustache, so he could search the studio. He later asked her to replace his mustache with one of her own making, after telling her an army was coming to search the studio. Don Aristide then arrested her, convinced that she'd hidden the microfilm in his mustache. It mattered little that the microfilm was finally found cemented to the Senora's toenail. The French detective's methods were brilliant. So brilliant, in fact, that he was hired by the studio to write and direct movies!

"The Nose of Don Aristide" is a comedy, more notable for its satire of the idea of the "master sleuth" than for its mystery.

Brown did not publish another short mystery story until June 1953, when "Witness in the Dark" appeared in *New Detective*. A longer version of the story, entitled "The Cat and the Riddle," was discovered in Brown's files in 1990 and published in *The Pickled Punks* collection. The story is not one of Brown's best, and seems to have been written in order to work out an impossible situation: why would a stray bullet have traces of blood, silk, and feathers on it, unless it passed through a rooster wearing silk pajamas? A police procedural for the most part, "Witness in the Dark" is enlivened by its humor and by the interplay between police detective/narrator George Hearn and his wife, Marge, who trade quips about a classic quotation from British literature while discussing the crime at hand. The length of the unpublished version suggests that *New Detective* cut Brown's story severely; it is a telling comment on its quality that not much was lost.

After this series of rather undistinguished short mystery stories that appeared while Brown's creativity was flowering in the novel and with science fiction, "The Little Lamb" appeared in the August 1953 *Manhunt*. It is brilliant and chilling, hitting the reader on a variety of levels and adding to other works of Brown's by comparison.

The story begins as artist Wayne Gray grows increasingly anxious when his wife Lambeth ("Lamb") hasn't arrived home by 8:00 p.m. When she's not home by nine he sets out on foot toward town, without finding her along the way. He visits the Waverly Inn, a bar, where the jukebox blares loudly and no one admits to having seen Lamb. He pulls the plug on the jukebox so that he can telephone another bar and hears someone say "Maybe at Hans's." Wayne's suspicions grow when Charlie and Eve Chandler quickly leave the bar.

Wayne walks home and sulks awhile, then grabs his gun and heads for Hans's house. He searches the house while Hans fixes drinks and finds a locked closet. Hans shakes as Wayne shoots off the lock. Wayne opens the door and sees Lamb, naked, then shoots Hans six times.

The naked Lamb in the closet is only a painting, though, and Wayne cuts it from its frame and walks home. As he walks, he hears Lamb's voice in his mind reminding him that he had killed her that afternoon when she told him of her affair with Hans.

"The Little Lamb" is a fine story of psychological suspense, using art and artists to delve into an insane mind. Wayne narrates, beginning calmly but growing more and more paranoid until it is finally revealed that he is insane. His artistic references, to both painters and poets, give the reader clues to his mental state. He mentions Van Gogh's *The Starry Sky* and says "it looked frightening, but then again he was crazy when he did it" (*And the Gods Laughed* 384). He recalls William Blake's "Little lamb, who made thee?" and thinks it has an unintended obscene connotation. He also quotes T.S. Eliot's "The Love Song of J. Alfred Prufrock" and thinks:

Damn Eliot, I thought; the man saw too deeply. The useless striving of the wasteland for something a man can touch but never have, the shaking of a dead geranium. As a madman. (392)

Beyond the suspense, beyond the mystery, "The Little Lamb" also asks questions about art and the artistic temperament. Wayne at one point compares his paintings to Hans's; Hans's paintings look like photographs while Wayne's are abstract—objects are seen and filtered through his perceptions. At one point he tells Hans, "Outdoors is in your mind" (393) when Hans remarks that Wayne paints outdoors subjects. To Wayne, the only valid art is that which is filtered through the mind— its creations are "truer" than representational attempts at recreating reality.

It would be a serious misreading of "The Little Lamb" to see Wayne Gray as Fredric Brown and Wayne's opinions about art as Brown's. Brown examined the insane mind in many of his works, including this one, and here he is putting forth one side of the argument between representational and abstract painting, between naturalistic or realistic fiction and the more transcendental sorts of Romantic poetry. Brown's knowledge of art and literature is showcased in this story, and it is one of many tools he uses to masterful effect.

"The Little Lamb" makes much of its setting, in a small southwestern town and the hills surrounding it. At the time it was written, Brown had spent several years in New Mexico, and may have just moved to a then still very southwestern southern California. His next published short mystery story has a similar setting, in the small town of Tesqua, New Mexico, but is much less harrowing.

"Premiere of Murder" (*The Saint Detective Magazine* May 1955) has the feeling of a pulp story (it begins, "The first shot woke Delaney"), and is very engaging due to good characters, an unusual setting, and a likeable plot. It concerns the events in Tesqua, New Mexico, where Delaney is the town marshal. During a stage show preceding the midnight premiere of *Carnival of Death*, a movie written by Delaney's friend Lew Godey, Toni "Luscious Lush" Lavalle shoots and kills her co-star and fiancee, Dake Correlli, with bullets that should have been blanks. Delaney takes the cast to La Fonda de Tesqua, a bar, to conduct his investigation, but he's unable to determine who put the bullets in the murder weapon. Eventually, he deduces that the movie's director, Bill Wiley, is the guilty party, having been blackmailed by Dake.

The novel's setting recalls the New Mexico of *The Far Cry*, where Fred and Beth Brown lived from 1949-51. The movie is set in a carnival, and the stage show that precedes it shares this milieu. "Premiere of

Murder" appears to be a story that Brown tossed off, probably between novels—it's entertaining and shares many of his favorite motifs, but it is of little consequence.

Brown's last published short mystery story—other than those tied to novels—was "Murder Set to Music," in the January 1957 *Saint Detective Magazine*. It is a lot of fun, and it is perhaps the first appearance of "hipsters" in the author's work—the beat generation would have some influence on later writing like *The Murderers* and "The Missing Actor," the last Ed and Am Hunter story.

The tale is told by Ralph Oliver, a musician, who runs a used car lot with his old friend Danny Bushman. Ralph goes to pick up Danny, as they plan to see Tommy Drum's combo play that night at the Casanova Club. He finds Danny badly beaten and claiming that his assailant was a large, masked man. Ralph sees Danny safely to the hospital, then goes to the show.

The next night, saxophone player Mick O'Neill is found beaten to death in his motel room and Ralph agrees to take his place in the combo. After plenty of twists and turns Danny is shot and killed, and it is revealed that he had heavy gambling debts and resisted an arrangement to allow the used car lot to be used to unload stolen cars.

Again recalling Brown's better pulp stories, "Murder Set to Music" is fun to read and complicated enough to qualify as a good mystery. It has a jazz background, and its themes are music and trust—the reader must decide for himself whether Ralph's inability to prevent Danny's death was subconsciously a way to make a play for Danny's wife Doris, whom Ralph once loved. The story is good and fairly long; the fact that Brown didn't turn it into a novel is surprising, and possibly due only to its lack of unique features.

So ended one phase of Fredric Brown's career as a writer. He had made a name for himself in the early 1940s by churning out dozens and dozens of mystery stories for a great variety of pulp magazines, and this training had both bolstered his income and let him develop a style all his own. By the mid-1940s, detective pulps were dying out, and the great success of Brown's first novel made him take a different direction with his writing. Some of his greatest short mystery stories were written in 1947-48, but by 1949 he had clearly lost interest in the form. He only published a few short mystery stories after 1950, and none at all after 1957.

But this is not to say that his writing as a whole declined along with the decline of his interest in the short mystery. In fact, the opposite is true: he nurtured an interest in the quickly growing sub-genre of science fiction and became known as the master of the ironic "short-short," stories a page or two long that end with a twist. Of course, Brown also wrote a large number of mystery novels—including seven in the Ed and Am Hunter series—and it is in this direction that his mysterious and suspenseful tendencies flowed in the latter two decades of his writing career.

Chapter Seven
Novel Directions

After *The Dead Ringer* and the virtual end of his first marriage, Fredric Brown began branching out with the first of his novels to feature characters other than the nephew-uncle detective team of Ed and Am Hunter. For *Murder Can Be Fun*, published by Dutton in October 1948 but written in 1947, Brown returned to a story he had written in 1941 and published in the October 1942 issue of *Detective Story Magazine*, "The Santa Claus Murders." The difference between the story, which was Brown's longest piece of fiction prior to *The Fabulous Clipjoint*, and the novel vividly demonstrates the growth of Brown's writing abilities during the 1940s.

Murder Can Be Fun begins with a gimmick, as a man in a Santa Claus suit walks into the office of radio executive Arthur D. Dineen and murders him. Bill Tracy reads of the murder in the newspaper and finds it "*damnably* interesting" (5), especially since he worked for Dineen and wrote a script that spelled out the exact details of the murder method before it happened. The problem is that he had not shown the script to anyone!

Tracy is also the writer of *Millie's Millions*, a popular radio soap opera in which the heroine is regularly subjected to awful situations. Humorous details of the radio show intertwine with Tracy's concern over the possibility of his role in the murder until another man is killed; Frank Hrdlicka, the janitor in the building where Tracy lives, is murdered and stuffed in the building's furnace. Unfortunately for Tracy, this method follows the script of another of the unproduced shows for his radio series called *Murder Can Be Fun*!

The police are informed, and Tracy acts as an unofficial private detective looking to clear his own conscience, figuring that if he can determine who read his scripts he will know who murdered the two men. After a long subplot involving a pretty secretary named Dotty whom

Tracy trains to write scripts for *Millie's Millions*, his deductions lead him
to investigate the Dineen house, where he is nearly run over as the killer
drives away. In the house he finds a police officer killed by another
method he had cooked up for one of his scripts. The killer turns out to be
Dick Kreburn, one of the stars of *Millie's Millions*, who killed a jeweler
for diamonds and learned they'd been hidden in a dog collar mailed to
Dineen for his dog, Rex. The murders were part of an elaborate cover-
up, and he had the bright idea of using Tracy's inventive murder
methods when he got a look at one of the scripts without Tracy's
knowledge one day.

The plot of *Murder Can Be Fun* is not easy to summarize so
briefly, and it can only be done by omitting much of what makes the
novel so enjoyable. Tracy's dreams, for instance. In his early short
stories, Brown used the occasional dream sequence to good effect, and
Ed Hunter's dream of his sister in *The Fabulous Clipjoint* is overtly
sexual and speaks volumes about the psychological war waging in his
mind.

Chapter nine of *Murder Can Be Fun* begins with one of Tracy's
dreams, which he has after passing out in an alcoholic stupor. The dream
is so clever and funny that a portion of it must be reproduced:

They shouldn't have happened to a dog, those dreams. They didn't; they
happened to Tracy.

The pink cloud, with a very blonde and very dimpled and very decollete
Dotty enshrined upon it, and Tracy trying to climb up to her and the little green
devil pushing him back with a very sharp overgrown salad fork, screaming,
"Not without the General's permission. Not without the General's permission."

And, in the way of dreams, Tracy's mind asking the question without his
lips saying it, and the imp shouting, "Motors, you fool, General Motors. You've
got to get the General's permission to get on this program, for he's the sponsor,
and you can't be a professional."

"A professional what?" Tracy wondered, and the imp yelled, "A
professional anything. This is an amateur hour and you can't get up there if
you're a professional." And he jerked a thumb at the decollete Dotty behind
him. "Know what *she* is? This is an amateur hour, and she's an *amateur houri!*"

And the little green devil must have dropped the fork, for there he was
holding up a big placard that read LAUGHTER—only Tracy didn't laugh. (99-
100)

The idea that dreams could be interpreted according to certain guidelines was making inroads into the American popular consciousness in the 1940s, and Brown latched onto this to enrich his novels and have fun with his characters. This dream of Bill Tracy's mixes his desire for the stenographer, Dotty, with his concerns about radio advertising, and throws in a great pun for good measure. It continues for another two pages, and by the end Tracy envisions all of the novel's characters as pieces in a giant chess game. He had played chess with the janitor, Frank Hrdlicka, not long before he was murdered, and the metaphor is an apt one for this novel in which unseen figures seem to control the events beyond all reason.

Another of the controlling forces in the novel is alcohol—the characters drink an awful lot of it and it affects their abilities to function. Tracy gets drunk or drinks in eleven of the novel's 14 chapters and is recovering in the other three! Brown was known for his drinking, and the characters in his novels often spend part of their time in bars, but I don't think anyone ever approaches the sheer ability to consume liquor and still function that Bill Tracy shows in *Murder Can Be Fun*. Lawrence Block, in his introduction to the 1987 collection, *The Case of the Dancing Sandwiches*, remarks that he once read *Murder Can Be Fun* and tried to pace Tracy, drink for drink:

> One night I brought home *Murder Can Be Fun* and bottle of Jim Beam. I hadn't quite planned it that way, but whenever the lead character took a drink, so did I. Thinking back on it, it's a miracle I lived to tell the tale. (7)

Another bright spot in the novel has to do with Brown's satire of the radio business. Tracy writes for the soap opera *Millie's Millions* and hates it; he also hates the control wielded by advertisers, as his dream shows! At the novel's end he quits his job as a scriptwriter, gives up drinking (except for beer, suggesting that his heavy drinking was due to disgust with his job), and proposes to Millie, who helped him solve the murders. He tells his friend at the *Blade* that he'll be returning the next night to write for the newspaper, clearly a more "pure" and respectable form of writing in Tracy's (and thus Fredric Brown's?) eyes.

The last aspect of *Murder Can Be Fun* worthy of note is its use of Lewis Carroll's *Alice in Wonderland* and *Through the Looking Glass*. On numerous occasions Tracy thinks of situations from these books, and the chess game played in *Through the Looking Glass* is never far from his mind as he tries to sort out the events and crimes. Brown's use of these works would wait another few years to flower fully, however, in *Night of the Jabberwock*.

Murder Can Be Fun is almost exactly twice as long as the story upon which it is based, "The Santa Claus Murders," and it uses the added length to flesh out the story in interesting ways. Both story and novel begin the same way, and both are told in the third person by an omniscient narrator who only refers to himself as "I." Chapter two of the story is expanded to fill two chapters in the novel by adding some discussion about detective stories and the radio business, and chapter five of the novel is mostly new, including the character of Stan Hrdlicka, the bartender/brother of the murdered janitor. All references to Lewis Carroll's works are new in the novel, as are the references to chess and the dream sequences. "The Santa Claus Murders" is basically a straight crime story, a very fitting novelette for a 1942 pulp. The additions Brown made when expanding it to novel length did not change the plot significantly, yet they rendered it more complex and mysterious than the original. *Murder Can Be Fun* does not entirely shed its pulp origins, and it thus relies more on plotting and invention than Brown's first two novels, *The Fabulous Clipjoint* and *The Dead Ringer*, which are more character studies than anything else. It is a complete and creative rewrite, and the additions made during expansion show where Fredric Brown's interests were leaning in 1947.

The reviews of *Murder Can Be Fun* were positive—Brown was awarded the Edgar for *The Fabulous Clipjoint* the month this novel was published, and the wave of popular acclaim may have influenced its reception. Issac Anderson, writing in The New York *Times* Book Review, summarizes the complex plot quite neatly and concludes, "Unless our memory is at fault, this is by far the best thing that Frederick [sic] Brown has done up to this time. It bids fair to be the most ingeniously plotted detective story of the year." *The Saturday Review of Literature* thought it "fair," and *The New Yorker*'s critic called the novel "Fast and funny," while *Kirkus Reviews* remarked, "So-so humor and a fair to middling job." Curiously, despite the strong New York *Times* and *New Yorker* reviews, *Murder Can Be Fun* has been barely discussed in the 40-plus years since its publication. Newton Baird dismisses it as a "lesser work" ("Fredric Brown" 208) and, other than a paperback reprint in 1949 (with the much poorer title, *A Plot for Murder*), it didn't see the light of day until mystery reprinters Carroll & Graf brought it out in paperback under the original title for Christmas 1989. And even that edition went unnoticed, save for a small note in the New York *Times* Book Review that quoted Issac Anderson's 1948 review.

The novel is not Brown's best, but it certainly rewards the reader with a lot of entertainment, humor, and a clever plot. After completing *Murder Can Be Fun*, Brown wrote the science fiction classic *What Mad Universe* and *The Bloody Moonlight* before embarking on one of his greatest works, *The Screaming Mimi*.

I've read *The Screaming Mimi* a few times, and it's one of the reasons I developed an interest in Fredric Brown. Each time I read it it's a different novel, but I remain convinced of its fundamental brilliance. If *The Fabulous Clipjoint* sabotaged the classic form of the private detective novel, *The Screaming Mimi* takes the mystery thriller in new and frightening directions. As the novel opens, we meet William Sweeney, the "hero," who is a wino sitting on a park bench with his friend God, unable to sleep. Brown begins in a roundabout way, using the raconteur style he had perfected in short mysteries like "The Laughing Butcher":

> You can never tell what a drunken Irishman will do. You can make a flying guess; you can make a lot of flying guesses.
>
> You can list them in their order of probability. The likely ones are easy: He might go after another drink, start a fight, make a speech, take a train...You can work down the list of possibilities; he might buy some green paint, chop down a maple tree, do a fan dance, sing "God Save the King," steal an oboe...You can work on down and down to things that get less and less likely, and eventually you might hit the rock bottom of improbability: He might make a resolution and stick to it.
>
> I know that that's incredible, but it happened. A guy named Sweeney did it, once, in Chicago. He made a resolution, and he had to wade through blood and black coffee to keep it, but he kept it. Maybe, by most people's standards, it wasn't a good resolution, but that's aside from the point. The point is that it really happened. (7)

Brown immediately qualifies these statements by noting that "truth is an elusive thing...seldom that simple" (7). Sweeney is the uninvolved party who becomes involved in horror seemingly by accident when he walks several blocks and witnesses a strange scene: a crowd is gathered outside the glass door of an apartment building, where a vicious dog protects a beautiful blonde who lies face down on the floor. Police crease the dog with a bullet after the girl staggers to her feet and the dog tears her dress off—they see that she's been cut by a knife. Sweeney walks back to the park and vows to sleep with the girl.

This first chapter is powerful, and Brown writes beautifully. He echoes Theodore Dreiser early on as he sets the time: "Two o'clock of a summer night...." (8) recalls the opening line of *An American Tragedy* ("Dusk—of a summer night..." [19]), and *The Screaming Mimi* is strangely Dreiserian in the way it deals with the big city (Chicago) and the lives of those who are drawn along by a seemingly chaotic fate within its borders. The streets of Chicago vibrate through this novel, and it becomes immediately clear that Brown knows them intimately. I've always been fascinated by Sweeney's walk in chapter one; he begins at Bughouse Square, which is actually the park behind Chicago's Newberry Library, and makes a big circle by walking along various streets that can be followed on a street map. Even the building in front of which he stops can be pinpointed: it's on North State Street, between Huron and Chicago Avenues. This precise detailing of setting demonstrates Brown's intimate knowledge of Chicago (which is also the location of the Hunters' office and most of the action in their cases), and it's even more impressive because he wrote the book in New York City in the winter of early 1948.

Sweeney is the other major character established right away (after Chicago). We learn a lot about Sweeney. He's an Irishman. He's a drunk. He worked for the *Blade* as recently as three weeks ago but is now to the point where he sleeps on park benches. He knows his way around Chicago. He hasn't changed clothes in a week. He hates everybody, especially himself. When Brown writes "The Great Sweeney Walking Across the Night" (11), the capitals are not really necessary to make the ironic point. Sweeney is so depressed that the wheels of a streetcar rolling by sound "like the end of the world" (12). Even though his friend God argues that "A guy can get anything he wants, if he wants it bad enough" (9), the idea of Sweeney successfully carrying out his vow to spend a night with the blonde he sees is ludicrous. And yet Brown begins the novel by saying the vow will be kept. It's up to the reader to find out how.

The chapter ends as Sweeney's transition begins. God gives him confidence, and he begins to dust off and reshape his crumpled, dirty hat. He refuses a drink from God's bottle and says, " 'No thanks, pal. I got a date' " (20).

Sweeney cleans himself up in chapter two. After dawn breaks ("Dawn was different" [21] says the narrator), he rechecks the accident scene to prove it wasn't imagined, then visits a friend and collects money owed on a bet. The man is a lowlife and Sweeney treats him as such, demonstrating that Sweeney is not a very nice man when he's sobering up. He gets his apartment back by paying his landlady part of what he owes her, and begins to regain his job by phoning in an eyewitness story about the girl and the dog. The chapter ends as Sweeney listens to Mozart and decides that, to keep his vow, he'll have to hunt The Ripper, a serial killer who has been blamed for knifing the girl he saw the night before. Unfortunately, Sweeney has "a horror—almost a phobia—of cold steel, cold sharp steel" (21). Brown's perverse humor comes into play as chapter three begins: "Sweeney headed for the *Blade*" (37). The narrator then points out the pun, delighted with himself for making it. Brown is clearly at home with his newspaper reporter characters, and he has his narrator describe Sweeney's appearance in depth.

Chapter Three begins to develop the mystery, as Sweeney learns he was never fired from the paper, investigates previous Ripper murders, and arranges to see Yolanda Lang, the blonde he vowed to spend the night with, who does a "Beauty and the Beast Dance" at the El Madhouse club. Sweeney investigates the Ripper and Yolanda concurrently, all the while fighting the DTs: he must stuff his hands in his pockets in chapter three "because he had a hunch the shakes were going to come back" (49), and in chapter four he fights weariness, a "throbbing headache" (57), and wishes for sleep, though he knows "you always woke up to confusion and complication and the thousand little unpleasantnesses that periodically mount up to one vast unpleasantness from which only immersion in alcohol could bring surcease" (57). In other words, Sweeney is having problems. Like Bill Tracy in *Murder Can Be Fun*, he's an alcoholic, and his sickness first interferes with his life and later endangers it.

In chapter five, the novel's title is finally explained when the mystery leads Sweeney to a small black statue of a woman screaming. It's nicknamed "The Screaming Mimi" partly because its catalog code number is SM-1, but those initials also stand for "sado-masochism," as Sweeney remarks: " 'The thing is an orgy of masochism; it would appeal, in my opinion, only to a sadist' " (73). One of the Ripper's victims, Lola Brent, sold a "Screaming Mimi" the day she died.

Sweeney's alcoholic fog begins to cause him doubt in chapter six, when he finds his knife and razor missing. Is he the Ripper? If only his mind weren't blank for so many drunken periods! The next few chapters detail more of Sweeney's investigation, climaxing in chapter ten when he finally gets to see Yolanda's stage act. The dance is set up nicely, with Sweeney, the cops, and various other characters gathered at El Madhouse to see Yolanda and her dog Devil on stage. To a throbbing drumbeat, Devil leaps at Yolanda and unzips her dress with his teeth, leaving her nearly naked. Sweeney watches intently, and Brown describes Yolanda in very sexy terms, but the scene isn't the highlight it should be. It recalls the peep show in *The Dead Ringer* but lacks the emotional connection in the earlier book between Ed Hunter and Rita; sadly, Yolanda is such a non-character that it's hard to get too worked up. As Sweeney says of the act, " 'Probably symbolic as hell, but symbolic of what, I don't know' " (recalling Ed Hunter's reaction to the dead midget's poetry in *The Dead Ringer* [135]). Yolanda's power over men is clear, however, and that becomes important later on.

There is an interesting passage in chapter eleven that both sheds light on Sweeney's (not very nice) character and perhaps gives a hint of the author's thoughts: while investigating Dorothy Lee, another victim of the Ripper, Sweeney discovers a number of personal details and thinks:

Damn it, he'd probably passed her on the street half a dozen times. He looked at the picture again and wished that he had known her. Of course, if he had known her, he'd have found her just another uninteresting stenographer, stupid, vain and self-centered, who preferred Berlin to Bach and *Romantic Confessions* to Aldous Huxley. But now violent death had transfigured her and those things didn't seem to matter. Maybe, really, they didn't matter. (153)

Sweeney isn't exactly a good samaritan, and he's smart enough to realize that the dead girl was "transfigured" by "violent death" and thus became of interest to him. The last line mitigates it somewhat, but not completely. When Sweeney investigates Yolanda Lang's contract and finds a loophole, he blackmails Harry Yahn, the owner of El Madhouse, by threatening to tell Yolanda's manager, and receives $1000 and a punch in the gut for his trouble. Curiously enough, Sweeney then takes a cab to Bughouse Square (telling the driver, " 'I wish to commune with God' " [176]) and gives $100 to Godfrey, his bench partner, saying he's "tithing with God" (179). Sweeney is neither innocent nor pure, and his motivations are uncertain throughout *The Screaming Mimi*. His search for the Ripper is not a story of good versus evil; it's really more a story of an average man with experience in one level of Hell voluntarily making a descent into another for seemingly selfish reasons.

The novel takes an interesting turn in chapter 14 when Sweeney discovers that the artist who carved The Screaming Mimi, Charlie Wilson, is now a drunkard who shot another Ripper four years before. That Ripper, named Pell, had escaped from an asylum and terrorized Charlie's beautiful blonde kid sister Bessie as she was taking an outdoor shower. Charlie shot the Ripper and Bessie went mad; she died later in a private asylum. Sweeney journeys to rural Brampton, Wisconsin, to learn all of this, and eventually visits "Crazy Charlie," wondering if he might be the current Ripper. Charlie tells Sweeney that the statue he carved was modeled after Bessie and punches him upon learning he's a reporter.

This chapter takes the story outside the city of Chicago and into the rural Midwest, where killers may roam undetected and people take showers outdoors. Like Ed Hunter in his first three novels (and like the heroes of other, later Brown novels), Sweeney can only solve the mystery that confronts him by leaving the city and following a lead into the heart of America to find the "misplaced clue."

Charlie Wilson appears to be a victim; he's a talented abstract painter who finds his own work "horrible." When Sweeney talks to Jake Henderson, a bartender in Brampton, he hears that Charlie is not a great artist because he makes no money, and balks at bringing up "Van Gogh and Modigliani and a few others who'd been great artists and had made less than 500 bucks a year out of it" (185); Sweeney's thoughts prefigure those of the mad artist in Brown's later story "The Little Lamb" who is passionately concerned with the difference between abstract and representational art.

Charlie Wilson, Sweeney, Bessie Wilson, Godfrey the drunk— there is a lot of wasted life in *The Screaming Mimi*. Perhaps its theme can be found among these lost souls; they are so broken and beaten by forces of brutality and chaos that they cannot consistently realize their potential. El Madhouse is the world in microcosm, where sex, money and insanity meet and are regulated and repeated for entertainment and profit. Sweeney is a misfit like Charlie Wilson, partly because money doesn't matter to either.

Chapter 16 is a breather before the novel's conclusion, as Sweeney arranges for a picture of The Screaming Mimi statue to be printed on the front page of the *Blade* the next day, certain that the person who bought the statue from Lola Brent is the Ripper. In chapter 17, the paper comes out and Sweeney learns that Doc Greene, Yolanda's sleazy manager, has been captured as the Ripper. This would seem to end the story, but it doesn't—it only ties up all of the loose ends with a false conclusion. Sweeney figures this out after going to State Street, where Doc Greene was apparently knocked through a window to his death by Devil, Yolanda's dog. The statue is found with him and in pieces; Yolanda is nowhere to be found.

The last chapter of *The Screaming Mimi* is one of Brown's best, and it's curious that he wrote two versions—the one published and another that he apparently also sent to the publisher with the knowledge that it would be turned down.

In the published version, Sweeney tracks Yolanda to a room she's rented under an assumed name. He confronts her with his deduction that she is Bessie Wilson and that the doctor who put her in a private sanitarium and reported her dead is Doc Greene, her recently deceased manager. At the moment she was attacked Bessie went insane and became the Ripper in her mind, with a fixation for killing beautiful blondes. When Doc Greene figured it all out he tried to shock Yolanda with the attack in the lobby that Sweeney witnessed at the beginning of the novel, but this radical treatment failed.

What happens next is pure Fred Brown. Yolanda takes off her clothes and holds a carving knife, becoming "a nude high priestess holding the sacrificial knife" (244), and Sweeney quickly realizes that she remains transfixed only by his voice. He then launches into every speech and quotation he can think of, from the Gettysburg Address to nursery rhymes, and manages to continue speaking through the night until the police finally arrive the next morning.

The novel ends with Sweeney returning to the bench at Bughouse Square and sharing a bottle with God. The reader is left with the impression that the events of the novel have had little effect on Sweeney. He started out as a drunk on a park bench and ends up on his way toward returning to that state. Brown critic Newton Baird faults *The Screaming Mimi* for this dark vision and negative ending, but I think it is perfectly in keeping with the themes of wasted lives and despair in the novel. Bessie Wilson is a victim, just like Lola Brent and Dorothy Lee, the young women she murders. When it becomes clear that she is the Ripper, the reader feels immediate fear for Sweeney, but there is no real evil on the part of Bessie Wilson—she is merely another pawn in a wild chess game of fate that always seems to end in checkmate.

In the alternate ending to the novel, Yolanda kills Sweeney and he finds himself in Heaven, sharing a park bench with the *real* God, who promises him that Yolanda will arrive in two years and that in the meantime he may occupy himself with other heavenly delights. This fantasy ending turns a tough crime novel on its ear (something Brown would later do quite successfully in the middle of *Knock Three-One-Two*), and it is delightful and much in keeping with Brown's leanings toward science fiction and fantasy in the late 1940s. Yet it doesn't really fit the dark themes of the novel, themes that are developed consistently from the first page. *The Screaming Mimi* is a brilliant portrait of a world gone mad, in which there is no rhyme or reason to who survives and one might as well pass the days as a crook, a dancer or a drunk on a park bench.

The reviews of *The Screaming Mimi* were good. Elizabeth Bullock in The New York *Times* called it "fast, smooth, and well-plotted," and *The New Yorker*'s reviewer called it "tough, funny, and plausible in a dreadful kind of way." The New York *Herald Tribune*'s reviewer called the novel a "very absorbing yarn" ("Mystery and Adventure" 42), and *Kirkus Reviews* wrote, "the pace here is fast, the pitch high." The novel was bought by the Dollar Mystery Guild, a book club that paid slightly higher rates than the Unicorn Mystery Book Club, where all of Brown's earlier mysteries had been reprinted. This book club edition is still fairly easy and cheap to find. In her autobiography, Beth Brown noted that the novel brought high royalties (*Oh, for the Life* 137), and in 1951 it was sold to a Hollywood studio as a vehicle for well-known stripper, Lili St. Cyr. It was finally filmed and released in 1958, with Phil Carey and

Anita Ekberg. The film has been vilified by every critic who ever mentioned it, but it has recently begun to be available on videotape and is beginning to be seen as a good example of late 1950s film noir kitsch by students of the era. Brown himself hated the film (E. Brown, Letter to Newton Baird).

There have been a number of critics who have had something to say about *The Screaming Mimi*. In America, Newton Baird wrote the only sustained words on the novel, calling it one of Brown's best works but faulting it for its unhappy ending. In England, H.R.F. Keating made some perceptive comments about the passage of time in the novel in his introduction to a 1984 collection of which it was a part. And in France, where criticism of American popular culture has tended to be incisive, Jean-Pierre Deloux placed *Mimi* in the middle of his long thesis about Brown's works as expressions of a Romantic quest. The thesis is rather farfetched, but it is entertaining and should be read by anyone seriously interested in Brown's work.

Finally, another French critic, Daniel Compère, discussed *Mimi* in his study of Fredric Brown and Robert Bloch titled "Alice au pays des maléfices" (1984). In this fascinating article, Compère uses quotations from Lewis Carroll's *Alice* books as jumping off points in a discussion of various themes in the two authors' works.

One thing is certain—*The Screaming Mimi* is a powerful novel, perhaps existential in the way it presents a world whose inhabitants are tossed about at random as if by a wind of chaos. The novel ends without a resolution of the fundamental questions it poses, and Brown's refusal to provide a false "happy ending" only reinforces the harsh and brilliant tone he sustains throughout.

After completing *The Screaming Mimi* at the end of 1948, Fred and Beth Brown made a short trip to the Midwest before moving southwest to Taos, New Mexico. Brown wrote and published the fourth of his Ed and Am Hunter novels, *Compliments of a Fiend*, before embarking on a very experimental work, *Here Comes a Candle*.

In her autobiography, Beth Brown remarks that Fred plotted *Here Comes a Candle* on bus rides to and from the Denver library, where he went to research how television scripts were written. The Brown's were living in Taos at the time, and this novel was written there. Unfortunately, *Here Comes a Candle* is more fun to write about than it is to read. It concerns Joe Bailey, a young man tortured by the memory of tipping off the cops that his dad was taking part in a robbery and thus causing his father's death in a shootout. In a quest for acceptance he becomes involved with organized crime; he eventually tries to go straight with a nice girl, but they both come to a bad end due to Joe's obsession with the nursery rhyme of the novel's title.

Perhaps bored with the standard novel format, Brown decided to write *Here Comes A Candle* using experimental techniques. It consists of 25 chapters of "The Story" divided into six sections of a few chapters each, as well as six inter-sections, done in the following formats: radio play, screenplay, sportcast, teleplay, stage play, and newspaper article. The novel is very nicely printed on better paper than any of Brown's prior novels; it is as if Brown and Dutton decided they had something special here that deserved royal treatment. Instead of being labeled "A Guilt Edged Mystery," as Brown's earlier mysteries all had been, it is labeled simply, "A Novel." There is a table of contents page, the design and graphics are very modern, and the book is larger in size than Brown's prior books. Clearly, Dutton tried to package *Here Comes A Candle* as a serious novel—there's no list of prior works and no indication that it belongs in the "tawdry" category of a "mystery" or a "thriller."

The story takes place almost entirely in Milwaukee, where Brown had lived in the 1930s and 1940s, and (as with Chicago) he knows the setting inside and out. The plot is as old as they come, and its lack of originality is the novel's biggest problem. Joe is torn between the glamorous life of a criminal, symbolized by the flashy Francy Savigne/Scott, and the secure but dull life of an honest working man, symbolized by Ellie Dravich. What little interest there is in the novel comes from Brown's small touches. Joe Bailey, the doomed hero, loves science fiction; in chapter three, he reads the lead novel in the September 1948 *Startling Stories* and dreams about its scantily-clad space girls. Though Brown doesn't say it, the reader familiar with his work knows that Joe is reading "What Mad Universe," Brown's landmark comic novelette.

Brown begins *Here Comes A Candle* by setting the date as August 26, 1948, and giving details of what was going on in the world that day. This technique is interesting in retrospect but would be put to more effective use in *The Office*, Brown's second and much better attempt at a straight novel. The sense of time pops up obtrusively throughout the novel, mostly in the person of Krasno, a friend of Joe's who can't seem to stop talking about Communism and Capitalism (he prefers the former). There are also numerous referrals to the impending war with the Soviet Union and the danger of atomic explosions. Like Krasno's constant talk of Communism, these passages seem forced, as if Brown felt that he had to discuss serious, political issues if he wanted to write a serious novel.

Of course the obvious standouts in *Here Comes A Candle* are the inter-sections. The first two are promising: the radio play is a flashback to Joe's visit to a psychologist at age 15; Brown provides details of Joe's mental problems that stem from his belief that he caused his father's death. The truth is sad—Joe's mother went out and Joe's father went with two friends to rob a movie theater, leaving little Joe asleep. When the boy wakes up afraid from a nightmare and alone, he goes outside and finds a cop. He tells the cop where his dad is and they go there; they arrive as his dad runs out after committing robbery, and Joe sees him shot and killed. Brown was familiar with radio scripts, since a number of his stories had been produced on the air, and this section is entertaining.

The next inter-section is a movie screenplay, and it is a flashback to the events of the night Joe's father died. The scene is tragic and effective. The third break is a radio sportcast, and its point is humorous—it chronicles Joe's first crime in robbing a gas station. Unfortunately, the pattern of expository flashbacks that was set in the first two inter-sections is lost, and a sportcast is just another type of radio play, so Brown seems to be running out of ideas.

The fourth inter-section is a video, in which a doctor probes Joe's brain to project a dream onscreen. Brown does an excellent job of recreating the surrealistic progression of events in a dream and demonstrates the turmoil in Joe's twisted psyche. Inter-section number five is a stage play and is similar to part four in the way Joe's thoughts are played out by the characters involved. Finally, the novel ends with a newspaper account of Joe's murder of Ellie and subsequent suicide; the style makes it anticlimactic and ruins the scene that the whole novel had built toward.

Here Comes A Candle is wildly uneven. There is a clever bit of plotting at its center, involving Joe's fear of candles and hatchets that stems from a night in early childhood when he awoke to see his father tangled in his curtains, trying to chop ice away from his windowsill by candlelight. But this and all the other clever bits are overwhelmed by the novel's unjustified length and by the bag of tricks Brown uses in an attempt to jazz up a rather dull story. It's true that the various approaches allow Brown to examine Joe Bailey from many unusual angles, but the novel would have been much better if he weren't trying so hard.

Critical reception of *Here Comes A Candle* was mixed. Writing in *The Saturday Review of Literature*, Milton Crane called it "rather below Mr. Brown's usual level of achievement" and "a distressing bore." Nelson Algren's piece in The New York *Times* wasn't much better; after a snide retelling of the story he calls Francy and Ellie "lifeless as dressmakers' dummies" and writes that "Joe's ultimate choice is simply one of brunette over blonde." In an unusual move, the *Times* then published a longer discussion of the novel on August 26, 1950, in which William DuBois treats it as a "psycho-thriller" and gives a very positive review. Other reviewers were in agreement that the novel was flawed (most disliked the inter-sections), and their reviews ran the gamut from "fast paced narrative and sound psychological angles" to "mixed up" (Doyle 22).

After the special sendoff that Dutton gave *Here Comes A Candle*, the book seems to have fallen flat. It never sold to a book club, and Bantam's single paperback edition in 1951 is the last time it was published in America. In his series of articles in *The Armchair Detective* in the late 1970s, Newton Baird discussed the novel favorably, admitting its flaws in part but asserting that it was, overall, very good. Beth Brown listed it among those novels of Fred's that she particularly liked (Intro. viii), and J. Grant Thiessen offered "high praise" in an obscure 1976 appreciation, as did William F. Nolan in his introduction to *Before She Kills* (1984). The 1978 reprint of the novel in France sparked some criticism on that side of the Atlantic, as well; both Jean-Pierre Deloux and Daniel Compère include it in their interesting 1984 Brown studies.

Yet *Here Comes A Candle* is not a very good novel. Compared to *The Screaming Mimi*, *What Mad Universe*, and *The Far Cry*—all of which were written within a year or two of it—it is a very poor effort indeed. Critics and friends of Brown have attempted to make it into something it isn't, perhaps feeling that Brown tried so hard to be original that he and the novel deserve some sort of accolade. It doesn't hurt that the novel has been essentially unavailable in America for over 40 years—it's hard to argue about a book you've never seen.

Brown's next novel was not as original as *Here Comes A Candle*, but it was much more memorable. *Night of the Jabberwock* was written immediately after it, while the Browns were still living in Taos. It is drawn from two old pulp stories published in 1944—"The Gibbering Night" and "The Jabberwocky Murders"—and they are carefully woven together and expanded to form a seamless whole. Beth Brown wrote that her husband got writer's block after writing one chapter and had to take a long bus trip to El Paso to finish plotting it.

Plot is a standout of *Night of the Jabberwock*, which concerns the events that befall Doc Stoeger, the 52-year-old publisher of the tiny Carmel City *Clarion*, on a summer Thursday night. The novel begins with echoes of "Monday's an Off Night" as Stoeger laments the lack of news in the little Illinois town. As the night progresses, a string of newsworthy events occur, each of which Stoeger is talked out of printing for one reason or another. A divorce story is toned down and replaced with one about a church rummage sale, then the rummage sale is canceled. A man is injured in an explosion at the fireworks factory but his wife asks Stoeger to kill the story so as not to endanger the man's job. Throughout, Brown does a marvelous job of evoking the small town of Carmel City. Best is Doc's walk home from Smiley's bar in chapter two; as he passes stores and homes he recalls personal details that give meaning to each building. He sees the undertaking parlor "through which both of my parents had passed, 15 and 20 years ago" (30), as well as "the house in which Elsie Minton had lived—and in which she had died while we were engaged, twenty-five years ago" (30). Stoeger is a man who thinks life may have passed him by, but who will learn this night that it has not.

The first of the two major plot lines in *Night of the Jabberwock* concerns gangster Bat Masters, who happens to drive through Carmel City and ask Doc Stoeger where he is. Doc recognizes the criminal and is kidnapped and nearly killed when he and Smiley the bartender are driven out of town to a quiet spot. This plot is lifted from the short story "The Gibbering Night," and it ends in chapter six.

The other plot line, the one that most people who've read the novel remember, deals with a curious little man named Yehudi Smith who knows all about Lewis Carroll and leads Doc into a bizarre series of incidents culminating in Smith's own death. The "Jabberwock" of the novel's title comes from Lewis Carroll's *Alice in Wonderland*, and Doc Stoeger is a scholar on the subject, having written *Lewis Carroll*

Through the Looking-Glass and *Red Queen and White Queen*, two obscure monographs, while working on his Ph.D. decades before. Stoeger is surprised that Smith has heard of his work, and he's even more surprised when Smith tells him he's a member of the Vorpal Blades, an organization devoted to the belief that Lewis Carroll was writing fact, not fiction, and that he discovered another plane of reality in which the *Alice* books were true.

The novel is a lot of fun, and its roots show—the pulp touches only add to the entertainment. Doc drinks too much and too often and it affects his perceptions and his judgment, as is often the case with Brown's heroes. But he's a likeable guy, and the reader roots for him not to give up his small town newspaper, certain that he'll eventually see that his life isn't as worthless as he might think. There's a conflict with the town sheriff that recalls *The Bloody Moonlight*, and Brown begins the novel with a dream, as he did *The Fabulous Clipjoint*:

In my dream I was standing in the middle of Oak Street and it was dark night. The street lights were off; only pale moonlight glinted on the huge sword that I swung in circles about my head as the Jabberwock crept closer. It bellied along the pavement, flexing its wings and tensing its muscles for the final rush; its claws clicked against the stones like the clicking of mats down the channels of a Linotype. Then, astonishingly, it spoke.

"Doc," it said. "Wake up, Doc." (9)

This mysterious tone continues throughout the novel and enriches it considerably. Doc encounters another imaginary figure in chapter thirteen, when he sits in Smiley's bar and converses with an imaginary Yehudi Smith to work out the murderer's identity after the little man has been killed.

The novel's conclusion recalls Brown's several pulp stories that dealt with pyromaniacs. Al Grainger, the wealthy and eccentric illegitimate son of banker Ralph Bonney, is the killer, seemingly angry at Doc for calling him a bastard in jest too many times. Doc tapes Grainger to a bed and threatens to set his room on fire to force a confession out of him. This is a pulpy and rather forced way to end a terrifically enjoyable novel, but it doesn't ruin the fun. The novel's coda wraps everything up neatly, as one by one Doc is allowed to print all of the stories he formerly had been told to kill. The novel ends as Doc finishes making up the paper, has three quick drinks, and passes out, exhausted but happy. As Francis Lacassin so cleverly observed, "Penelope's tapestry is restored in a single stroke" (260).[1]

Night of the Jabberwock is one of Fredric Brown's most popular and critically acclaimed novels, perhaps because it combines the positive qualities of his other work with an overwhelming sense of fun. Reviewers at the time of its publication were full of praise, and when it was reissued in 1984 as part of a series of mystery classics the reviews were even better. In her 1973 introduction to *Paradox Lost*, Beth Brown called it one she particularly liked, and Francis Lacassin, in his 1974 article on Brown, called the novel "a small, underestimated masterpiece of detective fiction, certainly Fredric Brown's masterpiece" (258).[2] Lacassin discusses the novel in depth, and it is clearly his choice for the best of the six Brown mysteries published in French up to that point. Newton Baird seems to have a love/hate relationship with the novel: he praises its plotting but finds it flawed and seems to fault it for explaining all of its unusual events so rationally ("Paradox and Plot" 157).

Other writers have felt compelled to praise the novel: H.R.F. Keating called it "a conspicuous example of Brown's skill with plot" (viii); Marcia Muller wrote that it was "a perfect example of Fredric Brown's somewhat eccentric view of the world" (Pronzini and Muller 94); Joe R. Lansdale believed it to be "one of the best and most original mysteries I've ever read" (6); and Jean-Pierre Deloux spends a good part of his long article, "Mouvement brownien," comparing *Night of the Jabberwock* to Eastern and Western mythical traditions and deeming it a "masterpiece" that "occupies a place all by itself in detective fiction" (10-11).[3] Popular opinion on this novel must prevail; it is a very entertaining and magnificently plotted tale that represents the essence of one aspect of Fredric Brown's many talents.

Between 1947 and 1950, Fredric Brown published four mystery novels featuring Ed and Am Hunter, a science fiction novel, a good number of short stories, and four non-series mysteries—*Murder Can Be Fun, The Screaming Mimi, Here Comes a Candle*, and *Night of the Jabberwock. The Screaming Mimi* is the strongest of the lot, but *Murder Can Be Fun* and *Night of the Jabberwock* are entertaining variations on stories he had previously written for the pulps. *Here Comes a Candle* is a failed experiment that deserves reading for its small touches but is rather dull overall.

This four-year period was one of great change for Fredric Brown: in 1947 he was married to Helen Brown and living in Milwaukee with his family; by 1950 he was married to Elizabeth Charlier and living a bohemian life in Taos. He wrote some of the best fiction of his life, and even his most mundane work was interesting. Brown would have a few more productive years, but his body of work in the 1940s had been immense—over 100 stories and seven novels. In contrast, by 1960, his writing career would be nearly over and he would be settled (for the most part) in the southwestern city he would inhabit for the rest of his life. Before all of that, however, he would write some more masterful novels and short stories.

Chapter Eight
The Southwest

In 1949, Fred Brown and his wife moved to Taos, New Mexico, and began living a bohemian life in a small house in what was then a tiny and very rural town. While living there, Brown wrote a considerable number of science fiction stories, several novels, and a novella, *The Case of the Dancing Sandwiches*. This novella is unique among Brown's fiction because it was published in book form and because Brown began expanding it to novel length but gave up along the way.

The Case of the Dancing Sandwiches first appeared in the Summer 1950 issue of *Mystery Book Magazine*. In her autobiography, Beth Brown remarked that the novella sold to this magazine for $400 (131). It was then sold to Dell Publishing Co. for $1000, and they published it with the subtitle, "A Murder Frame-Up That Didn't Jell," as a paperback original in November 1951 in their new line of 64-page paperbacks. The book sold for ten cents and has become the most sought-after collector's item in the Brown canon, now worth over $100—more than one thousand times its original price. The story was again reprinted in *Triple Detective*, as well as the anthology *Carnival of Crime* and a limited edition volume published by Dennis McMillan in 1985.

The story begins as Carl Dixon dances with lovely Dorothy Tremaine in a club. He recalls meeting her brother, Vic, weeks before and being invited to the opening of Ancin and Vic's, a new roadhouse Vic and his partner were opening in New Jersey. Carl feels some guilt when he thinks of his fiance, yet he spends the evening flirting with Dorothy and getting drunker and drunker.

What Carl doesn't know is that he's a pawn in an elaborate con game being run by Jerry Trenholm, alias Vic Tremaine, who kills Tom Anders, a man who betrayed him years before, and leaves the gun and the body in the same car with Carl.

Carl is tried and sent to jail, unable to trace Ancin and Vic's, Dorothy, or Vic. Months later, Carl's fiance, Susan Bailey, contacts Peter Cole, a New York City police detective, to recommend a private investigator on the case in an attempt to clear Carl's name. Carl takes a personal interest in the case and discovers the truth; meanwhile, he and Susan fall in love and, as soon as Carl is freed, she leaves him for the detective.

The Case of the Dancing Sandwiches is perfect for its length; there is no filler, and the story is kept going just long enough to be satisfying. Brown notably switches perspectives several times, beginning different chapters with completely new characters and then weaving them into the situation that has already been established. Chapter one is told from Carl Dixon's point of view and paints a relatively innocent portrait of the events. Chapter two is told from the point of view of Tom Anders, and he begins to reveal the complex web of disguise and deception that entraps Carl. Chapter three features Jerry Trenholm's point of view and explains the final double cross. The first three chapters thus use a complicated method of exposition to depict a crime and its diverse causes.

Chapters four through eight are told from the perspective of Peter Cole, and it is his job to piece together the puzzle set up for the reader's eyes only in chapters one, two, and three. Finally, chapter nine begins with the perspective of Claire Evans (alias Dorothy Tremaine), and sees the story to its conclusion. Although the novella is narrated in an omniscient, third-person voice, the switching of perspectives foreshadows Brown's later interest in multiple first-person narrators, as in *The Lenient Beast.*

The characters are all quite good, as are the plot and the gimmick, which is tied to the curious title. Brown uses the New York/New Jersey location well and is very crafty in the way he switches reader sympathy from Carl Dixon to Peter Cole, so that it is quite pleasant at the end when Susan decides she loves Cole, not Dixon, who wouldn't have had this trouble had he not cheated with Dorothy! We are given least insight into Peter's and Susan's minds; in fact, chapters four through eight read like a straightforward mystery story. The variations in narrative technique of chapters one, two, three, and nine make the novella memorable, and the total result is a satisfying, unusual mystery that has a special place in Fredric Brown's oeuvre.

As he often did, Brown began expanding *The Case of the Dancing Sandwiches* to full novel length several years later. He never finished it, however, and the existing nine chapters were published with the novella in Dennis McMillan's limited edition volume. The novel version is quite different, and appears to have been written in about 1956, when Brown was living in Tucson, Arizona. The story's setting is changed to Tucson, and Brown eschews the narrative experiments of the novella for a more leisurely pace and a much fuller development of characters.

In chapter one, for instance, Carl Dixon is invited to meet Dorothy, and they only visit one bar before the chapter ends. What was explained briefly in Dixon's thoughts is now shown; the result is more depth. As in *Here Comes A Candle*, where Joe Bailey reads the pulp version of "What Mad Universe," Carl Dixon relaxes with "a pocketbook mystery novel...about a complicated and elaborate frame-up, with murder as a side-line, and he couldn't get much interested in it. Things like that didn't really happen" (13). The irony is obvious because the reader suspects Carl will get involved in just such an unlikely situation; to the reader familiar with Fredric Brown's fiction, it's doubly ironic because this pocket book sounds suspiciously like the Dell paperback, *The Case of the Dancing Sandwiches*!

The expansion continues in chapter two, as the reader is given more details of the events surrounding Jerry Trenholm's betrayal of Tom Anders years before. Chapter four further details Jerry and Claire's plan for Tom's murder. Chapter five is most interesting: Jerry Trenholm, who is only sketched briefly in the novella, is given full biographical treatment. Brown is clearly interested in the formation of the criminal mind, but happily he is much less long-winded than he was in his analysis of Joe Bailey's development in *Here Comes A Candle*. Jerry is "atypical as a criminal" because "he had not drifted into crime but had deliberately chosen it as a career" (46). He grew up in St. Louis and both his mother and father died within a short time of each other while Jerry was a sophomore in high school. Jerry was then allowed to live at a room and board in St. Louis and his Uncle Walter paid his bills by mail. All of this parallels Fredric Brown's own experience, and the autobiographical echoes add weight to the character.

Soon after his parents' death, Jerry read two very influential books: Dale Carnegie's *How to Win Friends and Influence People* ("the perfect con man's manual" [47]) and Dostoevsky's *Crime and Punishment* (he thought Raskolnikov's conduct appallingly stupid). Jerry didn't make many mistakes; he studied hard and "in twenty-two years he had taken only one fall" (45), when he was betrayed by Tom Anders. Brown's decision to expand his novella in part by delving into the genesis of his criminal's mind recalls William Faulkner's changes to his first draft of *Sanctuary*, wherein he added a chapter softening the character of the criminal Popeye by detailing his harsh upbringing. In both cases, the additional material alters the reader's perceptions of criminal and crime; in the unfinished novel, *The Case of the Dancing Sandwiches*, we cannot forgive Jerry for killing Tom but we can at least understand his motivations.

In chapter seven, the novel makes the switch to Peter Cole's investigation, and Brown makes further expansion by adding details to Cole's character and fleshing out the Arizona setting. Peter quotes the biblical Solomon's "*How beautiful are thy feet with shoes*" and calls it a "ridiculous mistranslation; obviously it should have been *How beautiful are thy sandaled feet*" (70). This same quotation and commentary appear in *The Office*, published in 1958, leading to the supposition that the novel version of *The Case of the Dancing Sandwiches* may have been written near that time as well. In addition to expanding Peter and Susan's investigation into the crime (they visit bars and travel around Arizona looking for Ancin and Vic's), Brown adds a marvelous new character to the story: Willie Neutzel, a retired, arthritic private investigator Peter hires to look into Tom Anders's background. Described as "a neat graying little man who looked more like an ex-actor than an ex-cop" (122), Neutzel chats engagingly with Peter and Susan, and one wishes for more of his quirky personality; Brown might have intended using him in the rest of the novel to help Peter and Susan discover the motive behind Tom Anders's murder.

But the novel ends suddenly and without warning, obviously unfinished, just as Peter and Susan have located Ancin and Vic's and unlocked the mystery of its name. It's possible that Brown ran out of steam when he ran out of plot from the novella to expand upon; had he continued the novel, he would have had to take the story in a new direction, probably involving an investigation into Tom's background that eventually led Peter and Susan to Jerry Trenholm, the intelligent killer. It's a shame Brown didn't write the rest, for Jerry would have surely been a worthy rival for Peter Cole and Willie Neutzel. Luckily, the unfinished manuscript survived to give a taste of what might have been.

As a paperback original, *The Case of the Dancing Sandwiches* was never given the privilege of a book review, and it has been basically ignored by critics (it has apparently never been published in France). Newton Baird mentions it briefly, but, other than Lawrence Block's 1985 introduction to the volume that first published the unfinished novel, *The Case of the Dancing Sandwiches* has been forgotten by everyone but collectors seeking the rare paperback.

Both versions are engaging reading, and the change from novella to unfinished novel demonstrates Brown's considerable ability to use narrative experimentation and settings to enrich a very clever tale. The novella is set in New York and was probably written in Taos, not long after Brown had moved there from Manhattan. The unfinished novel takes place in Arizona and was almost certainly written after Brown had moved to Tucson. In between New York and Tucson lay Taos, New Mexico, the setting of perhaps Brown's most brilliant thriller and next novel (after *Death Has Many Doors*, the fifth installment in the Ed and Am Hunter saga), *The Far Cry*.

The novel begins with a paragraph in italics, followed by an extremely subtle time change that recalls Virginia Woolf's experiments in compression of time in *To the Lighthouse*:

Sudden terror in her eyes, Jenny backed away from the knife, her hand groping behind her for the knob of the kitchen door. She was too frightened to scream and anyway there was no one to hear, no one but the man who came toward her with the knife— and he was mad, he must be mad. Her hand found the knob and turned it; the door swung outward into the night and she whirled through it, running. Death ran after her.

Eight years passed.

Then:

What happened started quite casually, as most things do. It started on the eighteenth of May, a Thursday. (1)

In only a few lines, Brown details a brutal past murder, brings the story up to date, and slows the narrative pace in order to begin telling the story of George Weaver. George is a real estate broker who suffered a nervous breakdown and has been told to take a rest cure—he decides to spend the summer in serene Taos, New Mexico. George has a "gaunt face" and his eyes have a "haunted look" (2); he has spent six weeks in a sanatorium and his two young daughters have been sent to a camp for the season. George doesn't like his wife, Vi, and writes to her unhappily.

George's friend, writer Luke Ashley, shows him the house where Jenny Ames was killed. It is a lonely house—the last one on a dirt road well outside of Taos—and George decides to rent it. The real estate agent lets him stay for free if he'll fix the place up; he hopes an inhabitant will break the jinx that has prevented its sale for eight years. Luke tells George that the murder was "a Lonely Heart murder" (12), and George wonders: "Isn't every heart lonely, always?" (14). The scene is set for disaster in the first chapter; Brown's writing is at its most powerful, and he describes the beginning of George Weaver's rest cure with a terrific sense of foreboding.

At the end of the first chapter George is already drinking hard; he is hung over and shaky as chapter two begins. Various people are hired to clean and repair the house, and some of them recall Jenny's murder. Even at this early point, George is growing obsessed with Jenny's death; there are several points where he could avoid investigating her background, but as each bit of information presents itself he is drawn in, as if a web is being spun around him. His destiny seems controlled by a higher force— he is inexorably drawn toward tragedy. Brown ironically makes George a godlike figure: "Weaver looked over his domain and found it good..." (16), yet he is unable to keep himself sober—only four pages after sobering up he is again drinking himself into "a sullen stupor" (18). In fact, two of his first five nights in Taos he goes to bed drunk.

George's troubled relationship with his wife, Vi, is also expounded upon in this chapter. She sends him a letter, and it's a writer's nightmare:

Dear Georgie—[He hated being called Georgie and had managed to break Vi of the habit of doing it verbally, but she still wrote to him that way whenever they were apart.]

Im glad you found a place you like and hope your feeling good by now, I wish it had been Santa Fe because we both lived there and liked it once and had friends there, I guess it was mostly your friends but if Taos is what you want its all right by me, I dont know just yet what day I will come but it will be about a week yet and Ill write again and let you know in a few days, meanwhile the girls are fine... (19)

George angrily analyzes her poor writing and mentally accuses her of having neither a keen mind nor good taste. He recalls meeting her when she was working as a waitress and trying to convince her to attend night school; after their first child was born, he gave up on trying to improve her.

Alongside the depressing relationship with Vi, the temptation to delve deeply into Jenny's murder becomes greater. Luke wants to write a true crime story about the murder and offers George $150 to investigate it in Taos. George is bored and lonely, and a murder investigation is an irresistible diversion. As the chapter concludes, the night grows dark and so does George's mind: "Darker than he dreamed" (24).

George becomes a detective in chapter three, in which he interviews Pepe Sanchez, a young man who witnessed Jenny's attack but didn't realize it until her body was found two and a half months later. He also speaks to Callahan, editor of the local newspaper, *El Crepusculo*, and studies details of the inquest. He learns that Jenny met George Nelson through a lonely hearts club and came by bus to marry him. She was murdered the day she arrived. Nelson was never found, nor were the two suitcases Jenny brought with her.

In addition to the plot details, this chapter is highlighted by its portrait of the Sanchez family and their home, where Spanish-American handmade furniture is interspersed with American bric-a-brac, the junk being the more prized because it is American. Sanchez makes Weaver uncomfortable with his extreme deference, and Brown begins to explore the relations between whites and Spanish-Americans, a problem he would examine again in *The Lenient Beast*. In the midst of his investigation Weaver again tries to forget Jenny; his weakness leads him to get drunk and pass out in his own vomit. He wakes up and continues his search; no matter how he fights, he cannot avoid being drawn into the story of Jenny Ames's murder.

In chapter four, Brown uses italics to allow Weaver to mentally ask direct questions of Jenny, and he fears that his interest is turning into a compulsion—he thinks, "Was his interest psychopathic, abnormal?"— (43) but he convinces himself that it's not. Weaver discusses the case with Callahan, the editor, who says that Nelson was a painter whose paintings "looked to me like something an insane man might do" (51). He also wonders if Nelson was a homosexual, as well as tubercular. In a passage that recalls Brown's science fiction, Weaver wonders about Jenny:

The stars, the silly, far, twinkling stars. Somewhere he'd read that the nearest one was eight light-years away. That meant that the light he was seeing it from now, tonight, had left it eight years ago, perhaps on the very night—He shook himself a little. It was all right to let himself get interested in—this—but he couldn't let it *get* him, like that.

He went back into the house and decided that for once he was going to bed early and reasonably sober. He did. (53)

Clearly, George is romanticizing Jenny Ames, and his obsession with her is making him less lonely and depressed; he goes to bed "early and reasonably sober" for a change. As the novel progresses, Jenny will become George's imaginary, perfect companion, in sharp contrast to the all too real and horrible Vi, his wife. The dichotomy, of course, has a tragic result.

The next chapter has George discovering three paintings by Nelson in the shed behind the house:

They were all pictures of mountains, but they were mountains in such shapes and colors as mountains have never been. They were mountains that writhed in dark agony against spectral skies. They were mountains of another dimension, on another world under an alien sun. (55)

The paintings are described in almost exactly the same way that the painter in Brown's subsequent short story "The Little Lamb" describes his own paintings, and both characters share a twisted mind and a brutal murder. Brown uses their artistic expression to portray their tortured spirits and, after seeing Nelson's paintings and thinking about what they mean, George Weaver "lost all inclination to get out his own water colors" (55).

With Vi's impending arrival, George also thinks more about their awful marriage. Their sex life is over, and he is repulsed by her:

But damn, damn. Vi, he had seen within two years of marrying her, was incurably stupid, almost aggressively stupid and dull. Nothing, almost literally nothing, could penetrate the carapace of her indifference to everything worth while in literature, art, music, living. Nothing above the level of sheer unendurable trash. Love pulps, soap operas, cloying popular ballads—she chewed them all contentedly as a cow chews a cud. She needed, wanted, nothing more; these things were her life, these things and drinking and the eternal eating of candy—box after box of it—that had put forty pounds of weight on her since their marriage, forty flabby pounds that made her body, once slender and desirable, almost as gross and bovine as her mind. (61-62)

What a brutal description of a woman, not to mention a wife! Weaver wishes he could leave her, "if only he could earn enough money—" (61). Knowing something of the circumstances between Fredric Brown and his first wife, Helen, it is impossible not to see George Weaver as autobiographical in this instance. Both Brown and Weaver had two children, and Brown and Helen appear to have had little in common. They did not sleep together for many years before their divorce and, like George, Brown waited until he had money to leave his wife. Most strikingly, Brown met his wife through the mail, much as George Nelson met Jenny Ames. In a sense, *The Far Cry* is Fredric Brown's autobiographical attack on his ex-wife; he sets up Jenny Ames as perhaps the idealization of Helen when he first met her, then portrays Vi as the reality of his recently divorced spouse. Of course, the portrait of Vi in the novel is highly subjective and filled with vituperation, and I'm not suggesting that it's an accurate description of Helen Brown; it's simply a fictional extrapolation of the author's extremely biased perception. With this in mind, *The Far Cry* may be read as Fredric Brown's attempt to exorcise the memory of his first wife by splitting her into two characters and having George Weaver's soul torn apart by the difference between them.

George's investigation continues. He speaks to Carlotta, a woman who met Jenny on the bus the day she arrived, and idealistically concludes by thinking of Jenny: "Quite probably you were a virgin, inexperienced in love"! (68). George's fantasies about Jenny are implicitly sexual by this point. When Vi finally arrives, his disgust with her grows as he is more and more torn between unpleasant reality and safe fantasy. He is so obsessed with Jenny that he is unable to put words on paper describing Nelson's attack—the italicized paragraph that begins the novel is repeated here, but for George, "the words wouldn't come" (83). Time passes slowly for George in Vi's presence; she drinks heavily and he worries:

Sometimes he had dreams, almost nightmares of the kind that had started his breakdown and had sent him to the sanitarium back home. (87)

Learning the location of Jenny's grave, George visits and photographs it, ostensibly for the story he's supposed to be writing but really to feed his own developing fetish. Even as he approaches the grave he continues to battle his obsession:

> There's nothing for you here, he told himself. Go back. Go back to Vi, to what you have. Go back to the light, to the life that you know, the life that isn't so horrible but that you can face it and continue to live.
>
> This is death, out here in the dark. Jenny Ames is dead, eight years dead, and death is darkness; darkness is death. Go back to the light.
>
> Go back to life and light; no matter what that light shows, it is better than death and darkness.
>
> Is it? (108-09)

Sadly, horribly, for George Weaver, the phantom of a dead girl he never met is better than the corporeal reality of his own wife.

Brown speaks through George as the character ponders the reason for the lifeless prose in his story about Jenny Ames:

> The crime of murder is a meaningless thing, a mere statistic, unless the victim of that murder can be presented as a human being with a background and a history. (112)

To help fill in the details, George seeks and finds Jenny's two suitcases, buried behind a little hillock a hundred yards to the east of the house. He thinks about where Nelson may have hidden them and spots the hillock, then walks "in a slow spiral around it" twice until he sees a depression under which he finds the suitcases. The image of George pacing around the barren soil in search of the past is arresting; he is literally going in circles—spiralling down to Hell, perhaps—in the cause of following his obsession.

Naturally, George treats Jenny's suitcases and their contents with fetishistic reverence, separating the deteriorating items with the care of an archaeologist. He places each item "reverently on his spread coat" and carries the load "like a baby back toward the house" (131). He examines the contents in the shed and makes himself sick by first drinking to forget the cold and then passing out in the closed and overly heated shed. This is George's descent into Hell—he drinks and loses his senses, and the act of going through Jenny's suitcases is like a crime, a hidden act of desire and violation done secretly in the night. George consoles himself by thinking, possessively, "Don't you *have* more of Jenny Ames than anyone else?" (132).

The novel reaches its first (and false) conclusion when George tracks Jenny back to the small town of Barton, California, using a remark in one of the letters he finds in her suitcase. He drives to Barton and talks to locals, learning that Jenny's parents were repressive and that she embezzled money from her father's bank and ran away to meet Nelson, whom she had once met when he visited her town. As in *The Screaming Mimi, The Fabulous Clipjoint*, and many other Fredric Brown mystery novels, the main character reaches a point in his investigation where he must travel out of his immediate area to find the "misplaced clue" and the final pieces of the puzzle. Here, the trip leads to Barton, California, and a confrontation with Jenny's mother, a harsh woman whose lack of concern about her daughter's murder angers George. By coincidence, George then learns that Nelson's life ended in a Tucson, Arizona sanitarium, where he paid for tuberculosis treatments with money he may have taken from Jenny. At this point, the mystery is solved and the novel could end, but it doesn't. The real conclusion must involve George Weaver and his wife, Vi, the only real characters driving the novel.

After George visits the sanitarium in Tucson, things take a strange turn. George gets drunk, and then: "There must have been hallucinations ..." (160) as George seems to imagine himself arrested, thrown in jail, and released on a charge that he can't understand. Convinced these events were in fact hallucinatory, George returns to Taos, picking up Vi on the way, and discovers that one of Jenny's precious letters has been stolen from his house. All his questions are answered when Sheriff Tom Grayson (George's rival in wanting the glory for solving Jenny's murder) arrives to tell George he really *was* arrested in Tucson—Jenny's mother thought he must have killed Jenny and sent the police after him. A call to Taos solved that problem, but Grayson then tells George that Jenny's mother described her as 5' 3" and blonde, while the body identified as Jenny's was 5' 5" and brunette! Either Jenny escaped and is alive, or there was more than one murder. Whatever the case, George snaps and becomes convinced that Vi is Jenny grown old and fat. He grabs a kitchen knife to kill her, and the novel ends with a repetition of the shocking paragraph with which it began.

George's descent is complete in this final chapter. He wonders "am I going crazy" (166), worries that he's "a fetishist" (167) and thinks "God, was he becoming an alcoholic?" (168). He fights his obsession but loses when he learns Jenny may be alive, and in a clever moment of psychic transference sees Vi as Jenny:

> Vi was five feet three and blonde. He'd met Vi three months after Jenny Ames had escaped from Charles [sic] Nelson. She'd been working as a waitress in Santa Fe, only seventy miles away on the main highway. She had no relatives. She'd been twenty-two.
>
> Vi was Jenny. Jenny was Vi. (175)

Tempting? Yes. Believable? Only to a lunatic, which is what George has become by the end of the novel.

The Far Cry ends as it began, with an image of horror. Weaver yearns for Jenny Ames, picturing her as the young, ideal Vi whom he had loved once, briefly. The novel charts his doomed search for this lost, innocent love. By the end, Vi has become a human monster in George's eyes and his murder of her symbolizes his attempt to destroy the corrupted Jenny Ames—he believes Vi has destroyed the purity of his youthful ideal and left him with nothing, not even the certainty of a body in a grave beneath a cottonwood tree where he could plant his illusions. He becomes George Nelson (note the identical given names), the man he obsessively hates for killing Jenny eight years before, and repeats the murder that has consumed him.

When *The Far Cry* was published in 1951, the reviews were universally strong. Curiously, after the original Dutton hardcover and a subsequent book club edition, Bantam brought the novel out in paperback in 1953 and promptly forgot about it. The novel was reprinted in Spanish (as *El grito lejano*) in 1963, then in French (as *La fille de nulle part*) in 1979, and finally again in the U.S.A. in 1987 and 1991. As a consequence, the novel has always been fondly remembered by critics (Elizabeth Brown lists it among her favorites) but little discussed in detail. Newton Baird makes a few praiseworthy remarks in "Paradox and

Plot," and Jean-Pierre Deloux's comments in "Mouvement brownien" are perceptive but brief. The most interesting writing relating to *The Far Cry* comes in Elizabeth Brown's autobiography, a large portion of which is devoted to her and Fred's years living in Taos. The Browns took the train to Santa Fe, not intending to remain in Taos; Vi takes the train to Santa Fe, and neither she nor George plan to stay. The carpenter the Browns hired to build furniture was named Ellis DeLong, as is the carpenter George Weaver hires to repair his house (this may be false memory on the part of Mrs. Brown, however; Walt Sheldon, who lived in Taos at the same time, has doubted other details in her book). The Browns drank at El Patio and La Dona Luz, as does George Weaver. Fred got hooked on painting, and George Weaver also tries his hand at painting until he sees George Nelson's work. Brown also mentions Frank Waters, editor of the local paper, *El Crepusculo*; in *The Far Cry*, the paper is the same but the editor is named Callahan. Most importantly, the house George Weaver rents is the house of Brown's friend and co-writer, Mack Reynolds, in Arroyo Seco, about seven miles from Taos (64).

Fredric Brown wrote *The Far Cry* in 1950-51, while he and his wife were living a happy, bohemian life in Taos, New Mexico. Yet the marriage it portrays is a troubled one, and the protagonist—George Weaver—is far from content. I think this is Brown's most subtly autobiographical novel, and he was far too careful a writer for this not to be intentional. It's dangerous to take the idea of the *roman a clef* too far, because *The Far Cry* is certainly fiction as far as its mystery plot is concerned. The dichotomy between Vi Weaver and Jenny Ames is fascinating, however, and Brown uses the southwestern setting so well as a backdrop that the novel is one of his most successful, its writing among his best.

At about this time, a small Chicago publishing house named Shasta issued Brown's first collection of short stories, *Space on My Hands*, which featured a selection of Brown's science fiction. He then began work on *We All Killed Grandma*, one of his weakest novels and the last one he would complete in Taos.

According to Beth Brown, Fred began *We All Killed Grandma* in 1951, wrote a portion of it, and changed the title to *Hangover in Red*. He experienced writer's block in the midst of the novel and solved it with one of his customary bus trips (this time, to Albuquerque), finally finishing the novel by mid-year. The book sold to Dutton, as always, but when the proofs came back for author review the publisher had mistakenly labeled them with the original title, *We All Killed Grandma*, and Fred "had to rewrite a small part of the book to justify the original title" (*Oh, for the Life* 94).

This confusion is evident in the lackluster novel, which concerns Rod Britten, who has total amnesia of everything that happened before midnight the Monday before, when he found his wealthy grandmother murdered. *We All Killed Grandma* is an experiment in exposition in which very little happens; the murder has already occurred as the novel opens, and Rod becomes a detective of sorts in trying to piece together what he has forgotten in order to solve both the murder and the more pressing question of why his wife Robin is suddenly cold to him and unwilling to reconcile their marriage. Unfortunately, the "investigation" is just endless talk in which Rod asks one person after another what happened. In this way, he rebuilds his life and identifies the murderer. Occasionally, an evocative passage like this one stands out, as Rod sits alone in his apartment waiting for a police lieutenant to arrive:

> It was a warm muggy night, with flashes of heat lightning in the distance. An unusually warm night for May, even late May. If this was a fair sample, it was going to be a hell of a summer.
> I didn't like it outside, in the hot, flashing night. I was glad to get back to my room and finish the cool drink I'd made. (104)

But, overall, the book just plods along until the conclusion, by which time the murder has ceased to be of much interest. The real focus of the novel is on Rod's marital problems and his attempts to reconcile with Robin. They do, in the end, and Brown concludes with another nicely written passage:

> I guess I forgot that I had a car there. I turned and walked away down the long sidewalk into the rain. I walked nineteen steps before I heard her voice, "Rod, wait!" and the click of her heels on the concrete, and I turned and breathed and lived again. (224)

Unfortunately, the rest of the novel does not live up to this last line.

Reviewers in 1952 were kind to Brown in general, probably because of his good track record. More telling is the fact that *We All Killed Grandma* has not been reprinted in America since the 1953 Bantam paperback, and was only finally published in France in 1978, as part of François Guerif's reissue series of Brown's novels. Critics have ignored it; even Newton Baird and Jean-Pierre Deloux, the two most perceptive writers on Brown's mystery fiction, barely mention it. Perhaps the best assessment was made by critic Anthony Boucher, writing in the May 25, 1952 New York *Times* Book Review:

Fredric Brown's WE ALL KILLED GRANDMA (Dutton, $2.50) seems not so much a first draft as a hasty attempt to rewrite a pulp novelette to book length. Brown's novels have varied from superlative to disappointing; but hitherto his most uneven stories of murder and of science fiction have at least been startlingly original. This one is simply a standard stock case of arbitrary amnesia, such as flourishes only in murder novels, with action and detection notably absent. I suppose you can't blame Brown for resting his dazzlingly inventive mind; the next one will probably be a honey.

He was right.

Fredric Brown began his next novel, *The Deep End*, in Taos, but, as Beth Brown related, he ran into problems completing it. He started plotting the novel in October 1951, but various trips around the country and a developing interest in moving to Los Angeles made demands on his time. He at first wanted to finish the novel before moving but had barely started it by December and decided to go ahead and move right after the Christmas holidays.

Fred and Beth Brown bought their first house together in early January 1952, settling in Venice, California. Always easily distracted, Fred put off writing *The Deep End* and grew interested in fixing the house, watching television, hob-nobbing with the surfeit of writers in the area, and trying to maintain the goldfish pool in his yard. He had barely begun *The Deep End* by March 1952, but he buckled down and wrote it in the spring, finishing sometime in June.

Brown's last three novels—*We All Killed Grandma*, *The Far Cry*, and *Death Has Many Doors*—were all originals, not based on any short stories and never condensed for magazine publication. For *The Deep End* he returned to his occasional practice of mining his own earlier work, this time choosing to expand a novelette he had published in 1946 entitled "Obit for Obie."

According to Brown's logbook, "Obit for Obie" was completed and sent to Harry Altshuler on November 6, 1945 (between "Madman's Concerto" and "A Voice Behind Him"); the 20,000-word novelette sold quickly to *Mystery Book Magazine* on December 8, 1945, for $600 and was published in the October 1946 issue, only a few months after *The Fabulous Clipjoint* made its first appearance there as "Dead Man's Indemnity." Brown may have intended making a novel out of the story sooner; his logbook lists the sale as "1st ser. to Mys. Bk.," a code he used when selling his novels to magazines before they were published in book form. It's true that the subsequent success of *The Fabulous Clipjoint* led to pressure to follow it with another novel featuring Ed and Am Hunter; perhaps Brown simply put "Obit for Obie" aside during the vast changes that occurred in his life between 1945 and 1948. Whatever the case, it is a brilliant novelette and one of his best mysteries.

Narrated by reporter Joe Stacy, the story takes place in an unspecified small city. It begins as Joe is assigned to write the "sob-story" obituary on the death of high school football star Obie Westphal, who was killed on the tracks of the Blue Streak roller coaster at the Whitewater Beach amusement park. No sooner does Joe finish the story than he's told to kill it—the dead man is Jimmy Chojnacki, another high school boy, who must have stolen Obie's wallet and been wrongly identified.

From a bar, Joe sees Obie's parents visit the funeral home and learn that their son is not dead; Joe is troubled by the shocked look on Obie's father's face and returns early from a vacation fishing trip to look into the death on his own. A little investigation makes Joe suspicious of Jimmy's death, especially since several other high school boys have met with accidental death in the last few years. He shadows Obie and sees him walk to the train jungles on the edge of town, and a visit with Obie's father leads Joe to discover that Mr. Westphal suspected that Obie intentionally pushed his sister from a tree years before, paralyzing her.

After speaking to Obie's doctor, Joe is convinced the boy is innocent—until someone rings his bell in the middle of the night and he almost dies falling over a typewriter that has been placed at the top of his dark stairs. As the story ends, Joe and Pete Brenner, a friend of the dead boy's, follow Obie to the train jungles, where Joe pretends to be a hobo and chats with Obie, barely escaping with his life when Pete knocks Obie to his death just as Obie was struggling to kill Joe. Joe is able to reuse the obituary he wrote a week before, and heads for a bar to get drunk and forget his harrowing experience.

"Obit for Obie" is one of Fredric Brown's great early suspense tales. It is as mature as anything he wrote and perfect for its length as a novelette; each character is as developed as he needs to be and the plot is quick and sure, drawing the reader along faster and faster toward a tense, harrowing conclusion.

In 1951, when Brown decided to expand the novelette to novel length, he had a difficult job ahead of him. The novelette is very tight and suspenseful; how would he expand it to considerably greater length without diffusing the suspense and pace that made it so good? He solved the problem in an ingenious way, by changing the focus of the story and developing characters and situations that were minor in the pulp version.

In *The Deep End*, Joe Stacy becomes Sam Evans and time becomes very important, as Brown experiments with a new way of organizing his story. Instead of the chapters of the novelette, he divides the novel into ten sections, each section detailing the events of one day, from the Saturday Jimmy Chojnacki is killed beneath the roller coaster to the Monday nine days later when Sam returns to work and writes his revised obituary for Obie Westphal. This technique is tremendously successful in a naturalistic sort of way; by letting the reader know what day is being described, Brown makes the story easier to follow and emphasizes the irony that the entire story occurs during Sam's week-long vacation. At one point, Sam even remarks about the importance of time in a mystery story:

> I remembered that detectives in stories always carefully time the observed movements of a suspect, so I looked at my watch. It was twenty-seven minutes after four o'clock, if that matters. (106)

The comment is ironic in the context of a novel that is so carefully worked out according to the time of its events. Brown often used compressed time sequences to good effect in his novels, and Jean-Pierre Deloux discusses this technique in his article, "Mouvement brownien."

Another major theme in *The Deep End* involves marriage, betrayal, trust, and infidelity, concerns which are absent from the novelette. As the novel begins, Sam Evans and his wife Millie are near divorce and are spending a week apart on separate vacations. In the novelette, Joe remarks that he and Millie "are smart enough to figure that a week's vacation from each other once a year—well you know what I mean" (97). Things are quite different in the novel, as Sam's thoughts after he speaks to Millie right before she leaves indicate:

And the phone clicked in my ear before I could put it down. The click seemed to have an oddly final sound.
I put down the phone and sat staring at it, feeling a little empty inside, wondering how final that click had been. Was it going to be the end of things between us? (12)

As in *The Far Cry*, a tale of suspense and murder occurs in and about the confines of a failing marriage. Yet Sam Evans (unlike George Weaver) is healthy and sane, and his lustful, extramarital obsessions direct themselves toward Nina Carberry, with whom he "had had a very important first experience" (24) as a senior in high school. Nina is all grown up now, and Sam runs into her unexpectedly when he visits the mother of the slain Jimmy Chojnacki. Sam gets excited at first glance: "her body didn't look schoolteacherish, not by miles. It had filled out, and in the right places..." (46). Sam visits Nina at her apartment and sleeps with her, and they spend Monday, Tuesday, Wednesday, and Friday nights in bed together. This is in sharp contrast to their brief meeting in "Obit for Obie," where Nina blushes at the memory of the time she and Sam met in the high school basement. By Saturday morning, Sam suspects that Nina has a hidden attachment to Obie and confirms this by reading her diary. She discovers and curses him, and their affair ends.

On Sunday morning Sam is nearly killed, and he realizes he loves Millie "to hell and back" (200)—he calls her and warns her not to return until the danger Obie represents is gone. Sam has been tempted and has succumbed, yet it only serves to strengthen his love for his wife and speed their reconcilement. The subplot involving their marital problems and Sam's affair with Millie enriches the novel both by deepening Sam's character and by demonstrating how even a good man can be guilty of betrayal.

Two other items in the novelette receive interesting expansion in the novel. One is Jimmy Chojnacki, the boy killed by the roller coaster. Sam investigates his background more fully, including meeting his mother and learning of his ambitions. Jimmy's mother gives Sam a picture of the boy, leading Sam to think:

> Jimmy Chojnacki had been a good-looking boy. His face was a bit weak, but not vicious...A dreamer and a thief. Well, François Villon had combined those qualities and had done a good job of it. Maybe Jimmy Chojnacki would have, too. If he'd had a chance. (90)

Comparing the dead boy to a great French poet says quite a bit about Sam's intelligence, his background, and his compassion. It also suggests quite strongly where the author's sympathies lie.

The other item to be expanded in *The Deep End* concerns Obie's sister. In "Obit for Obie," Sam visits a psychiatrist who casually clears Obie of all abnormality and infers that Armin Westphal, Obie's father, harbors an unwarranted guilt complex over crimes he imagines his son has committed, including causing his sister to fall from a tree as a child and become paralyzed for life. In *The Deep End*, the girl died in the accident, and Sam visits old Doc Wygand, a friendly, retired doctor who goes into great detail about the Westphal family and suspects Sam may be correct in his suspicions about Obie. The difference is one of complexity—in the novelette, Obie seems innocent until the end, when he tries to kill Joe. In the novel, Obie's guilt is forever clouded, and Sam wavers between believing the boy to be what he appears (a clean-cut kid) and what he may be inside (a tiger).

The Deep End is not a hasty patch-up job of adding new characters and scenes to make a novelette long enough to publish as a novel. It is instead a brilliant recreation of a story that was told economically the first time around. The structure is changed, characters are more fully developed, scenes are longer, and new themes are introduced. Both "Obit for Obie" and *The Deep End* are examples of Fredric Brown's best work: the first is typical of his fine achievements in the mystery story at the beginning of his career as a novelist; the second is an excellent example of the sort of novel he was capable of writing during his mature period.

Although "Obit for Obie" has never received critical attention, *The Deep End* has been written about as much as or more than almost any other Brown work. Reviewers at the time were mixed in their opinions. Anthony Boucher, in The New York *Times* Book Review, called its "sharp prose and narrative movement...Brown at his best," while *The New Yorker* unfairly called Brown's style "vivacious, if not always grammatical" and remarked that "the book may divert you mildly." The novel's publication history is brief—after a Dutton edition on December 1, 1952, and an English edition in 1953, the 1954 Bantam paperback was its last appearance in English until 1983, when Jacques Barzun included it as one of his series of hardcover facsimile reprints of "50 Classics of Crime Fiction, 1950-1975." This prestigious reprinting was followed by a paperback edition the next year. Foreign editions have also been scarce: other than an Italian version in 1954, there were none until the novel was published in France as *Rendez-vous avec un tigre* in 1978.

Critical notice has been perceptive. Newton Baird devoted an entire section of his late 1970s series "Paradox and Plot" to *The Deep End*, calling it "Brown's masterpiece of psychological detection, as well as his best novel..." (151). Jean-Pierre Deloux also discusses the novel in some detail in "Mouvement brownien"; both he and Baird are fascinating in their analysis of the theme of guilt in the novel, and Deloux follows Baird with the thought that Sam Evans, the hero, may be as psychologically troubled by guilt about his marriage as Obie Westphal is about his sister's death.

* * *

The four works discussed in this chapter represent Fredric Brown's early mature period. They show him experimenting with plot, narrative, setting, and theme, and they were written during a period when he was living as a bohemian for the first time in his life in Taos, New Mexico. During these years, Brown was also writing a considerable amount of science fiction, which must be discussed before moving on to the four great novels of his later mature period.

Chapter Nine
Science Fiction Stories

As early as 1938, Fredric Brown tried his hand at science fiction. Throughout his early pulp period he wrote a handful of science fiction stories in the midst of writing dozens and dozens of mystery stories. Upon moving to Taos in 1949 he began spending time with Mack Reynolds; the association corresponded with a boom in science fiction magazines and Brown responded with an increased number of stories of this type. By the mid-1950s he had stopped writing stories (other than short-shorts) except on occasion, and the last decade of his career includes but a few science fiction stories, just as his output of short mysteries dwindled.

Part I: 1938-1945

According to his logbook, Brown's first attempt at writing science fiction may have been a story called "The Eyes Have It," completed by December 17, 1938, and submitted directly to *Amazing Stories*, which quickly rejected it and returned it to him on December 30. The gap in Brown's logbook for 1939 and the first part of 1940 makes it impossible to determine whether any other early science fiction stories have been lost; during this period, he wrote his first one to be published, "Not Yet the End," which was accepted by his new agent Harry Altshuler and sold to *Captain Future* for publication in the Winter 1941 issue. The story is short and ironic, the precursor of his later short-shorts. It deals with the theme of "first contact" and describes the results of a failed alien invasion. The aliens, Kar-388Y and Lal-16B, approach Earth intending to capture men to keep as slaves on their home planet. They land, pick up two "people," and fly off, but their tests reveal the "men" to be below acceptable levels of intelligence even for slave labor and the aliens depart in search of another planet. Meanwhile, on Earth, two men in a newsroom decide to run a story about the disappearance the night before of two monkeys from the zoo! The twist ending is funny—the end of the world is avoided by the aliens' careless error and the world does not know that it has been saved. As Douglas J. McReynolds points out in his essay on "The Short Fiction of Fredric Brown," one of the major themes of Brown's science fiction is "...the unpredictable natures of possible extraterrestrial invasions" (1955). This is true in his first science fiction story, and it remains a concern through his last completed science fiction novel, *The Mind Thing* (1961).

Alien invasion is also a factor in "The Hat Trick," in which the subject is treated more like a fantasy. The story's climax occurs as two young couples sit in an apartment and one of the men, Bob Evans, taunts the other, Walter Beekman, into doing his famous "hat trick." When Walter pulls a huge, hideous black rat from a hat, the others are so shocked that they do not remember the event the next time they meet. At the story's end, Bob meets Walter in a bookstore where the latter works and gives him a book about aliens living in disguise among men, which Bob dismisses as "hooey." The implication is subtle but sinister: Walter is an alien on Earth with unknown powers, living in disguise among men for an unstated purpose. Yet nothing is said explicitly, no science is discussed, and no motive or consequence is given for this seemingly successful alien invasion. Brown thus uses science fiction elements in a dark fantasy, and the urban, almost bohemian atmosphere of the story is in keeping with Thomas Clareson's remark that *Unknown Worlds* (in which the story appeared) "Infused fantasy into the mundane streets of the modern world" (694).

By 1945, Brown had written *The Fabulous Clipjoint*, and his prose was mature as well as more lyrical than it had been in his earlier stories. In January of that year he published "The Waveries," an elegiac story describing a different kind of alien invasion. As the story begins the invasion is complete, and the narrator (an unidentified "I" who disappears once the tale is underway) says he will tell the story of the waveries by telling the story of George Bailey. In short, the waveries are invisible, wave-like alien beings that gradually absorb all the electricity on Earth and force mankind back into a pre-electric lifestyle. These aliens are not malicious, like those in "Not Yet the End," nor do they interact with human beings, as does Walter in "The Hat Trick." Instead they are invisible, and no contact is ever made between them and the inhabitants of Earth. They merely arrive, absorb electricity and stay, yet their presence causes enormous changes in people's lives.

Scientific discussion enters into this story in the form of explanations of the Heaviside layer and the various effects of the waveries, and Brown details the world economic changeover from electric to nonelectric existence in a mere three and one-half pages, but these discussions are not the point of the story. The consequences of the changes caused by the waveries' arrival are what matter, and these consequences are most eloquently shown in Brown's evocation of the changing lives of George Bailey and those around him. Brown thus presents a portrait of a benevolent alien invasion and, in the three stories I have discussed, his portraits of aliens are never cruel: aliens are humorous and incompetent in "Not Yet the End," subtle and potentially dangerous in "The Hat Trick" (but so subtle as to leave nothing certain), and unconcerned with human events in "The Waveries." Brown's three treatments of this theme in his early stories represent three of the author's strongest talents: humor, terror, and an almost meditative philosophical prose.

A similar theme to that of Earth's invasion by aliens involves the visits of earthmen to other planets and their interactions with the aliens they encounter. Brown deals with this question in several early stories, and his developing approach parallels the changes in his treatment of the "invasion of Earth" theme. "The Star Mouse" is the first Brown story in which a representative from Earth journeys to another planet and meets that planet's inhabitants. In this story, however, the earthman is actually a mouse, Mitkey, who is the passenger in an experimental rocket designed by Professor Oberburger. Mitkey's rocket arrives on Prxl, a planet invisible to Earth where the inhabitants are one-half inch tall. The Prxlians raise Mitkey's intelligence level to that of a human, give him a machine to do the same for all mice, and send him back to Earth, where he surprises everyone before finally losing his intelligence.

The most interesting aspect of the story is Brown's treatment of the Prxlians, who are far ahead of humans in scientific achievement and have painted their world a light-absorbing black to keep it invisible and safe from attack. The Prxlians are kind to Mitkey and act rationally and beneficially toward their guest. Brown thus suggests that the inhabitants of other worlds may be superior in intelligence to earthmen and may need to hide from us for their own safety.

A much different picture of a visit to another planet is presented in "And the Gods Laughed," in which Hank, the narrator, tells what appears to be a tall tale about a previous expedition to Ganymede, where the natives were controlled by powerful beings who looked like earrings. Hank tells of how these beings gradually took over the bodies of all of his fellow crew members, but ends the tale by claiming it is only a story. Later, when Hank is alone, he reports to his fellows that the experiment in *embedding* the rings (which formerly had to be worn in the ear) is a success and that he will have no trouble taking over the ship. The aliens in this story are completely malevolent, casually killing men and taking control of their bodies before proceeding with their plans for world domination. The expedition to Ganymede and its results prefigure the paranoid science fiction of the 1950s, and the trick ending works well. "And the Gods Laughed" is thus the science fiction counterpart to "The Hat Trick," hinting at alien possession of human bodies for potentially evil ends.

Two of Fredric Brown's stories on this theme are mainly humorous: "Nothing Sirius" presents a world inhabited by small beings that look like cockroaches, while the planet in "Placet is a Crazy Place" is a physical nightmare. In "Nothing Sirius," Captain Wherry and his family discover the planet Nothing Sirius, a name they choose because it is inside the orbits of the first and second planets of the star Sirius. On the planet they see such strange sights as a giant ostrich with a bow-tie, birds that fly with the aid of propellers, and a long-dead friend of theirs who introduces them to a beautiful movie starlet. Finally realizing that these are all illusions, they return to their ship and receive a telepathic message from the cockroach-like creatures that are the planet's only inhabitants: they feel that they could not abide humans on their planet due to fundamental incompatibility and ask the ship to leave and send no more people in its place.

The story is very funny, and its main point is that aliens may find humans just as repugnant as we find them. As in "The Star Mouse," the aliens cannot live side by side with human beings and thus shun discovery. Although they cause no harm, the "cockroaches" are far ahead of humans scientifically and want nothing to do with us.

Brown's other humorous tale on this theme, "Placet is a Crazy Place," is really just a bit of wordplay drawn out into a short story. The planet Placet has already been colonized by humans and no sentient aliens inhabit it. Placet itself is a problem, though, for its physical differences from Earth play havoc with the men and women who live there. The only alien is the planet itself and, like the waveries, it causes great changes in the people it affects yet is indifferent to human affairs.

Perhaps Brown's best science fiction story, "Arena," also addresses the theme of man's meeting alien beings on a far planet and couches it in the form of a battle of wits and skill. "Arena" has received serious critical attention and stands out as the author's most powerful statement on one possible outcome of the meeting between a human and an alien, the "Roller," who is completely evil. They are placed on an unknown planet's barren desert by an omniscient alien who sees that the conflict between the two races about to take place will destroy both. In the best gladiator tradition they are ordered to fight, the loser's race to be annihilated. There are thus two important aliens in "Arena": the omniscient being and the evil Roller. Although Gary K. Wolfe faults Brown for his simplistic portrait of the omniscient being (*The Known and the Unknown* 35), Rosemarie Arbur notes that the story

dramatizes the evolutionary end, not just the process. In its own telepathic 'words,' an absolute mentality, independent of time, space, and even individual personality as we know it, informs us that evolution for mentality—the path we humans evidently have taken—has been fully achieved by at least one sapient race... (84-85)

The omniscient being is thus another example of an alien far superior to man, and this time that superiority approaches godhood. It is a pagan godhood, however, because this god allows a problem to be settled by a gladiatorial battle.

The Roller, on the other hand, is clearly inferior to the man in the story in every way except his ability to fight and survive. Looking like a red ball with tentacles, the Roller is described as "utterly alien, horribly different" (*The Best of Fredric Brown* 15), and whenever it approaches Carson, the earthman in the story, it gives off "an almost tangible wave of hatred" (15). There is no communication between the two, and the alien's only concern is with killing Carson. Gary Wolfe makes much of "the opposition between the known and the unknown" ("The Known and Unknown" 103) in the story, and it is clear that, in this case, man's encounter with another race results in nothing but war. However, the main problem in the story—that of discovering a way to pass through the invisible barrier that separates the two combatants—is only solved when

Carson realizes he must lose consciousness in order to achieve the other side. Perhaps Brown here suggests that man can only defeat hatred (represented by the Roller) by passing through a barrier that is closed to conscious men—the barrier against accepting the different, the unreal, the unexpected.

Fredric Brown's approaches to the meeting between humans and aliens in space are varied, from the beneficial yet hidden Prxlians to the superior "cockroaches" of "Nothing Sirius"; from the malevolent "earring gods" who steal men's bodies to the Roller, a creature of pure hate. The single thread running through these works is the suggestion that any aliens we meet will probably be superior to us, if not indifferent (other than the Roller, which is superior only in its capacity for hatred) and that most likely we will have more difficulty dealing with their differentness than they will have dealing with ours. In "Arena," Brown presents a member of a race that has evolved to a purely mental state and, to this being, man is a small figure to be viewed almost for sport. Brown thus cannot be accused of writing stories that promote human racial ethnocentricity; rather, the variety of his stories suggests his fundamental openness to the possibilities inherent in meeting alien beings, whether the consequences be humorous or terrifying.

In addition to man's meeting actual beings from other planets, Brown's early science fiction stories often deal with the consequences of advances in technology on present and future people. Douglas J. McReynolds claims that one of Brown's central themes is that "the basic machines of mid-twentieth century American industry—drill presses, lathes, linotypes, and the like—are more valuable to civilization's future than are the electronic gimmicks which this or any other technology might manage to produce" (1955), and this is certainly evident in "The Waveries," in which the elimination of electricity results in a happier populace. However, these "mid-twentieth century" machines are sometimes problematic, as in "Etaoin Shrdlu," in which a linotype machine acquires a mind of its own. Gary K. Wolfe cites the story as "one of the earliest...[in which] everyday machines" are suddenly animated and turn "on their masters in some sort of mechanical revolt" (*The Known and the Unknown* 151). Although, as Amelia A. Rutledge notes, the machine in "Etaoin Shrdlu" is "a substitute for the usual bug-eyed monster" (81) of science fiction stories, the story is more fantasy than science fiction and the linotype machine—which takes to heart the ideas of every book it sets in type—grows more difficult the more human it becomes, until it is finally neutralized after it reads a book on Buddhism and decides to devote the rest of its life to contemplating its cam-shaft!

A more dangerous encounter with technological advances occurs in "Death is a White Rabbit," which appeared in a detective pulp (*Strange Detective Mysteries*, January 1942) but contains science fiction elements that anticipate Brown's later novel, *The Mind Thing*. The story is tasteless, but its villain, a scientist who can control the minds of animals and uses them to attack his enemies, suggests the dangers of technology gone mad. A futuristic variation on this theme is found in "Daymare," in which Rod Caquer, a police lieutenant on the moon of Callisto, foils a mind-control plot hatched by powerful official Barr Maxon. The story is set in the future and includes all the trappings of a technologically-advanced world, yet in this society some knowledge is forbidden. This knowledge is collected in Blackdex books, which include a description of how to construct a Vargas Wheel, an apparatus that gives the person wearing it the power of instantaneous mass hypnosis. A complex story, "Daymare" is partially concerned with the dangers of advanced science, and the Vargas Wheel, so dangerous that its use is prohibited, provides an example of an invention that does more harm than good.

On a lighter note, Brown uses another piece of headgear in "The Yehudi Principle," in which Charlie Swann demonstrates the title principle to his friend Hank: the wearer of the headband in this story can command that a thing be done and it will be done by a little man who is not there. Unfortunately, Hank tells the little man to "shoot yourself" (in his drunken pronunciation of "suit yourself"), and Hank and Charlie hear a shot outside their apartment, after which the headband no longer works. "The Yehudi Principle" demonstrates the possibility of man's misuse of technologies that should be beneficial to him and suggests that, with advanced science, small accidents may have large consequences.

In another humorous story, "Pi in the Sky," a soap manufacturer uses a device to rearrange the stars in the heavens to form a slogan advertising his soap. Brown's message is that the greatest scientific advances may end up being used for the most base purposes and, in 1987 (when the story takes place), man is clearly unhappy with the advertising clutter that scientific advances like radio have brought him.

Brown thus rebels against a simple acceptance of technological advance and cautions the reader against its possible misuse. In none of the stories mentioned does mankind benefit from an unusual invention; rather, technology consistently causes him problems. Douglas J. McReynolds is correct in seeing Brown as denying the value of scientific progress in his early science fiction stories, and this characteristic of the author aligns him once again with the philosopher and debunker of scientific certainties, Charles Fort.

Charles Fort's writing showed an extreme distrust of science, and Brown, in the detective story, "The Spherical Ghoul," pays his debt to Fort's thinking. Fort's greatest influence, however, was on writers in the science fiction field, and Brown was among them as well.

"The Angelic Angleworm" is Brown's most extensive treatment of Charles Fort's theories, and in certain passages Brown even imitates Fort's prose style. The story's plot concerns Charlie Wills (perhaps a play on Charles Fort's name?), a printer whose life is shaken by a series of seemingly inexplicable and unconnected events. He sees a worm sprout wings and a halo and fly off, he suddenly acquires a bad sunburn on a rainy day, he sees a wild duck in a museum case where Roman coins are on exhibit, he finds a Hawaiian lei on a golf course while looking for a golf ball, he passes out as he enters a jewelry store. Each of these events is explained away by Pete Johnson, Charlie's friend, who represents the rational perspective that refuses to accept the possibility that there is anything unusual behind the occurrences. Finally, in the hospital, Charlie tries to commit suicide when he realizes that the events are connected by periodicity and that another is due very soon. It is not until he figures out the underlying connection between the events that he is able to correct things; at the end of the story Charlie visits Heaven, where he tells the Head Compositor that a matrix in the linotype machine up there is defective from wear and is slipping out of place every 50 hours and ten minutes. The defective matrix is repaired (it had moved the letter "e" in various words and thus caused the metamorphoses—for example, "angleworm" became "angelworm") and Charlie's problems are solved.

"The Angelic Angleworm" is one of Brown's early stories and the author's firm hand is felt throughout, spinning out strange occurrences but never losing control of the narrative. In the passages where Charlie thinks through the events, Brown seems to adopt a Fortean prose style—

short, choppy sentences, repetition of words, and heavy use of dramatic tricks to drive a point home. The story's conclusion somewhat agrees with Fort's theories: all of the strange events are attributed to a mistake made by the heavenly Head Compositor, thus suggesting a higher state of order or perfection in which all seemingly bizarre events fit a logical order. This higher order is beyond man's ken and represents the force of total order that Fort insists is the only way to explain and include all of this world's anomalies.

"The Hat Trick," which Brown published in the same issue of *Unknown Worlds* as "The Angelic Angleworm," deals with the Fortean premise that man cannot accept that which is inexplicable and thus must treat it as an unreal event. In this way, Brown gives another nod to Fort's insistence that modern man, conditioned as he is by the teachings of science, is mentally unprepared to accept the strange or unusual. This theme reappears briefly in "Paradox Lost," when Dopey, a time traveler, tells Shorty McCabe, the story's protagonist, that "Normals" (like Shorty) are unable to accept being faced with anything out of the ordinary.

Out of the ordinary occurrences are found in several other science fiction/fantasy stories in Brown's early period, especially those that deal with devils or demons. In "How Tagrid Got There," an unpublished fantasy written by July 18, 1941, but never sold, Tagrid meets several monsters on his quest, including a witch and a wizard whom he is able to outsmart. In "Armageddon," the devil himself appears when a Tibetan lama accidentally knocks a prayer wheel from its mooring. The devil takes the place of Gerber the Great, a stage magician in the middle of a performance:

Quietly, then, the magician began to chuckle. In the overtones of that soft laughter was all of evil. No one who heard it could have doubted who he was. No one did doubt. The audience, every member of it, knew in that awful moment who stood there before them, knew it—even the most skeptical among them—beyond shadow of doubt. (*The Best of Fredric Brown* 200)

The devil's appearance is absurd yet frightening; Brown's skillful use of fantastic elements enriches the mood of his tale. The linotype machine in "Etaoin Shrdlu," another fantasy, also becomes possessed, and there is a suggestion that the "little guy with the pimple" who sets secret Eastern books in type on the machine and thus imparts it with a mind has connections not grounded in everyday reality.

Brown uses several demons in "The New One," in which Wally Smith's attempt to stop his own pyromania is hindered by the influence of several fire elementals, beings of pure thought who seem to inhabit a place like Hell. The malevolent dolls of "The Geezenstacks" (as well as the "witch" who ends the story on a note of doom) also seem to demonstrate demonic influence. In opposition to these characters are the inhabitants of Heaven that appear in "The Angelic Angleworm." It is clear that, in his fantasies, Brown found it convenient to use some of the traditional symbols of good and evil—angels and demons—while occasionally espousing Fortean philosophy through a catalog of unique and unexpected occurrences.

Brown thus deals with a number of themes in his early imaginative fiction, from contact with aliens to man's inability to cope with advanced technology, from Fortean strangeness to traditional fantastic elements of literature. While these themes are important, Brown's use of characterization in these stories should also be examined, and such an examination reveals (in a development parallel to that found in the author's early detective fiction) an evolution in which the author progresses from sketchy characters necessary to a plot to characters from whom the plot develops.

Brown's earliest surviving science fiction story, "Not Yet the End," is very short and is mainly a set-up and twist ending. The aliens are barely mentioned and the newsmen at the story's end function only as devices by which the punch line can be delivered. The characters in "Armageddon" are also sketchy, and Herbie Westerman, the boy-hero, is little more than a type. By 1942, however, Brown was beginning to flesh out the characters in his detective stories and, as "The Star Mouse" demonstrates, in his science fiction work as well. The story is longer than his earlier efforts and, although Professor Oberburger is one of Brown's silliest caricatures, Mitkey Mouse is shown to possess "human" characteristics, evolving in the course of the story from a dumb mouse into an intelligent thinker.

"The Angelic Angleworm" and "The Hat Trick," both published early in 1943, demonstrate Brown's growing ability to create characters and invest them with individual lives. In the first story, Charlie Wills undergoes a strenuous test of will and emerges victorious when he solves and corrects the series of mishaps that plague his life. In "The Hat Trick," although the story is not long enough for any of the characters to be extensively drawn, the interactions among the two young couples are quite realistic and the author makes each person in the group an individual. By the next year, Brown's ability with character was nearly at its peak in this early period and Carson, the heroic earthman in "Arena," is depicted in some depth; the entire story revolves around him and his mental abilities, he must progress through stages of induction in order to save himself, and his acts of kindness in sparing a talking lizard and in later putting another lizard out of its misery help provide the key to solving his problem.

Finally, in "The Waveries," published in January 1945 but written in May 1944, Brown is able to have a character state at the outset that he will tell the story of the waveries' invasion by telling the story of one man who experienced it. That man is George Bailey, a disgruntled radio writer who, like the protagonist of *Murder Can Be Fun*, drowns his self-doubt in alcohol. The story follows his reactions to the general changes caused by the arrival of the aliens and ends in a very lyrical passage. George has been discussing music with his friend Pete and still holds his cornet:

And with the shining silver thing in his hand he wandered over to the window and stood looking out into the night. It was dusk out and the rain had stopped.

A high-stepping horse *clop-clopped* by and the bell of a bicycle jangled. Somebody across the street was strumming a guitar and singing. He took a deep breath and let it out slowly.

The scent of spring was soft and sweet in the moist air.

Peace and dusk.

Distant rolling thunder.

God damn it, he thought, *if only there was a bit of lightning.*

He missed the lightning. (*Angels and Spaceships* 113)

This passage and others like it demonstrate that, by 1944, Brown no longer needed to rely on plot or gimmicks in his fiction, just as *The Fabulous Clipjoint*, written later that year, shows his ability to work with gentleness and depth in the novel form. His fiction had clearly progressed in the several years since "Not Yet the End"; by 1944, his prose was mature and flowed with the sure hand of a writer just reaching the height of his powers.

Throughout Brown's early science fiction there are many themes, and the small number of stories spread over a period of several years makes it relatively easy to spot signs of change and growth in his prose. Yet these stories were by no means always serious and, in fact, Brown is often cited for the humor in his early work. From the beginning the stories were funny: the aliens in "Not Yet the End" are incompetent, the portrait of Herbie in "Armageddon" is comic, the situation in "Etaoin Shrdlu" (even though the idea of a linotype machine growing sentient could be frightening) is presented with a light touch from start to finish: the machine sets type for love pulps and demands a mate; it sets Socialist copy and goes on strike. Brown later made a point of emphasizing the need for humor in science fiction: "man is more essentially a comic figure than a tragic one," he wrote, "especially when he faces the cosmos rather than the tiny world upon which he evolved." Brown concludes that to ignore the comedy in a situation is "to paint a flat, and not rounded, picture of the future" ("Why I Selected—Nothing Sirius" 103). Brown's other early science fiction stories range in humor from the sophomoric ("The Star Mouse") to the complex ("Paradox Lost") to the deeply ironic: in "Pi in the Sky," a vast array of characters run back and forth throughout the story in their attempt to discover the cause of the stars' realignment; at the end, the stars spell out "Use Snively's Soap" and the mastermind behind the gigantic advertisement collapses from a heart attack because his name is misspelled! The development of humor in Brown's early stories thus roughly parallels the development of character; however, the author always remains open to a pun or a pratfall, even when his stories are at their most subtly ironic.

One last point needs to be made about Brown's early science fiction stories, and that is their connection with his work in the detective pulps. The idea of merging science fiction and detective stories was new in 1941 when Brown began experimenting with the form, and consequently he is seen as one of its pioneers. "Death is a White Rabbit" (written in June 1941 and published in January 1942) appears to be the first example of his using elements of science fiction in a story published in a detective pulp, and "The Numberless Shadows" (written in November 1941 and published in September 1942) features a protagonist, Buck Henderson, who at several points jokes with his girlfriend Rita and makes up stories about people being aliens. As they sit alone in a room at the story's end, Rita asks, " 'is that the police?' ", to which Buck answers: " 'it's the Martian Royal Guard. You haven't heard, of course, but they landed in a spaceship yesterday on Long Island. They're after kangaroos'." Buck then describes the Martians: " 'They walk on their elbows and communicate with one another by their sense of smell...' " (*Who Was That Blonde* 54). Brown had written only a handful of science fiction and fantasy stories at this point, yet "The Numberless Shadows" demonstrates that his science fiction work was already spilling over into his detective fiction.

An interesting comparison can be made between "Red is the Hue of Hell" (written around New Year's Day 1942 and published in *Strange Detective Mysteries*' July 1942 issue) and "The New One" (written later in January 1942 and published in the October 1942 *Unknown Worlds*). In "Red is the Hue of Hell," Duncan is a recovering pyromaniac who reluctantly takes a job in the Hermes Powder Works because he feels it is his patriotic duty to help during the war. The factory is sabotaged and Duncan blamed for the fire until he learns that the culprit was actually a Japanese spy named Roberts. The story is a straightforward mystery with no fantastic elements, and its main strengths are in its plot, which makes good use of flashbacks, and its examination of Duncan's pyromania. "The New One" is similar: Wally Smith is a pyromaniac from birth who also takes a job at a TNT factory after Pearl Harbor. Like Duncan, Wally wrestles with his problem and nearly lights a fire to blow up his factory. The difference in this story is in its fantastic sequences, in which several fire elementals discuss the plan of Darveth, the head fire demon, to use his power to control a man. Throughout the story, as Wally edges closer to disaster, the narrative switches back to the fire elementals, who observe the events surrounding Wally Smith. In the end, he is prevented from lighting the destructive fire by the "new one," a newly-arrived elemental who beats up Darveth and prevents him from carrying out his plan. The elementals, Brown explains, are creatures of pure thought which exist because people believe in them, and their strength depends on the number of believers. The "new one" turns out to be Uncle Sam, who has appeared among the elementals in the wake of Pearl Harbor and is able to prevent Wally Smith's pyromania from doing any harm to the American war effort.

These two stories demonstrate Brown's ability to vary his fiction from detective story to fantasy by shifting the focus and providing either realistic or imaginative explanations for his characters' actions. In "Daymare," Brown actually synthesizes the two types of stories into one and creates a new hybrid. Sam Moskowitz has written that "this story presaged the entrance into the scientific detective field of a crack professional capable of homogenizing both the detective story and the science fiction story into an acceptable blend" (157). In the story, Rod Caquer is a policeman of the future in Sector Three City on Jupiter's moon of Callisto. He uses detective methods to solve the mystery in this technological society; several times he recalls reading the adventures of detective Wilder Williams during his childhood on Earth and finally solves the case through a combination of dogged clue-hunting and concentrated induction. As Douglas J. McReynolds notes, the protagonists in Brown's science fiction stories are like those of his detective stories—it is the "kinds of worlds and technologies with which they are involved that intrigues and arrests the reader" (1955).

Thus, Brown's early imaginative fiction is not always as far from his early detective fiction as it might seem on the surface. In his 1951 introduction to his collection *Space On My Hands* Brown wrote of his preference for writing science fiction: "Science-fiction stories are the least painful of all stories for me to write, and when I have put THE END on the final page of one, I feel greater satisfaction than with any other kind of story" (1-2). Coming from Brown, who wrote many more detective stories than science fiction or fantasy stories, this is illuminating. Brown goes on to say that the lack of "rules and limitations" in science fiction makes it "closer than any other fiction to being honest writing" and notes that the science fiction writer can

tailor his background, his universe, to the story he wants to write; he can thereby, achieve an integration and an integrity denied the writer who has only one universe to work in and who must twist and trim the products of his imagination to fit the inflexible mold of fact. (2)

Brown demonstrates this very quality of imagination in many of his early science fiction stories. While some critics see this early work as mainly humorous, it is more than that. Beginning his science fiction career with short stories that rely on plot gimmicks, Brown quickly expands in numerous directions, dealing with a variety of themes in fresh ways each time he returns to them. Unlike his early detective stories, in which he sometimes relies on formulas embellished by inventive details, his early science fiction stories seem to represent the author's flights of fancy. By 1944, he was capable of a story like "The Waveries," in which the best elements of his previous fiction are synthesized in a poignant tale with an emphasis on character. Fredric Brown's early science fiction work may not be extensive, yet it often shows the author at his best; the emotion of his poetry, the sense of character of his best detective fiction, and his mastery of plotting are combined with great imagination to produce a series of memorable stories that would only be surpassed in quality by the work that was to come.

* * *

Part II: 1946-1957

Fredric Brown's life and career changed significantly in the years following the completion of *The Fabulous Clipjoint*. He published no short science fiction in 1947 and, other than a novelette, which will be discussed in chapter ten, only one story in 1948. American life and publishing also changed significantly after World War II, when atomic explosions made science fiction and futuristic technology not only possible, but commonplace. As the post-war years wore on, science fiction grew more and more popular, with the first real publishing "boom" occurring from about 1949-52. Brown responded by writing more science fiction stories in a shorter period than ever before: from April 1949 to December 1951 he published 19 such stories, three novelettes, and a collection in book form. These stories ran the gamut, and reflected many changes in Brown's style.

In his stories published from 1948 to 1957, Brown returned to some of the themes of his earlier stories and introduced some new and topical ones as well. Aliens were still coming to Earth and meeting humans, usually with surprising results. In "Knock" (*Thrilling Wonder Stories* December 1948), the Zan arrive and kill all but two of most animal species on Earth, then put the survivors in a zoo on their ship for further study. Walter Phelan and Grace Evans are the last humans, and Walter tricks the Zan into abandoning the planet.

That story is told in the third-person "raconteur" style that Brown used so effectively in some of his short mysteries in 1947-48, and beginning and end contain these famous lines:

The last man on Earth sat alone in a room. There was a knock at the door.
(*The Best of Fredric Brown* 129, 138)

Of course, what is "a sweet little horror story" at the beginning is revealed to be not so horrible at the end; the person knocking on the door of the last man on Earth just happens to be the last woman on Earth! The alien Zan are unconcerned with life forms on Earth and quickly kill virtually all animals and humans. They have advanced technology and can create instant habitats for any animal, yet their advanced skill does not make them any less likely to kill. Unlike the waveries, the Zan know what they are doing when they cause mass destruction. In this way, they resemble the aliens of "Not Yet the End," though they are certainly less easily fooled.

Aliens come again in "All Good Bems" (*Thrilling Wonder Stories* April 1949), but in this humorous story they only stop by while their damaged ship is repaired. They appear in the guise of various friendly animals and visit a writer and his wife who resemble Fred and Beth Brown.

"Mouse" (*Thrilling Wonder Stories* June 1949) finds another alien masquerading as an animal; this time, a pet cat named Beautiful. The protagonist, Bill Wheeler, sees a ship land in New York's Central Park. The only thing found inside it is a dead mouse. Six days later numerous world authorities are assassinated and Bill deduces that the alien can possess bodies at will and that its base of operations must be his apartment, the place nearest its point of landing. He realizes his cat is possessed, and we learn he's correct in his assumptions.

The purpose of the alien in "Mouse" is unknown but its acts are chilling. Its ability to inhabit bodies at will recalls Brown's earlier story, "Death is a White Rabbit," and prefigures his later novel, *The Mind Thing*. Bill reasons that the alien plans to make mankind destroy itself to facilitate invasion; the alien recalls the earlier (and even more subtle) visitor in "The Hat Trick."

A single alien with malevolent intent arrives in "From These Ashes" (*Amazing Stories* August 1950), where a roving "Stranger" is sucked into the body of Johnny Dix, a dying soldier whose prejudices guide the Stranger into working toward a world where white men rule. Dix becomes dictator of the United States and puts the world on the brink of war before a clairvoyant boy manages to help the Stranger escape from Johnny Dix's body, diffusing the impending holocaust.

Continuing the trend of aliens hiding among us is "The Last Martian" (*Galaxy* October 1950), in which all living Martians teleport to Earth and inhabit human bodies. The unfortunate narrator is not a Martian, and when he discovers that most of the people he knows *are* he is understandably upset—until the Martians convince him that the whole thing is a product of his imagination. The story concludes as two Martians agree that the intruder will pose no threat to their impending takeover.

Finally, in "Dark Interlude" (*Galaxy* January 1951), an alien arrives without ill intent, only to be killed by prejudicial men. Unfortunately, Jan Obreen is not really an alien but a time traveler from the future, where all races have blended into one. His partially black heritage does him in when he falls for a white woman in the rural South of 1950.

Another set of aliens that are easily fooled arrive in "Man of Distinction" (*Thrilling Wonder Stories* February 1951); they kidnap Al Hanley, who is hopelessly drunk and behaves illogically. On that basis they decide earthlings are too stupid to enslave en masse and take Al back to their planet, Dar, where he becomes a star zoo attraction in a cage labeled "Alcoholicus Anonymous"! Once again, alien takeover is prevented by the aliens' poor judgment and misfortune in picking sample humans.

In "Cartoonist" (*Planet Stories* May 1951), Bill Garrigan is taken to the planet Snook by aliens who like his drawing ability (his way-out cartoons look just like them) and want him to be Royal Cartoonist to the Emperor. He is treated so well that he decides to stay! Clearly, the aliens here fall into the category of those who look very different than us and don't try to hide it; their intent is not bad, and Garrigan is pleased when he's kidnapped.

"Me and Flapjack and the Martians" (*Astounding* December 1952) features more Martians who plan to take over Earth because Mars is dying. They converse with Flapjack, the narrator's mule, who gives them a better solution, after which they leave with best wishes!

These nine stories of alien invasion do not generally show aliens in a good light. Some are chilling, implying that the aliens will have no trouble conquering Earth and will find only slight resistance. Others are comic, with aliens giving up their attempts at world domination due to the acts of clever humans or due to their own errors. The aliens are of much darker purpose overall than those in Brown's earlier stories, perhaps reflecting the paranoia of Cold War America at its height.

This paranoia is not as evident in the seven stories Brown wrote during this period dealing with human (or mouse) expeditions to other planets. These stories are both humorous and suspenseful, but they do not paint other-worldly inhabitants in as negative a light as those stories in which they invade our planet. The first such story is "The Undying Ones" (*Super Science Stories* September 1950), in which Earth ships destroy approaching alien ships because "any alien is an enemy" and must be destroyed on sight. A single spacemen, Lt. Don Ross, returns to space and learns that the aliens are peaceful and only want to get as far away from Earth as they can. Ross agrees to take them, ensuring their safety and his death. As opposed to the many "invasion of Earth" stories, this one portrays Earthmen in a negative light, anxious to kill intruders and fearful of the unknown.

"Honeymoon in Hell" (*Galaxy* November 1950) continues this theme, with an American man and a Russian woman marrying and traveling to the moon to try to conceive a male child after an unknown force prevents baby boys from being born on Earth. On the moon, the couple is kidnapped by aliens; they escape and return to Earth, causing East and West to forget the Cold War and work together against the aliens. It is finally revealed that the entire plot was worked out by a computer to prevent the Cold War from heating up, and Brown again demonstrates that humans may pose a greater danger to themselves than aliens ever could.

A lighter note is struck in "Device of the Turtle" (*Worlds Beyond* December 1950), when Rod Spencer and other explorers travel to Venus to capture a rare Venusian mud-turtle. Unfortunately, every time someone looks at the turtle he experiences a temporary lapse of memory, causing him to forget his purpose and walk away! The mud turtle is uninterested in human affairs and perfectly capable of protecting itself, and the fact that the explorers are kind rather than malevolent supports Douglas McReynolds's assessment of Brown's message: "the universe and the creatures which inhabit it are just crazy enough to go on surviving, and just resourceful enough to make that survival a relatively painless experience" (1956).

"The Gamblers" (*Startling Stories* November 1951) returns to the image of a man on the moon abused by aliens. He has been left there with insufficient provisions by aliens obsessed with gambling and intent on claiming Earth as a colony. Captain Thorkelson uses his wits to survive, able to return to Earth and warn mankind to prepare for attack in 40 years, when the aliens will return. The Tharn resemble the unfriendly aliens of the numerous "invasion of Earth" stories; this time, their stop on the moon provides mankind with the warning it needs to survive.

One of Brown's worst stories, "The Hatchetman" (*Amazing Stories* December 1951), continues the theme of excursions into space; this time, the "aliens" are Duplies, duplicate men who run Mars with an iron hand. The Duplies are defeated by the heroic acts of Matt Anders and are little more than evil twins of humans in a clumsily-handled Cold War allegory.

Brown wrote two more stories in this period set on alien worlds: "Something Green" (*Space On My Hands* 1951) and "Happy Ending" (*Fantastic Universe* September 1957). Obsession and insanity control McGarry, the spaceman abandoned on Kruger III in "Something Green," who talks to an imaginary alien pet and doesn't realize Earth was destroyed years before by an Arcturan attack. Similar manias bedevil Number One, the exiled dictator in "Happy Ending" who hides on Venus and is eventually killed by the Kifs, alien army ants that destroy everything in their path.

These seven stories are more thematically varied than the nine written on the "invasion of Earth" theme, and they predominantly show humans as malevolent, petulant, or insane, while aliens are usually portrayed as kind or indifferent. The change is significant—fear reigns supreme of the consequences of alien invaders, but when man ventures out into space he often shows himself to be unworthy of amicable treatment.

As Fredric Brown's science fiction stories of 1948-57 dealt increasingly more with the fears of alien contact, they dealt less with the consequences of advances in technology on present and future people. Only three stories share this theme, and in only one is it central. "The Switcheroo" (*Other Worlds Science Fiction* March 1951) involves an invention with which the user can exchange places with anyone he chooses. The inventor switches bodies with the governor, and a reporter takes the place of the president! This invention has the potential to cause mass chaos, but the tale is a humorous one and all is well by the end. "The Dome" (*Thrilling Wonder Stories* August 1951) tells the story of Dr. Kyle Braden, who has sat alone in a protective dome for 30 years since he heard a nuclear holocaust was about to destroy his native Cleveland. When he emerges from the dome he learns that the destruction never occurred and that, instead, friendly aliens came to welcome Earth into the interplanetary union, bringing with them the seeds of world peace and prosperity as well as near-immortality. Sadly, Kyle is too old to enjoy it and plans to return to the dome to die alone.

"The Dome" demonstrates the danger of acting too soon, for the technological advance that should protect Kyle ends up ruining his life. A similar dome appears in "The Gamblers"; it is under this dome that Captain Thorkelsen is left with limited provisions to await a rescue ship. The inventions in these three stories are fantastic and futuristic, not connected to any invention commonly in use in 1951, when all three stories appeared. They are therefore different than the early stories, like "Etaoin Shrdlu" and "The Waveries," where common inventions of the twentieth century have significant effects on modern man. Instead, they resemble "Daymare" and "The Yehudi Principle," in which the effects of fantastic technologies are examined. Still, Brown seems to say that none of these inventions are beneficial—the Switcheroo and the domes cause nothing but problems.

This unwillingness or inability to accept the new and unusual in scientific advances extends, in this period of Brown's science fiction work, to a repeated inability to accept or deal with revelations or situations that are highly unusual.

Brown's strongest statement on this theme is "Come and Go Mad" (*Weird Tales* July 1949), which Newton Baird has discussed extensively in his "Paradox and Plot" series of articles in *The Armchair Detective*. In short, the story tells of George Vine, a reporter who goes undercover in an insane asylum to check the sanity of the man in charge. Vine is an amnesiac, and his trip to the asylum gradually leads him into a revelation that man plays an insignificant role in the universe, which is ruled by three intelligences that combine to form God. Vine goes mad when he sees a cell of The Brightly Shining, one of the three intelligences, and realizes it's an ant. The story is complicated, weird, and wild, and the knowledge of the truth drives Vine insane.

McGarry, the spaceman stranded on Kruger III in "Something Green," is also insane as a result of the knowledge that Earth has been destroyed and he will never again see the object of his obsession, the color green. His madness makes him imagine an alien pet that he talks to throughout the story; when a rescue ship does come and he learns the truth he destroys the ship and retreats into his fantasy.

The reality in both of these stories is horrifying and the retreat from it understandable; in this way, they differ from the earlier stories on this theme, in which the unacceptable reality wasn't so bad ("The Angelic Angleworm") or was uncertain ("The Hat Trick"). Perhaps, in the wake of World War II and during the developing Cold War, Fredric Brown found it easier to postulate situations so extreme as to demand a mad response from rational men.

He also returned twice to the theme of angels and devils during this period, in "Rustle of Wings" and "A Word From Our Sponsor." "A Word From Our Sponsor" came first, in the September 1951 issue of *Other Worlds Science Fiction*. At 8:30 p.m. on June 9, 1954, a voice comes over the radio and says, "And now a word from our sponsor," followed by a different voice saying "Fight." The result is that people everywhere do exactly the opposite, and the narrator concludes: "There wasn't a war." The story is a sometimes tedious exercise in psychology in which Brown investigates notions of God (presumably the sponsor) and man's reactions in time of crisis. God never appears, other than as a voice heard on the radio, and "A Word From Our Sponsor" is thus less concerned with spiritual beings than with human perceptions.

"Rustle of Wings" is a charming little story that appears to have been written in March 1947 but not published until the August 1953 issue of *The Magazine of Fantasy and Science Fiction*. The style is similar to that Brown used in a number of wonderful 1947-48 stories, like "The Laughing Butcher" and "Knock," and the setting is a small Ohio town just after McKinley's assassination in 1901, as remembered by Johnny, the narrator. He tells of a poker game and a superstition that turned his grandfather into an avid churchgoer. The tale is pure fantasy without a tinge of science fiction, and it turns on the old saying, "speak of the devil...and you hear the rustle of his wings." "Rustle of Wings" has autobiographical echoes—Brown is from Ohio and was born five years after McKinley died—and the story is in the class of *The Fabulous Clipjoint* and *The Office* in that it is made up of vague memories brilliantly filtered through the creative mind. The fantastic elements recall the early story "Armageddon," but the tale as a whole is so haunting and yet pleasant that it belongs among Brown's best work.

By 1948, the beginning of this middle period of Fredric Brown's short science fiction, he was skilled at developing characters, and these two dozen or so stories do not demonstrate any real progression in his growth as a writer. They do introduce a new theme, however: that of social or political commentary. Brown's earliest (and perhaps best) story of this type is "Letter to a Phoenix," from the August 1949 *Astounding Science Fiction*. Written in the form of a letter to the reader, this story deals with Cold War fears in a science fiction context. The narrator is a near-immortal speaking from the distant future who assures men and women of our time that humanity's insanity makes it the only immortal species in the universe. Thought-provoking rather than exciting, "Letter to a Phoenix" has invited some critical discussion. Paul Brians, in his 1987 work *Nuclear Holocausts*, believes Brown writes that "the holocausts which periodically almost annihilate the human race are actually necessary to perpetuate the species, which—without this invigorating tonic—would die out like every other race in the universe" (13), and concludes that "no attempt is made to explain this extraordinary proposition" (147). Sam J. Lundwall claims the story "tells about the cyclic development of Man's civilization in a way somewhat reminiscent of Jules Verne's *L'eternal Adam*" (185). Finally, Douglas J. McReynolds, the most perceptive writer on Brown's science fiction, notes a "cosmic pessimism almost worthy of Mark Twain" and remarks that:

> Unlike most of Brown's pieces, "Letter to a Phoenix" is an upsetting story, largely because of the fundamental incompatibility between the sustained consolation in its narrator's voice and the existential horror waiting in the future that voice so calmly foretells. (1955-56)

Whatever its author's intent, "Letter to a Phoenix" is a discourse open to interpretation.

Clearly, the Cold War affected Brown's science fiction stories in the late 1940s and early 1950s; stories like "Honeymoon in Hell" and "A

Word From Our Sponsor" dealt directly with American-Soviet conflicts and often used aliens as a method of solving them. "Dark Interlude" treats racial prejudice in the rural South with irony, and "From These Ashes" and "Happy Ending" show the development and doom of fascist leaders. This body of socio-political tales is rather an anomaly in Fredric Brown's larger body of work, and the themes are hardly subtle or terribly original. Still, with the exception of "The Hatchetman," none is unreadable and most are excellent.

Brown's forte, of course, was humor—his agent Harry Altshuler wrote that "humor is almost the only thing Fred took seriously" (Letter to the author, 13 March 1989). Certainly, "All Good Bems" and "Mitkey Rides Again" are written for laughs, as are such stories as "Device of the Turtle," "Man of Distinction," and "Cartoonist." They are not as easy to classify as the tales that are linked thematically, but they are no less enjoyable.

In short, Fredric Brown's science fiction short stories published between 1948 and 1957 follow somewhat the boom in the publishing field that occurred in the early 1950s and its quieting down in the mid-1950s. He moved in the direction of socio-political tales during the hottest part of the Cold War; then, when things cooled off, his story output tapered off. By 1952, Brown was writing very few short stories of any type, and his science fiction was no exception—one story each published in 1952 and 1953, none from 1954 through 1956, and one in 1957. And even those three stories were probably written some time before publication.

* * *

Part III: 1958-1972

By the late 1950s, the pulps were dead and the market for science fiction stories was changing. Several digests (*Astounding* and *Galaxy*, especially) published the cream of the crop, and the top writers had been writing long enough to have developed their own followings. Men's magazines were becoming a respectable outlet for fiction in the wake of *Playboy*'s success.

Most of Fredric Brown's short fiction of this sort by this point was in the form of vignettes, which have their own special characteristics and will be dealt with in their own chapter. His writing output as a whole was slowing down, and he published no short stories in the science fiction or fantasy vein in 1959, 1960, or 1961 (except for a portion of a novel in the March 1960 *Fantastic Universe*).

From 1962 to 1965, Fredric Brown published four short stories with science fiction or fantasy themes; after 1965, he never published another. "Puppet Show" and "It Didn't Happen" appeared in the November 1962 and October 1963 issues of *Playboy*; "Tale of the Flesh Monger" appeared in the October 1963 *Gent*, and "Eine Kleine Nachtmusik" appeared in *The Magazine of Fantasy and Science Fiction* in June 1965.

In "Puppet Show," Brown returns to the theme of alien visitation, as an old prospector walks into Cherrybell, Arizona, from the desert, leading a burro with a nine-foot-tall red alien on its back. Garth, the alien, summons world leaders to the deserted area and proposes admitting Earth to the Galactic Union. He tests man's ability to accept aliens differing in appearance and reveals that the red alien was just a puppet, controlled by the old prospector. When the men express relief that a human is in charge, the burro reveals that it is the real alien, and is a bit concerned about the men's ability to accept different races. The tale is short and ironic, following Brown's series of stories dealing with mankind's first contact with an alien race. As so often happened in earlier stories, we fail the test in this last meditation on the theme.

"Come and Go Mad" is recalled in 1963's "It Didn't Happen," in which killer Lorenz Kane, a solipsist, believes he can murder at will and leave no trace. When he kills stripper Queenie Quinn and her body doesn't disappear he is puzzled; his lawyer and doctor reveal he's had a head injury and knows too much about the reality conspiracy—so they kill him and *he* disappears! In Brown's earlier stories the protagonist went mad upon learning an impossible truth. In "It Didn't Happen," Lorenz Kane's ego is so great that he can accept the unusual truth about reality, but his partial knowledge makes him dangerous to those in power. This final story on the theme of the consequences of accepting the impossible also recalls "The Last Martian" in its insistence that, while there is a conspiracy, it's not for everyone to know.

In the same month, Brown published "Tale of the Flesh Monger," which tells the story of Bill Wheeler, a down on his luck actor who goes on a spending spree with credit cards he finds in a discarded wallet. He meets the wallet's owner and strikes a deal—Bill will become famous while Roscoe (the owner) will get ten percent of everything. This is, of course, taken to the extreme—and the story ends with Bill in the gas chamber, wondering if Roscoe will take a cut of his death. Hollywood serves as the background for this humorous and ironic twist on the old idea of selling one's soul to the devil; the fact that Roscoe becomes Bill's supernatural "agent" is an amusing commentary on the person no writer can live with—or without.

Brown's final published story was the dark "Eine Kleine Nachtmusik," written in collaboration with Carl Onspaugh. In the story, Dooley Hanks is a clarinettist who searches the world for the Sound. He finds it in a small German town, where an old man plays an hautboy and girls flock for an orgy. Dooley kills the old man and plays his instrument, but it is hungry rats who respond this time in the sleepy town of Hamelin.

This fantasy mixes Brown's interest in music with classic Germanic horror; the setting is unusual, but it makes for a chilling story that mixes crime and fantasy in a fitting end to Brown's career as a published writer.

* * *

The dozens of stories discussed in this chapter represent the bulk of the work that has formed the basis of Fredric Brown's reputation as a writer of short science fiction. They were published randomly over a period of 25 years and followed his career as a published writer from near the beginning to the end. During that time, and also since Brown's death, all of the stories have been collected in various books, and it is these collections that are probably most familiar to his readers.

The first such collection was *Space On My Hands*, published in July 1951 by the small Chicago publisher, Shasta Books. It led off with an introduction by Fredric Brown, dated January 4, 1951, and written in Taos, New Mexico. The stories included "Something Green," written especially for the book, and eight others from the 1940s.

Later during his stay in Taos Brown collaborated with Mack Reynolds on *Science-Fiction Carnival*, published in 1953 by Shasta and including an introduction by Brown, his story "Paradox Lost," and thirteen stories by other writers—introductory notes to seven of which are also by Brown. The book was intended to show the humorous side of science fiction and was mildly successful.

Brown's next collection was the wonderful *Angels and Spaceships*, completed in a month in 1953 in California. He wrote another short introduction (dated July 3, 1953, and written in Venice, California), as well as eight new short-shorts which, interspersed between eight stories from the 1940s, give the book a strong thematic glue resembling that of Hemingway's similarly constructed collection, *In Our Time*.

Two collections were published as paperback originals by Bantam Books: *Honeymoon in Hell* (1958) and *Nightmares and Geezenstacks* (1961). These mixed stories from the early 1950s with a generous sampling of vignettes to present a truly varied picture of Brown's unique skills.

His last work was *Paradox Lost*, a collection of stories from the 1940s through the 1960s that was published in 1973, the year after his death. *The Best of Fredric Brown* followed in 1978, and featured an excellent selection of science fiction stories, from "Not Yet the End" to "Eine Kleine Nachtmusik."

On these six collections (excluding *Science-Fiction Carnival*) rests much of Brown's reputation as a science fiction writer. He never took himself very seriously, as is evidenced by his introduction to "Nothing Sirius" in the 1949 anthology, *My Best Science Fiction Story*; in it, he faults science fiction for being too serious too much of the time and praises its occasional comic tendencies.

Brown's remarks on his own work are important in placing his science fiction in his oeuvre as a whole. The form is one to which he returned regularly over the course of three decades; the majority of his work was in mysteries, but he claimed to prefer writing science fiction in his introduction to *Space On My Hands*. He began in the early 1940s hero pulps and followed the field through the early 1950s publishing boom and bust, ending up as a celebrated contributor to the increasingly respectable "slick" men's magazines of the early 1960s. He does not deserve a place among the truly great science fiction writers of his day, though—he never cared enough to try for one. Yet his stories remain in the memory, often for the same reasons that his short mysteries linger— their humor, their playful originality, their magical plotting—in short, for all of the reasons readers keep returning to the work of Fredric Brown.

Chapter Ten
Science Fiction Novels

In addition to his many mystery novels and hundreds of short stories, Fredric Brown also published five science fiction novels in his lifetime, and began work on another one that was published in an unfinished state years after his death. Of these six novels, two are straight comedies and among his best-known works; the other four range from a serious exploration of the politics behind the space program to a wild thriller about an insane—and invisible—mutant human.

What Mad Universe was Fredric Brown's fourth novel, first appearing as a novelette in the September 1948 issue of *Startling Stories*. According to his logbook, Brown wrote it in 1947: he received a $200 advance on May 14, 1947, from publisher Leo Margulies, and sent 10,000 words and a plot synopsis to Harry Altshuler on July 10, 1947. He received another $100 advance from Margulies on September 23, 1947, and sent the completed manuscript to Altshuler on October 8, 1947. It sold immediately, and Brown received his share of $800 on October 21, 1947.

In an article on Brown's early years as a writer, Harry Altshuler recalled Margulies's reaction to the novelette:

> Casually the story gave some inside info on how such magazines are put together, and editorial attitudes. "Fred is skating on thin ice here," Leo exclaimed to me, "but, oh, how that man can skate!" ("The Early Career" 24)

Startling Stories was a leading pulp of the day, and its September 1948 issue featured a garish cover painting of a purple monster hovering above Saturn and menacing a beautiful blonde, who wears only a gold bra, bikini pants, and boots. The contents include Brown's "Astonishing Complete Novel," a reprinted novelette by P. Schuyler Miller, three short stories, a seemingly endless column of fan letters, an article by "The

171

President of the United States Rocket Society," and a review of fan publications.

All of this is quite relevant to "What Mad Universe," whose hero is Keith Winton, editor of the "scientifiction" pulp, *Surprising Stories*. As the story begins he is at the country estate of L.A. Borden, "publisher of the Borden chain of magazines" (12). Keith passes up a gin game to work on the current issue's letter column, "Rocketalk," and reads a letter from fan Joe Doppelberg, who writes in the typically punning way of a young scientifiction fan of the late 1940s (though the story is set in 1952). Keith responds in the same punning manner and wanders outside. Suddenly, the first rocket to the moon—which has been launched that evening and which Keith expects to see hit the moon at 9:16 p.m.—falls back to Earth and crashes only two yards from the tree beneath which Keith sits.

The stage is thus set in the first chapter. Keith is the editor of a magazine similar to the one the reader holds in his hands, and he deals with fans and letters not much different than those in the back of the September 1948 *Startling Stories*.

In chapter two, Keith finds himself in a world strikingly similar to the one he knows, yet with even greater differences. Money has been replaced by credits, Earth is at war with Arcturus, and purple "Lunans" walk the streets without attracting attention. Keith only slowly begins to realize the change, while Brown begins planting clues to what has happened as Keith catches a ride from a farmer who "looked, Keith thought, almost too much like a farmer to be one" (17).

Keith becomes a fugitive, forced to solve the mystery of where he is and how he got there while avoiding capture and execution as an Arcturan spy. He takes a train into Manhattan's Grand Central Station and arrives as night falls; there, he finds thousands of frightened travelers on cots in the large station, afraid to go outside after dark. This is the "mist-out"—an artificially-induced total blackness that prevents Arcturan ships from locating and destroying Earth's great cities.

Venturing out into the streets, Keith runs afoul of the "Nighters," gangs of renegades and psychotic space vets who roam the streets "with locked arms, perhaps, from one side of the street to the other, so their prey couldn't escape" (30), tapping canes like an army of synchronized blind men as they go. The image is tremendous and Keith's fear is understandable when he finds himself alone on the street between swiftly approaching murderous gangs! He escapes by breaking a window just in time, but the point has been made: in the world Keith has fallen into, the city streets are unsafe at night, and woe to the man who unknowingly finds himself wandering them.

Much of Keith's confusion is explained away when he reads H.G. Wells's *Outline of History*, which reveals that space warp travel was invented in 1903 and that Earth is in the midst of a space war with Arcturus. Once he understands the world he's in, though, Keith must still determine two things: why he's there and how he can get home.

He tries to fit in for awhile, doing what he does best by writing stories for pulp magazines. He is contacted telepathically by Mekky, a spherical mechanical brain created by Dopelle, the greatest man in the universe and the leader of Earth's armies in space. Mekky hints at a resolution but is called into space to help at the front. After some more close scrapes, Keith realizes space travel is possible and decides to journey to Saturn to contact Mekky. Subtle clues to the mystery's solution continue to pepper the story; for example, when a WBI investigator pulls a gun on Keith he successfully disarms the man with a "gun jump," a trick that should only work in stories.

Night is again encountered in this otherworldly Manhattan, and with it, the mistout. But this time Keith is armed with knowledge and fearless:

Funny, he thought; he wasn't afraid. Maybe because now, tonight, he was the hunter and not the hunted. (57)

Keith hooks up with Joe, a former space-pilot and now shady character who helps him travel through the Holland Tunnel to New Jersey; there, Keith finds a small spaceship and travels in an instant to the moon. Keith gets out and looks around (there's air on the moon in this universe), but the experience

hadn't thrilled him as much as he'd thought and he believed he knew why. It was because—here, in this universe—it didn't seem completely real, however real this universe was. It was too easy. Much too easy. (64)

Brown thus provides further clues to the reader about the solution to the mystery of just what universe Keith is in.

In the next to last chapter, Keith pilots the ship to the war front near Saturn, where he's taken aboard the fleet's main ship and meets the great Dopelle, whose appearance provides the final piece of the puzzle:

"I know you now," Keith said. "I've got a clue to this set-up. You're *Joe Doppelberg*, a science-fiction fan of—of back there where I came from. Only you're older than he—and a thousand times handsomer and more intelligent than he and—you've got everything he wanted.
      "You're what he would have dreamed himself to be." (66)

Keith's knowledge of the Burton potentiometer, a device used in the rocketship that crashed at the start of the novel but unknown in this universe, provides Dopelle with what he needs to defeat the Arcturans, and Mekky explains where Keith is:

There are, then, an infinite number of co-existent universes—including the one you came from and this one. (67)

Mekky then tells Keith that he landed in this universe

Because you were thinking about this particular universe at the instant the rocket struck. You were thinking about your science-fiction fan, Joe Doppelberg, and you were wondering what kind of a universe he would dream about, what kind he would like. And this is it. (68)

The mystery is solved and all that remains is to get Keith back home, which is accomplished by letting him pilot the ship that defeats the Arcturans in a gigantic explosion.
      Brown slips one last in-joke into the story as Keith pilots the ship:

Inside his head, Mekky's voice said, "It's coming. I feel ether vibrations."
(69)

Readers of *Startling Stories* would have seen right away that Brown was kidding, because the letters column in that and presumably every issue was called "The Ether Vibrates." The story concludes with a twist—just before the crash, Keith was thinking of his own universe, but with slight improvements; when he returns, he's the publisher of the pulp he used to edit and he's beloved by Betty Hadley, the lovely fellow editor he has spent the entire story mooning over. "*This*, he thought, was a universe he'd really settle for" (71).

So ends a classic novelette. The philosophy behind it is almost Fortean: everything is true somewhere, so no anomaly can be dismissed. In his introduction to a 1978 reissue of the novel *What Mad Universe*, Philip Klass noted that the pulp novelette was the publishing event of 1948, and that the Joe Doppelberg character came from Walt Dunkelberger, a regular contributor of letters to late 1940s science fiction pulps. Brown worked briefly for publisher Leo Margulies in 1948, but the novelette preceded this, so Klass's suggestion that Brown's editing experiences were echoed in the novelette are clever but incorrect.

The rest of Klass's introduction is fascinating reading; he discusses the novelette and the subsequent novel, noting its connections with Brown's other science fiction and with his writing as a whole:

There are certain notes that Fred Brown struck again and again in his stories— the aliens he depicts are almost always utterly vicious; his characters drink constantly and will drink at the flick of a bartender's thumb; size, as between one creature and another, is almost always an issue; the story will pause at any time, in the midst of any action, for a pun or a word game—but the one *large* theme to which he kept returning was the question of reality, how we really know what we know, how much of it is, as he put it in "Come and Go Mad," "truth under the guise of falsehood."

This, the theme of *What Mad Universe*, was for Fred Brown the ultimate comic question, the investigation of the belief he voiced in "It Didn't Happen," that "the entire universe is the product of one's imagination—in my case, *my* imagination." He carried it about as far as his master, Lewis Carroll had done, when Alice said of the Red King, "He was part of my dream, of course—but then I was part of his dream, too!" (xvii)

These are the themes of "What Mad Universe," a delightful novelette that succeeds as humorous science fiction and manages to poke fun at itself all the while.

The success of "What Mad Universe" prompted Brown to expand it to novel length, and the longer version was published as Dutton's first science fiction book in October 1949. Since the novelette has never been reprinted, the novel is what most people refer to when they think of *What Mad Universe*. The time is moved from 1952 to 1954, and Keith is now the "Ole Rocketeer" instead of just plain "Rocketeer." Scenes are expanded in length, and one scene in particular is much longer: in the novel, when Keith strides into the mistout determined to hunt men and meets Joe, they go to a bar where the bouncer is a "proxie," a creature that

looked like a large turtle with tentacles like a devilfish, and with bright red luminous eyes like flashlight bulbs behind big red lenses. (136)

At the bar, Keith sells his "coins" to Ross, a fence, and drinks "moonjuice," the effects of which include a wild hallucination that sends Keith flying through space in his mind. The novel's plot follows that of the novelette.

What Mad Universe was well received on publication, both by the mainstream press and by reviewers in science fiction periodicals. It has had several paperback reprintings, in addition to a limited edition hardcover in 1978 that included the aforementioned introduction by Philip Klass. It is also quite popular; as early as 1953, Reginald Bretnor wrote that the novel had "persuaded more people to try science fiction than most other books" (89). Beth Brown remarked in her autobiography that movie producers were interested in filming the novel but that none could figure out how to film the mist-out sequences, and critics have generally agreed that it is a classic comic work, paving the way for other science fiction writers like Kurt Vonnegut and Robert Sheckley (110).

Perhaps most interesting of all is that Brown felt compelled to refer back to "What Mad Universe" in subsequent works. In *Here Comes a Candle* (1950), protagonist Joe Bailey falls asleep reading the September 1948 issue of *Startling Stories*:

He got interested in the lead novel and finished it before he turned in. He went to sleep thinking of bug-eyed monsters from far Arcturus and unbelievably beautiful Earth-girls riding space-ships and wearing unbelievably abbreviated costumes. (12)

This is, of course, shameless self-promotion, but it's also a lot of fun for readers who get the joke.

Another mention of *What Mad Universe* pops up in Brown's next science fiction novel, *The Lights in the Sky Are Stars*. Written between the end of 1952 and May 1953 in California, the novel was not based on any short story and never appeared in a shortened or condensed form. The mention of *What Mad Universe* comes when the protagonist, Max Andrews, recalls

a book I read in my teens, one of the early science fiction novels. I forget who wrote it but it was called *Mad Universe* or something like that. (142)

Max goes on to say that

You might get a kick out of it, while you're getting better, if I can find a copy, but I doubt if I can. It's probably been out of print for forty or fifty years... (143)

and that, when he was young, he once tried to rig sewing machines to invent an interplanetary space drive, as was done in the novel!

Dutton published *The Lights in the Sky Are Stars* in October 1953, and it has been reprinted several times since. It is divided into five sections, one for each year from 1997 to 2001, and follows 57-year-old rocket mechanic Max Andrews, who lost a leg in a rocket accident 30 years before, as he relentlessly pursues the Dream of seeing mankind journey into space. He becomes involved with Ellen Gallagher, a middle-aged politician who shepherds a bill through Congress to fund Project Jupiter, which will build a ship to travel to that planet. As the bill works its way toward success he and Ellen fall in love; she sees it passed shortly before she dies of a brain tumor. Max's plan to act as director of the project is then foiled when politicians learn that he lied about his background. He claimed to have lost his leg in an accident during a trip to Venus, but he actually lost it before the rocket ever left the Earth and never even made it into space!

Max descends into a drunken reel for a time and gets caught up in the celebration of New Year's 2000; his nephew's excitement over space exploration finally pulls him out of his mental pit and he watches as the rocket prepares to take off for Jupiter.

The Lights in the Sky Are Stars is an unusual novel for Fredric Brown, both structurally and thematically. Brown bucks convention by postulating a future in which people have lost interest in space travel and by featuring, as narrator and hero, a middle-aged, handicapped liar. In the 1997 of the novel, America is divided into two camps: Stardusters, the minority who support space exploration, and Conservationists, who feel it's a waste of taxpayers' money. As Robert Bloch remarked in his introduction to *The Best of Fredric Brown*, Brown "deliberately dumped on dreams and offered, instead, a raw reality," writing about politics rather than "the gung-ho glories of space projects" (5). Sadly, Brown's future was close to the truth, for, as Patrick H. Adkins remarked, "Brown foresaw the politics of space with eerie accuracy."

Character development is another strength of *The Lights in the Sky Are Stars*. Max narrates the story and is most fully realized; through the course of the novel, we learn his life story and his dreams of mankind reaching into space, and his final crushing brush with reality is effectively portrayed and not at all contrived, however surprising it may be. Ellen Gallagher is also a well-developed character, and her motives are complicated: she loves Max and believes in the Dream, but she's firmly grounded in political reality and understands the steps that she must take to make Project Jupiter succeed. Finally, there is M'bassi, a Masai mystic who was converted to Buddhism and seeks a spiritual method of traveling to the stars. He is a brilliant man and his death near the end of the novel suggests that he may have finally found a way to go where Max can only imagine.

Structurally, the novel unfolds in long sections that are broken into various "scenes" of a sort. The use of long sections (one for each year) rather than short chapters imparts a languid flow to the novel, which is actually rather brief. It is a single story from beginning to end, and the years run into each other, as years do in real life. In fact, the end of the section titled "1999" is taken up with Max's drunken perceptions and ends in mid-sentence. The sentence concludes as the beginning of the next section, "2000":

Suddenly it came to me what this was. Not just another damn new year after another Christmas; it was more than that. It came to me through the noise, through the gently falling snow, this is the turn of the century and the turn of the millenium, Jesus God, this isn't just another year, this is the year two thousand, the year *two*

2000

thousand! Something to celebrate, something really to celebrate! (198-201)

The excitement of the new year helps Max work his way out of his depression, and Brown's trick is extremely successful in conveying the way one millenium flows into the next in the sweep of a second hand.

Perhaps the most memorable things about *The Lights in the Sky Are Stars* are its optimism, its sense of wonder, and the feeling the reader gets of the sheer awe of the potential for man's expansion into space. This potential is what drives Max Andrews to lie, cheat, steal, and love in order to help propel the space program. It is also what saves him: when Max's hopes have been dashed and he has descended into drunkenness, he is pulled out by hope, hope which includes his nephew Billy, with whom he watches the preparations for takeoff of the Jupiter rocket:

Forty-three feet tall it stood, and beautiful. God, how beautiful. Sleek and slender, shiny and Oh God there aren't any words for a rocket, a new one-man rocket that's going where no rocket has been before, to another world, farther out. Nearer where we're going. (219)

This is typical of the sort of prose that fills *The Lights in the Sky Are Stars*. It naturally leads to questions about God, and Max, like Brown, is not a believer yet seems to want to be one; watching the rocket with Billy, Max thinks about man's potential, and the novel ends with these poetic and beautiful lines:

Here waiting in the breathless dark I feel humble before it and before you, before man and his future, before God if there is a God before mankind becomes one. (222)

This, then, is *The Lights in the Sky Are Stars*: a serious, almost poetic novel that concerns itself with issues both political and moral, that uses a languid, flowing structure to tell its story, that eschews the slam-bang, choppy action scenes of *What Mad Universe* in favor of a more thoughtful development of characters.

The novel has had several reprintings (the last in the early 1970s) and has received serious critical attention in most science fiction reference works. In a 1991 article, Patrick H. Adkins even went so far as to call it the best science fiction novel of 1953. Reviewers at the time said basically the same thing: a reviewer in the June 1954 *Galaxy* called it "richly human, exciting, tragic, and, in the long run, inspiringly imaginative" (Conklin 121), and a reviewer in that month's *Astounding Science Fiction* called the novel "Brown's best science fiction and certainly one of his best books" (Miller 145).

Brown would not write another work of such thoughtful optimism. Instead, his next science fiction novel began as a novelette in the September 1954 issue of *Astounding Science Fiction*. "Martians Go Home!" was probably written in late 1953, and it is an acknowledged classic comedy.

The "story," such as it is, is really a series of vignettes that occur when about a billion little green men from Mars descend on Earth. They are untouchable and can get in anywhere, leading to problems wherever privacy is concerned. They arrive at 8:14 p.m. on March 26, 1964, seemingly for no reason but to create havoc, and they disappear at 3:22 p.m. on July 18, 1965, without explanation. In the intervening months, they drive humans crazy, interfering in poker games, television productions, wedding nights, politics, and every other aspect of human behavior.

There's really no plot to "Martians, Go Home!" and the characters are stereotypes. Where Brown succeeds is in the writing; he chooses choice examples to show the effect of the Martian invasion. The story is hilarious from beginning to end, the Martians are unrelentingly nasty, and nothing we do has any effect! The Martians only give one hint to the source of their interest in humans: "Have you ever gone to a zoo and if so, why?" (16). The story is told in Brown's best "raconteur" style; the narrator is in control from beginning to end, telling a series of past events—this allows the humor to flourish because the reader knows that, somehow, the Martian problem will be resolved by the story's end.

An entertaining sidelight to "Martians, Go Home!" occurs when writer Luke Deveraux, whose attempts at writing science fiction are thwarted by Martian interference, decides to try his hand at writing westerns. He begins a story, "Guns Across the Gila," in this way:

As Don Marston drew nearer the figure that waited for him on the trail, the figure resolved itself into a grim-eyed hombre whose hands held a stubby carbine crosswise on the pommel of his— (44)

Only a die-hard Fredric Brown fan would think back to "Trouble Valley," published in the November 1940 *Western Short Story*. It was one of the two western stories Brown wrote in the days when he was just beginning to sell to the pulps, and its hero is gunman Don Marston. As with the mentions of *What Mad Universe* in subsequent novels, Brown is fond of in-jokes; this is one of his most obscure.

"Martians, Go Home!" is not a self-reflexive satire, like *What Mad Universe*, nor is it a thoughtful, serious work, like *The Lights in the Sky Are Stars*. Instead, it is pure fun, in which Brown delights his readers by postulating an outrageous situation and taking it to its extremes.

Not long after the novelette was published to great acclaim, Brown began expanding it to novel length for publication in book form. He finished the job in March 1955 and the novel was published in November 1955, barely a year after the novelette first appeared.

In turning a plotless, characterless series of vignettes into a novel, Brown faced an unusual challenge. A comparison of the short and long versions gives some insight into the differences between the two forms. The basic change is that, in the novel, Luke Deveraux becomes the central character, while in the novelette he had been just one of many unfortunate persons victimized by the Martians. While both versions begin with Luke, the novel introduces concerns about his wife, Margie, and suggests future developments regarding the hapless writer. Brown also writes scenes more expansively, giving up some of the clipped and choppy style that made the story so funny. Finally, the novel is filled with lists—on page 21, he lists weapons people try to use against the Martians; on page 46, he lists adjectives to describe the Martians (including at least one for every letter of the alphabet); etc. This has a humorous effect, but it also helps pad the novelette to novel length.

About 50 pages into the novel, Brown begins expanding Luke Deveraux's role. Unable to write, Luke is low on money and becomes an example of the troubled post-Martian economy. Luke answers a help-wanted ad to learn how to be a psychiatrist (a booming profession), but the class is, of course, disrupted by Martians. The novel continues as Brown intersperses chapters from the novelette with chapters and sections of chapters about Luke Deveraux. The overall effect is to make Luke the protagonist; the chapters picked up from the short version universalize his problems.

After trying to write a western, Luke lapses into catatonia. In the novelette, this is the last time we see him. In the novel, Luke is placed in General Mental Hospital, where he successfully completes his western and receives visits from his wife, Margie. Luke's doctor goes so far as to say that Luke's insane condition (he can no longer perceive the Martians) is preferable to sanity! Luke eventually acquires the solipsistic belief that he invented the Martians while trying to write a science fiction story. When he fails to de-invent them, he decides he must be at the same spot where he was when he invented them, and escapes to head for the desert.

The novel then follows several threads to a conclusion. The head of the United Nations kills himself after a world effort fails to drive away the Martians. A crackpot inventor in Chicago tries and fails with an "anti-extraterrestrial subatomic supervibrator" (155), and an African witch-doctor conjures up a juju to accomplish the same thing. The three efforts climax at the same time and the Martians disappear. No one knows what worked or why, but all agree to do everything possible to make sure they never return!

Martians, Go Home is extremely successful as a novel, just as it was as a novelette, yet the two are strikingly different. The novelette is a slam-bang comedy, without much plot or character development. The novel has a well-developed central character and deals much more with philosophical and psychological aspects of the Martians' visit. The novel concludes with an "Author's Postscript," by Brown, dated "Tucson, Arizona, 1955," which was absent from the novelette. In it, Brown replies to a letter supposedly written by his publisher insisting that he reveal where the Martians really came from. He replies that the universe and the Martians exist only in Luke's imagination, but since he invented Luke, where does that leave the rest of us? This conclusion pretends to offer a logical explanation but in reality it just tweaks the reader's nose and compounds the humorous solipsism found in the story proper. In other words, it's perfectly in keeping with the book it follows.

Reviewers lauded the novel: "a rare piece of satire," "the year's most entertaining logical fantasy," "bigger and better than ever" (by a reviewer in *Astounding Science Fiction*, who also wrote that Brown accomplished the expansion to novel length by "enlarging on the character and problems of Luke Deveraux"). A writer in *Science Fiction Quarterly* praised the novel and added, "Serious, constructive science fiction readers, stay away." The novel has had many reprints (a hardcover book-club edition and five paperback printings in the U.S. as of 1992), and its popularity never wanes; in the Spring 1977 *Algol*, a reviewer called it "one of the most charming bits of SF-whimsy ever written." It has received little critical attention beyond countless brief mentions in reference books and long plot summaries elsewhere; perhaps this is because, when all is said and done, a book as funny as *Martians, Go Home* is hard to analyze—it needs to be read to be appreciated.

For his fourth science fiction novel, *Rogue in Space*, Brown again returned to earlier, shorter works; this time, two related short stories he had published at the turn of the decade in two different science fiction pulps. In the first, "Gateway to Darkness" (*Super Science Stories* November 1949), Crag, a big-time crook and ex-spaceman, is jailed for a crime he didn't commit. He is tried and convicted to life on the Callisto penal colony, but he is offered a deal by Judge Jon Olliver. Olliver needs Crag to help establish a new political party, the Cooperationists, to end corruption in this future world run by the Guilders (workers) and the Gilded (wealthy). Crag escapes from jail and falls in love with Evadne, the judge's stunning wife. Judge Olliver asks him to steal a supposedly useless invention on Mars that will help the Cooperationists, and Crag successfully infiltrates the laboratory where the invention is kept and steals it.

The invention is one that collapses matter into neutronium, the heaviest substance known to man. Crag, Judge Olliver, and Evadne fly into an asteroid belt and land on an asteroid to test the invention. It works, and as the asteroid shrinks, the judge reveals his real objective: to dominate the universe by fear of planetary destruction. After a tense confrontation, Crag kills Olliver by shattering his helmet, and Evadne disintegrates herself with the invention rather than suffocate. The story ends as Crag stands alone in space, laughing as he puts the now orange-sized asteroid in his pocket.

Crag is the anti-hero of this exciting novelette—he begins as a criminal and ends as a hero whom no one will ever know. "Gateway to Darkness" is a very strong example of action-oriented science fiction with plot elements that could belong to a thriller; it shows that Fredric Brown was at top form in 1949, a master of plot, action, and character.

In one of his series of articles in *The Armchair Detective*, Newton Baird devoted a portion to a discussion of Crag, calling him "the most unusual and paradoxical central character in Fredric Brown's novels... a key to the author's overall concept of heroism" ("Paradox and Plot" 253). Baird's point is that Crag typifies the rogue-hero who rejects society and creates his own to replace it. Of course, in "Gateway to Darkness," Crag keeps busy rejecting society, but makes no effort to create his own. This occurs in the sequel novelette, "Gateway to Glory," published eleven months later in the October 1950 *Amazing Stories*.

Brown creates a deus ex machina in the form of an entity (named the Rogue in the subsequent novel) formed from the energy that had existed between atoms and molecules on the recently-disintegrated asteroid. The entity returns Crag's ship to him and sets out to explore the corrupt political system on Earth he has learned about from Crag. After the entity returns from its investigation, it tells Crag of its plan to create a new world from asteroid matter, a world to be populated by Crag and criminals like him, the only persons tough enough to survive.

Crag hesitates and returns to Mars, where he begins living a high life with the money he got from Judge Olliver. The life of debauchery sickens Crag, however, and the more he hears newscasts about the mysterious formation of a new planet in space (named Cragon by scientists, not knowing that the entity planted the name in their minds), the more interested he becomes in colonizing it. Finally, after a confrontation with police over some illegal Martian *woji* (a drink), Crag pilots a ship toward Cragon, in the company of two petty crooks and their girlfriends. Life on a new planet is hard work, however, and all but Crag soon leave. Happily, the entity reforms Evadne for Crag from her dispersed atoms, and they set off to populate their new world.

In "Gateway to Glory," Brown beats Stanislaw Lem to the idea of creating a sentient planet by many years (Lem's *Solaris* was published in 1961). And, as Newton Baird noted, although Crag is a criminal, he is the most admirable member of his society precisely because he has refused to succumb to its weakness and corruption. This corruption is perfectly represented by the Luxor Hotel, where Crag has access to every kind of sin imaginable—he finds a blonde, a brunette, and a

redhead waiting in his bed, and when he dismisses them a fey bellboy
arrives at his door!

The entity's collection of asteroids by switching their orbits recalls
Brown's earlier "Pi in the Sky," but in that story the trick was
accomplished by a machine on Earth rather than a being in space.
"Gateway to Glory" is an entertaining conclusion to the story begun in
"Gateway to Darkness" but is less action-oriented and somewhat more
obvious in its intentions. The change in Crag from criminal to
misunderstood hero is not entirely successful, and it is this change that is
at the heart of the problems with Brown's novel, *Rogue in Space*.

According to Elizabeth Brown, Fred began working on *Rogue in
Space* in late 1955, and took eight months to complete a novel he "hated
working" on (*Oh, for the Life* 277-78). It's curious that he took so long,
because the novel is little more than the two earlier novelettes patched
together with a few scenes expanded. *Rogue in Space* was published in
February 1957 by Dutton, and begins with a two-page chapter
introducing the entity:

> Call him a thinking rock, a sentient planetoid.
> Call him a rogue, in the biological sense of the word rogue: an accidental
> variation.
> Call him a rogue in space. (2)

The Rogue of the novel is thus a preexistent being floating through space
that happens upon Crag at just the right moment, unlike the Rogue of the
novelette, who is formed following the disintegration of an asteroid.

"Gateway to Darkness" follows, slightly rewritten and expanded;
Brown adds a few details to show the decadence of 23rd century life,
such as a stock of gay pornography found in an apartment Crag searches.
Crag's visit to Mars to steal the invention is also expanded, and Brown
uses the tired method of having Crag pick a fight in a bar with a security
guard in order to gain that guard's trust and land a job at the lab.

The first portion of the novel concludes quite differently than the
novelette—Crag disintegrates Judeth (the Evadne of the novel) at her
request and then dies alone in space. The second half of the novel is a
slightly revised version of "Gateway to Glory," beginning as the Rogue
planetoid "listens" with its senses as the three humans die. It then
resurrects Crag and the story proceeds as before. Brown further expands

the portrait of debauchery in Crag's world—dinner at the Luxor is accompanied by a live sex show, and every time Crag switches on a television he sees a young homosexual singing "Jet up! Jet down!" Crag kicks in the screen repeatedly in a not-so-funny running gag.

Finally, Crag tires of the world, in a passage that recalls a similar one in *The Screaming Mimi*:

> He walked. Across the night and across the city he walked, and felt his mind clearing and his strength returning. (109)

After some filler material, the story ends as did the novelette.

Rogue in Space is a dull novel, in which two novelettes of unequal quality are joined with a minimum of revision and a maximum of padding. Crag's character wears thin in the novel's second half, and the reader is given little reason to care what happens to him or anyone else.

Reviewers at the time were unkind in their assessment of the novel. Villiers Gerson, writing in the New York *Times* Book Review, said: "Crag is a wooden invention; his story makes so little sense that one wishes it had ended on page 98"—page 98, of course, is where Crag dies. A reviewer in *Astounding* agreed that the first half of the book is the best, adding that "the invasion of the secret citadel and theft of the disintegrator are handled so perfunctorily that you wonder why the first bum out of the gutter couldn't have done it between drinks."

Anthony Boucher, who was usually quite supportive of Brown's work, called the novel "a thumping error in judgment...God knows why Brown decided to blow up one of his least interesting stories to novel length..."—apparently, Boucher had never read "Gateway to Glory." Other reviewers were just as negative in their assessment of *Rogue in Space*.

Despite all of this, the novel received a book club reprinting and has seen three paperback printings in the U.S., as well as many in foreign countries. Critical writing has been scarce and mostly unfriendly. Nevertheless, Brown continued to write science fiction, publishing one more novel in his lifetime and completing a portion of another.

The Mind Thing first appeared as a novelette in the last issue of *Fantastic Universe* (March 1960)—unfortunately, since the magazine was discontinued after publishing part one, the serialization was never completed. The central idea of "The Mind Thing" is one Brown had used twice before: in a very bad story called "Death is a White Rabbit" (Westlake 7) and in a very good tale called "Mouse." "Death is a White Rabbit," completed by June 9, 1941, and published in the January 1942 issue of *Strange Detective Mysteries,* tells the story of Sandy and Rita, a couple who visit a mad professor named Ormond Allers who had done business with Sandy's company. They encounter strange behavior from a lion and learn that Allers is experimenting with animal mind control to use animals to kill. Discovering that Allers is in limbo while possessing an animal, they kidnap a possessed rabbit; when it dies, Allers will be released. Unfortunately, Allers stays under for too long, and dies when the rabbit dies.

"Death is a White Rabbit" is an awful story, with very distasteful descriptions of various animals killing themselves—it seems the professor can only possess one at a time and can only be freed by the host's death.

The idea was picked up in "Mouse," published in the June 1949 issue of *Thrilling Wonder Stories.* "Mouse" was discussed in the last chapter, and it involves an alien possessing first a mouse and then a pet cat named Beautiful.

Finally, the idea of animal possession is taken to the farthest limits in "The Mind Thing." In the portion of the novelette published in the March 1960 *Fantastic Universe,* an alien, the "mind thing" of the title, arrives on Earth and makes use of its ability to possess the bodies of living creatures. The story is very hard to like at first, since the evil, completely emotionless alien, whose corporeal form is like that of a turtle, kills sympathetic human characters in particularly nasty ways.

The first humans we meet are Tommy Hoffman and Charlotte Garner, high-school lovers who share an illicit afternoon in the woods outside Bartlesville, Wisconsin. While Tommy sleeps the mind thing possesses him and hides its own body safely; Charlotte awakens alone and goes home for help. When hers and Tommy's fathers search the woods, the mind thing makes Tommy slit his wrists with a jackknife, freeing the alien. In the next chapter, the mind thing possesses Tommy's dog Buck and frees itself by making Buck leap in front of a car.

The mind thing is a criminal exiled from a distant planet, and can only be killed through destruction of its physical body. It can enter any living thing that sleeps, and its goal is to return to its home planet with news of Earth that will lead to colonization and enslavement of its inhabitants.

The mind thing can also read the minds of its hosts, yet it makes many foolish moves. The first is to have Buck die beneath the wheels of the car of Ralph S. "Doc" Staunton, Ph.D., a brilliant physics professor at MIT with a curious mind and a strong will. In the novelette, after accidentally killing Buck, Doc stays in Bartlesville and learns of the recent, strange events, writing to his friend Dave Tabor for help. Dave is a reporter for the Milwaukee *Journal* whose "experience as a reporter... taught [him] how to talk to people and get information from them" (72). Dave reads the letter to his fiance, Jean Morris, and decides to go to Wisconsin to help Doc. And there the serialization ends.

With the cancellation of *Fantastic Universe*, the conclusion of "The Mind Thing" remained unknown until January 1961, when Bantam Books published the first edition of the novel as a paperback, which has never been reprinted in America. The first five chapters of the novel are almost exactly the same as those in the novelette, with occasional copy editing and some additional details in the sex scenes. Chapter six of the novelette, with Dave Tabor and Jean Morris, is scrapped entirely, and the novel continues with Doc conducting an investigation on his own. This is where the novel picks up interest, once Brown finally hits on a protagonist with whom the reader can identify. As the story progresses, the mind thing possesses and kills various hosts, both animal and human, and Doc begins to put the pieces together. In chapter 11, the mind thing appears to take possession of a cat's body so that it may observe human activity; this directly recalls the earlier story, "Mouse." Doc decides to dictate a detailed report on all of the strange events in Bartlesville and hires Amanda Talley, a wonderful character and local English teacher whom Doc thinks of as akin to "Stuart Palmer's female detective character, Hildegarde Withers" (79).

By this point, the mind thing—as a cat—is in Doc's house, observing him and realizing that Doc is its greatest enemy. Doc figures out that the cat is possessed, follows it, and sees it drown itself. The novel's conclusion occurs as the mind thing traps Doc in a small farmhouse, possessing one animal after another and having them kill themselves in front of Doc to keep him at bay. Doc and the mind thing know each other's objectives and Doc must avoid sleep in order to avoid possession.

Doc survives the night, even after the mind thing shorts out a generator and leaves him in darkness. Around noon of the next day, Amanda Talley arrives and Doc sends her for help, but first he has her tie him to a chair. Doc falls asleep and is possessed; he struggles against it and yells out the location of the mind thing's body, which Miss Talley then destroys, ending the menace.

Doc is found, but with the memory of having shared the mind thing's thoughts and learning the process by which man will reach the stars. The novel ends as Miss Talley stares at the stars in awe, looking forward to a journey into space. *The Mind Thing*'s resolution is clever and surprisingly positive, with a sense of wonder that recalls *The Lights in the Sky Are Stars*. The novel has a shaky start and is rather unpleasant for awhile, but once Doc Staunton arrives on the scene it picks up steam and ends as an exciting battle of wits between an alien and a human mind.

Since it was published as a first-edition paperback, *The Mind Thing* received little attention from reviewers. A positive review in *Analog* suggested that "This is close enough to what Hollywood can do so that a smart director just might play it straight," and the novel was apparently optioned for filming by Alfred Hitchcock, but nothing ever came of it. Other than a few mentions in science fiction criticism, *The Mind Thing* has been little remembered, although it has significant strengths and deserves to be read.

After *The Mind Thing*, Fredric Brown never published another science fiction novel in his lifetime. His career as a writer was nearing its conclusion, and he would write only a few more mystery novels before his health made it impossible to write.

However, Brown did begin working on one more science fiction novel, *Brother Monster*, completing 117 pages before giving up. The unfinished novel was finally published in a limited edition hardcover in 1986, with an introduction by Harry Altshuler that is quite illuminating. Altshuler discusses his visit to see the Browns in Tucson in 1970 or 1971, when Fred's emphysema "made everything too difficult. It took all the energy he could get up, just to walk from one room into another" and his eyesight was "deteriorating" (6-8). He had written a portion of *Brother Monster* by 1965 and put it aside; he let Harry read it and later mailed it to Harry to complete in collaboration, writing that he would "never finish" it.

The novel begins in an asylum for dangerous criminals, where psychotic killer Walter Fremont is kept. The writing is dense and beautifully evocative. Fremont ran amok at age 23 and suspects he received psi powers when his father was exposed to radiation from an underwater alien ship shortly before Walter was conceived. Chapter two opens with a marvelous passage about man's beliefs and superstitions, recalling similar passages in *The Office*. Charles Fort's writing on anomalies in science is discussed in detail, and Walter speaks of his exposure to and interest in Fort's writing, which tied in with his belief in his own psi powers.

Walter succeeds in turning himself invisible and escaping the asylum; after going to a nearby town and stealing clothes, he slaps his doctor's face before leaving for good.

Walter's brother George is then brought into the story. He's a science fiction writer working on both a juvenile science fiction novel and a straight article on the upcoming Mars Probe. When Walter escapes, FBI agents find George and pump him for information, allowing Brown to give more details of Walter's history.

Meanwhile, Walter makes his way to San Francisco, where he barely escapes capture in a very exciting passage. The unfinished novel ends after a fragment of chapter eight, as Walter loiters in San Francisco's Golden Gate Park, thinking about the police and the government's search for him.

Brother Monster ends suddenly and unfortunately, because the portion that exists is outstanding. It is beautifully written, with intriguing characters and the beginnings of a well-worked-out plot. The fragment is a fitting end to Brown's career as a science fiction writer, and it is tinged with mystery as well. The biggest mystery of all, of course, is what would have happened in the rest of the novel! Brown and Altshuler discussed a climax in which "Walter is viewed eventually as so dangerous that the whole forces of the nation and the world are brought to bear on the problem. And the irony of it is that squashing him lets loose the real menace. Squashing the flea lets loose the elephant. He is only a trigger which the stupid officialdom pulls" (Intro. 7). He also wrote that:

My idea—not worked out in detail—was an eventual confrontation of the brothers; Walter, the invisible brother, has by then turned against George and tries to kill him, gets killed instead. Then: one idea was to have George find that he too is a mutant, and he takes up where Walter left off. But that's just one possibility; don't consider yourself bound by it. (11)

Clearly, Brown develops two plot lines in the fragment that would eventually have to converge in a confrontation between the brothers. Unfortunately, Brown never finished the book, so the details are left to the reader to imagine.

* * *

From 1939 to 1965, Fredric Brown wrote dozens of science fiction stories and not quite six science fiction novels. Some were serious; many were funny. Many of the stories were variations on various themes, while the novels were usually more concerned with character and plot. For one reason or another, Brown's science fiction has gained him more recognition than his mysteries even though he wrote many more of the latter.

Yet, by today's standards, what Fredric Brown wrote might barely be considered science fiction, at best a primitive version of a subgenre that has seen an explosion of critical interest in recent years. Brown's concern with technology and terminology was only slight; instead, he often used science fiction settings to tell tales that might have been told equally well (or almost as well) in contemporary settings.

Brown's best science fiction lacks the depth of his best mysteries, but his mysteries have not received as much attention. That's a shame, because he wrote many outstanding mysteries, in both short story and novel form, including a foursome in the mid-1950s that are as dark and brilliant as anything he ever wrote.

Chapter Eleven
A Descent into Madness

In Venice, California, after having completed *The Deep End* in 1952, Fredric Brown began working on his eleventh novel, about which he wrote:

in the six months [in Venice, CA] I've started only one new novel and had reason—irrelevant here—for making that a carnival-background story. ("Where Do I Get My Plots?" 181)

The novel was to be called *The Pickled Punks*, and Brown seems to have spent the summer of 1952 writing it; Beth Brown wrote that it set a precedent for him by only taking three months to write and that he was done by early October.

Brown seems to have been happy with the novel, and he decided to use it to try to get a better deal with his publisher, E.P. Dutton & Co., since his contract had run out. *The Pickled Punks* was sent to Harry Altshuler, who presented it to Dutton, but they would not agree to increase Brown's rates. Frustrated, Brown began working on *The Lights in the Sky Are Stars* while Altshuler tried to find a publisher for *The Pickled Punks*. New Year 1953 came and went, and the novel was finally sold to Dell Publishing Company, to appear as one of the first in their prestigious new line of paperback originals. Brown did the revisions Dell requested and received a $4000 advance; he also allowed them to change the novel's title to *Madball*. Soon after, Dutton reconsidered its position and offered Brown a new contract.

Madball is a brilliant, forgotten novel about the seamy side of life among carneys and crooks. It is told by an omniscient narrator in the third person and begins as carney Mack Irby returns to the Wiggins and Braddock Combined Shows, the carnival with which he travels, after having been in the hospital for six weeks due to a car accident that killed his partner Charlie. Just prior to the accident, Mack and Charlie had robbed $42,000 from a bank and hidden it on the carney lot; with Charlie dead, the money belongs to Mack.

There is none of the hopeful romanticism of *The Dead Ringer* in *Madball*—the carnival is sordid and so are those who travel with it. The "Mystery of Sex" exhibit is a big draw, but all the "marks" find inside is a two-headed calf fetus and a selection of pornographic books for sale. The "posing-show" girls are all whores (unlike Rita in *The Dead Ringer*); Jesse Rau, who runs the ball game, is a homosexual child-abuser; and so on. Carney slang is used in both speech and narration and the total effect is to create an awful, unpleasant world.

Chapter two abruptly switches perspective; whereas chapter one was seen through Mack's eyes, we now see through the eyes of "The Murderer," an unnamed carney who bludgeons Mack with a tent stake and pays off Dolly Quintana to prevent her from telling anyone that she saw him leave the tent where the murder was committed.

Mack was sleeping with Maybelle Seeley, a girl from the posing show who had gone for a walk before he was killed. Fearing the police, she goes to see Dr. Magus, the carney mentalist, for an alibi for the night. Magus is the most likable character in the seamy world of *Madball*; he tends to speak in poetic ironies and insists on searching Maybelle to make certain she didn't rob Mack; although she is naked, "He missed no inch of surface, no nook or cranny" (19). The narrator continues by pointing out that:

And Maybelle, all of whose amours had been with younger and less experienced men, learned a few things that night that she had never known before.

Young lust and then experienced lechery, with a murder in between. All in all, quite a night. (19)

The novel's fourth chapter is told from Dolly Quintana's perspective and it is a portrait of a woman brutalized and fearful. Her husband Leon, with whom she shares a knife-throwing act, has sworn to throw acid in her face if she ever leaves him, and his lovemaking is more like rape. Even Dolly's prayers go unanswered; her plea for rain is rewarded in this way: "The sun came out bright and the day was pleasant" (24).

As the police investigation into Mack's murder begins, we learn more details about the carneys: Doc is 52 years old, born in 1900, and was four months' shy of earning his Ph.D. at age 23 when he was thrown out of school after having earned a Master's in psychology. The Mystery of Sex, a highlight of the carnival, consists of fetuses in glass jars—it's also called a "punk show" and the fetuses are "pickled punks" (30), hence the novel's original title. Doc Magus remarks that the fetuses are rubber fakes themselves, demonstrating further the tissue of lies that makes up the carnival.

Throughout the novel, Brown uses a clever tactic to keep the murderer's identity hidden from the reader while still developing the character from two directions. As Evans, or "the murderer," we read his thoughts and actions as he tries to get the money Mack hid. As Burt, he is merely another carney, whom Doc describes as "the guy who gives you the dirtiest look" (31). Not until the novel's end is it revealed that Burt Evans is the murderer—the revelation is a surprise and yet not wholly unexpected, since the character has been right before the reader's eyes the whole time.

Yet another character's perspective is used in chapter five— Sammy, the halfwit adolescent who sets up the balls for Jesse Rau's concession game. The chapter has a childlike perversity that makes it one of the most disturbing of the novel. Jesse drinks and abuses Sammy, who arrived at the carnival a year before after escaping from an institution to be taken on and sodomized by Jesse. Sammy is curious about sex and has been teased by Trixie, a posing show girl, yet he is so innocent that he spends every dime he's given on cotton candy. He finds pornography in Evans's tent and his curiosity grows; he becomes obsessed with the need for "paper money"(41), which he thinks is necessary to get sex.

Chapter seven finally reveals Dr. Magus as the novel's "detective"—he deduces that Mack had a secret that got him killed, then figures out the nature of the secret. The novel continues along two lines, in alternating chapters, as Magus investigates Mack's bank robbery in order to locate the hidden stash while Evans plans Dolly's murder to eliminate her as a witness against him. Magus is a clever investigator who uses his training in psychology and powers of observation to elicit deep-hidden information; Evans is a methodical plotter who uses people's weaknesses against them to further his own ends.

An important moment occurs in chapter 13, when Magus consults his crystal ball for help in finding the missing money—he's just drunk enough to think it might work and recalls past times when the crystal ball led him to things. The crystal is called a "madball" in carney slang, and this is what he sees:

> There was a sudden bright flash of light in the crystal, then for a brief moment black darkness. Dr. Magus blinked, and again the crystal was as it had been before, reflecting his own distorted face and the interior of the mitt camp curving upon itself like an Einsteinian universe. (81-82)

A touch of the supernatural, this premonition is never explained—it is an anomaly that must simply be accepted, as in Charles Fort's philosophy. The event catches the reader and Dr. Magus off guard, and the fact that Magus later dies in the bright flash of an explosion only increases the impact of this foreshadowing scene.

Soon, Evans plays God by setting up a date between Dolly Quintana and Joe Linder and then speaking through a slit in Leon Quintana's tent to tell him where his unfaithful wife lies. Leon murders Joe and Dolly in his rage and no one ever knows Evans was involved. The slate is wiped clean when Leon commits suicide in jail by biting open a vein in his own wrists—nothing in *Madball* is done pleasantly.

There follows a glimpse into Evans's past, making him seem like the summation of Brown's best killers to date—a composite Fredric Brown murderer. He recalls "the time when he'd mugged the lush in the alley back of Clark Street in Chicago" ([113] recalling the death of Wally Hunter in *The Fabulous Clipjoint*) and also the time "He'd pushed the brakeman off the moving train in sudden anger" ([113] recalling Obie Westphal's death in *The Deep End*). Yet Evans is more evil than the earlier killers; his murders are purposeful and he is never caught, while the murders in the earlier novels were both ambiguous.

Madball is a central novel in Fredric Brown's *oeuvre*; it deals with one of his favorite settings, includes characters who seem to be composites or types of characters in earlier novels (Dr. Magus is in the tradition of Brown's drunken investigators, like Sweeney in *The Screaming Mimi* and Doc Stoeger in *Night of the Jabberwock*), and even the conclusion is lifted from *Here Comes a Candle*. But before that conclusion, the various characters and plot lines must be moved into place by the omnipotent author. Magus travels to the Glenrock hospital where Mack recovered after his car accident; posing as Mack's father, Dr. Rance Irby, Magus pulls out all the psychological stops to win over an old nurse and get her to tell him about Mack's ravings, thus revealing the location of the money. After this the novel really picks up steam, the pace increasing as Brown worries less about demonstrating how sordid the carnival is and instead concentrates on story, characters, and style.

A play on Wordsworth opens chapter 21 as "Sammy wandered lonely as a cloud" (129), and it is Sammy's wanderings that set up the novel's conclusion as Brown weaves a tight web around his characters and leaves their destinies certain. Sammy's confused sexual desires lead him to spy on Evans and Trixie in Evans's tent; when he's discovered, he is thrown out of the carnival by his protector Jesse, "Out into the night, the lonely night bright with moonlight and dark with dread" (140). Dr. Magus clears the way for his search of the rubber fetuses ("pickled punks") in which Mack's money is hidden, and Sammy wanders, hungry, into Evans's tent, where he finds a gun. Sammy is unable to fully comprehend his situation but fights against the memory of the road he once walked, as Brown evocatively describes:

> Far off in the night, in the direction in which Jesse had pointed, a freight engine whistled mournfully. The road, the hungry road. The road that had been before Jesse and the carnival. Hunger and freight cars clacking through the night, and running from brakemen and policemen, hiding and shivering in the cold. (149)

By this point, the chapters in *Madball* are very short, and alternate between Dr. Magus and Sammy like crosscutting in a film to heighten the suspense as the stories come closer and closer to converging. Sammy discovers a box of money in Evans's tent and meets Trixie, who heads for a hotel with the boy, intending to steal the money. Evans learns that Sammy has been seen by his tent and rushes there; Magus cuts into the pickled punks and dies in a booby-trap explosion, fulfilling the prophecy of the flash of light in the madball. Brown eulogizes the novel's most likable character in this way:

> Weep no tears for Dr. Magus. He died the best of deaths. He died without ever hearing the sound of the explosion that killed him, died so suddenly that

there was no time for either pain or realization. He died without *knowing* that he died, and in a moment of supreme satisfaction and happiness. What more could he have asked or wanted? (168)

Dr. Magus dies violently but happily, setting him apart from the other carneys in the novel who die in horrible ways.

Burt Evans is finally revealed as the murderer in chapter 29, which begins:

Weep rather for Burt Evans, owner of the unborn show, the murderer now of five people... (169)

Evans hears the explosion in his tent as he drives off in pursuit of Sammy and Trixie; he realizes he'll be caught and vows to get the money and get away. In his haste he speeds by two policemen who give chase and he is quickly killed in an ensuing car crash.

The final chapter of *Madball* focuses on Sammy and Trixie in their hotel room, in a twisted version of the situation faced by Joe Bailey and Ellie Dravich at the end of *Here Comes a Candle*: Sammy is a halfwit boy, lusting after a deceitful whore who spikes his drink while he's supposedly taking a bath. He sees this, however, and tries to scare her with Evans's gun, shooting her by mistake. As people hammer on the hotel room door Sammy is concerned that Evans not get his money back, so he sets fire to it and the novel ends as the blaze grows.

Madball is a novel that pushes everything to the limits. It's sordid but fascinating, as Brown experiments with multiple points of view to paint a portrait of a world gone mad (a mad ball, in a sense), where evil compounds itself into infinity and where the brilliant and the foolish reach equally horrible ends. No one in *Madball* is happy and nothing ends well; it is surely one of Brown's bleakest novels, beginning an investigation into the dark side of human nature that would characterize his work in the mid-1950s.

Madball was published as Dell 1st Edition #2E with a print run of 255,000 copies in August 1953 (Lyles, *Dell Paperbacks* 203) and received virtually no attention. The paperback series was thought to be of high quality, yet Ralph Ellison, whose groundbreaking novel *Invisible Man* had been published only a few years before, complained that Brown's novel was "in bad taste" (Lyles, *Putting Dell on the Map* 41).

One review appeared in the New York *Times* Book Review; Anthony Boucher gave the book qualified praise, calling the carnival background "much better than the story."

Since then, *Madball* has disappeared from view. A paperback reprint appeared in 1961 and there have been a handful of foreign editions, but it has earned no critical notice. Apparently never published in France (at least, not as of 1984), no French critic has discussed it, and American critic Newton Baird listed it among those novels he felt were of lesser merit and did not warrant attention. Yet Art Bourgeau, in *The Mystery Lover's Companion*, rates it higher than any other Brown book listed (22), and Frank McSherry, in a 1971 published letter, calls it "perhaps his best mystery novel" (61).

Madball did have one other incarnation: as a novelette, under Brown's original title of "The Pickled Punks." In 1953, well after the novel was completed, *Manhunt* magazine offered Brown $1000 for a version of *Madball* cut to 20,000 words. He spent a few weeks cutting the novel, only to have *Manhunt* refuse the shorter version on the grounds that it had too much sex! The short version eventually sold to *The Saint Detective Magazine*, where it appeared in the June-July 1953 issue and actually beat the novel into publication. According to Beth Brown, *The Saint* had its mailing permit revoked for daring to publish such a scandalous story (*Oh, for the Life* 233).

The novelette differs from the novel in that Brown reveals Burt Evans as the murderer right from the start. Several short chapters are combined and aspects of the novel are absent, such as Jesse's sexual abuse of Sammy. "The Pickled Punks" is strong on plot, character, and setting, but *Madball* is a *tour de force*.

After completing *Madball* in October 1952, Fredric Brown wrote the science fiction novel *The Lights in the Sky Are Stars*. He then wrote the novelette "The Wench is Dead" for *Manhunt* and cut *Madball* to novelette length for publication as "The Pickled Punks" in *The Saint Detective Magazine*. Later in 1953, the Browns moved from Venice, California, to El Segundo, California, where Fred completed his next novel, *His Name Was Death*, before the end of the year (*Oh, for the Life* 222-41).

His Name Was Death was published by Dutton on June 1, 1954, and, although it is not as sordid and dark as *Madball*, it is a wild ride through the mind and milieu of another fascinating murderer. The novel is barely 139 pages long in paperback and is divided into nine unnumbered sections, each of which begins with a name: "Her name was Joyce Dugan," "His name was Darius Conn," etc., until the final section, which begins: "His name was Death."

The novel opens innocently enough at four o'clock on a Friday afternoon, as young widow Joyce Dugan finishes her day's work in Darius Conn's print shop by making a date with old boyfriend Claude Atkins, for whom she cashes a check with $10 bills from her boss's safe. This simple act sets a series of deadly events in motion because the bills are counterfeits Conn has been using in an elaborate scheme. Conn discovers the loss and decides to recover the money from Claude; in the meantime, he recalls having murdered his wife the year before after finding that she had been with another man. He was never caught for the murder and his subsequent success in the counterfeiting scheme makes him feel invincible.

The first two sections are told in the third person, from the perspectives of Joyce Dugan and Darius Conn. Conn is portrayed as a slight, 41-year-old printer with bifocals and asthma—slightly reminiscent of Fredric Brown himself, who was only six years older. Conn thinks himself meticulous, yet he's a fool; his disguise is easily seen through and he leaves a clear trail of all his actions. He believes himself to be the perfect criminal, yet, as the novel's conclusion will reveal, his destiny is guided by the police officer who was his wife's lover and who allows Conn to go on unmolested until his moment for revenge presents itself. Throughout the novel, however, the reader believes that Conn's life is ruled by fate, both good and bad.

The third section is told from the perspective of Claude Atkins, who further ruins Conn's scheme by loaning $50 of the counterfeit money to his fiance, Rose Harper. Claude is well portrayed as a young man on the verge of a marriage commitment; at one point, a voice inside Claude warns him to avoid becoming *"tied down, like those other poor suckers, watching dimes—"* (41). Section four follows Darius Conn in his disguise as William Pierce as he plans and carries out Claude's murder. His belief that all loose ends have been tied up is shattered when he checks Claude's wallet and finds $50 missing. In the process of planning the murder, Conn reveals through his thoughts that he has a philosophy about murder: it's clean, safe, and merciful when the victim doesn't suffer. After killing his wife Myrtle he developed an interest in true crime stories and became fascinated with the idea of the Perfect Criminal, after which he models himself. He prides himself on his skill, but it seems luck is his guiding force; he finds a receipt in Claude's wallet that helps lead him to the missing $50.

Brown does another nice job of characterization with Claude's girlfriend, Rose Harper, from whose perspective the fifth section is told. She's a pleasant young girl on the verge of marriage, working as a waitress but wanting something else. *His Name Was Death* is actually a novel about people; it recalls *The Case of the Dancing Sandwiches* in the way different characters' perspectives are utilized both to move the plot along and to develop their characters more fully. The novel is a masterpiece of suspense as well: at the fifth section's end, the reader knows that the caller at Rose's door is not her fiancee Claude but rather the murderous little printer, Darius Conn.

Section six begins in a way that both frustrates the reader and increases the suspense: Brown skips the murder entirely and picks up Conn's actions the next day. It is only after several pages that Conn recalls killing Rose the night before:

She had died, as Atkins had died, without warning. Suddenly and unexpectedly and without knowing that she was being killed, spared even a fraction of a second of terror before oblivion. Yes, it made him feel better, much better, that he'd been able to do that much for both of them. Their deaths had been even more merciful than Myrtle's; she had been unconscious while he had strangled her, but she had had a fractional second of knowledge that he was going to strike and hurt her before the blow had landed. Neither Atkins nor the Harper girl had even that. (87)

Conn becomes further convinced that he is invincible, having committed three perfect murders; but, while his conscious mind is sure, his unconscious troubles him in one of Brown's best dream sequences.

In the dream, Conn argues with bank teller Jennings, whom he confuses with his father. Jennings wants Conn to pick up two women at a lodge and Conn discovers he's at a lodge meeting and that the bartender is the Royal Tiger (Brown had previously used tiger imagery in *The Deep End*, calling murderer Obie a tiger). One of the girls, a brunette, tells Conn "Printer Stink," and he then goes for the blonde, who turns out to be his late wife Myrtle. She is naked and taunts him; he then finds he is naked as well. He runs then drives to the storage company where he had checked his counterfeit plates; on the way, he drives off the road and into a cemetery, where he feels himself being pulled toward the graves. At the storage company, an Episcopalian minister brings out, instead of his checked bags, the naked corpse of Myrtle and begins reciting marriage vows!

This dream is an excellent example of surreal writing; the events flow in a progression that follows only dream logic, blending religious, criminal, and psychiatric elements into a chaotic whole that demonstrates the horror seething beneath the surface of Conn's calm exterior and hints at the disaster to come.

Joyce Dugan returns in the seventh section as she reads of Claude's and Rose's murders in the paper and decides to wait till morning to call the police. Joyce goes to the movies and sees *Sorry, Wrong Number*; ironically, it portrays a woman who doesn't know she's being stalked by a murderer. Joyce also continues to mourn her late husband Joe, suggesting that one of this novel's themes is the problem of dealing with lost loved ones: Conn has lost Myrtle, Joyce has lost Joe, Claude and Rose lose each other. Perhaps Conn's murderous impulses are driven in part by his anger at losing Myrtle—he kills Claude and Rose as they are on the verge of marriage.

Conn's luck begins to turn against him in the novel's next-to-last section; his plan to take his counterfeit money out of the bank and hide it in storage is failed because the bank is closed for Lincoln's Birthday. Returning to his printer's shop he grows concerned as Joyce questions whether she should go to the police to tell them she gave Claude the counterfeit money; he sends her out on an errand for the afternoon and makes plans to kill her that night. As events begin to point toward Conn's being caught his nervous thoughts are printed in italics:

> *Danger danger.*
> *Think, be calm, think.*
> *Don't breathe yet; this isn't over yet.* (117-18)

One further detail in this section links Conn the printer to Brown the author: Conn's father died when the boy was 18 and his mother died when he was 20 (120). Brown's parents also died when their son was a teenager.

The novel's final section begins ominously:

His name was Death, and he waited for Darius Conn. (137)

Death, in this instance, is Sergeant Charlie Barrett, who waits in Joyce's room for Conn to come through the window. When Conn arrives, Charlie tells him that he knows every crime Conn has committed and that he's been waiting for this opportunity; he was Myrtle's lover and he knew Conn killed her. He shoots and kills Conn then walks toward the hall phone to report shooting a prowler.

The conclusion to *His Name Was Death* is a tremendous surprise— Charlie has figured in the novel and was even friendly with Conn, but his revelations are astonishing. The final section is told from his perspective and his guilt is complex: he murders Conn with premeditation, yet he's a police officer and thus will succeed as the only *real* perfect criminal of the novel. The pitiful, mentally-unbalanced Conn is hardly the successful criminal he believes himself to be; in truth, the only character who succeeds in the end is Death itself.

His Name Was Death is not the descent into darkness that *Madball* was; rather, it is not unlike *The Far Cry* in its investigation of the results of an unhappy marriage (between Conn and Myrtle) and in the terrific suspense that mounts and mounts until a shocking conclusion.

The reviews of the novel in 1954 were overwhelmingly praiseworthy, from James Sandoe's comment that "Mr. Brown is an ingenious craftsman and likes to pin himself within special disciplines" (a comment that might apply to Brown's entire career), to Anthony Boucher's remark in the New York *Times* that "You'll be compelled to read through in one sitting to one of the very few endings that have genuinely surprised me in a long time."

Critical writing on the novel has, surprisingly, been sparse. Francis Lacassin, in his 1974 article "Fredric Brown ou Alice de ce côté du miroir," notes the "density of action...contained in a relatively short space of time" (256);[1] the events of the novel take place over the space of about three and a half days, from late Friday afternoon to Monday evening, though Lacassin mistakenly sets the time frame at 24 hours. He also notes the "excessive speed of the action" (257)[2] and remarks on the presence of the absurd in this novel, claiming that Conn's meeting Claude in a bar before the novel begins results in an incident "that, by grotesque consequences, transforms the story into a waking nightmare" (261).³ Lacassin's article is fascinating; unfortunately, subsequent critics have ignored *His Name Was Death*. Newton Baird lumps it along with *Madball* among novels of lesser merit that don't warrant discussion in his allotted space, and Jean-Pierre Deloux sadly gives it only a brief mention in his landmark 1984 article, "Mouvement brownien."

His Name Was Death apparently received two hardcover printings by Dutton in 1954, and was then reprinted as a Bantam paperback in 1956. It made a rather curious appearance in the December 1958 issue of *Swank* magazine, a then-relatively new men's magazine that featured pictures of naked women and stories that varied in quality. The novel is condensed in the magazine version and retitled "Who Was That Blonde I Saw You Kill Last Night?" and the title is the best thing about it; descriptive passages, characterization, inner thoughts, and narrative description are excised to make the novel short enough to fit the magazine. There's even a breakout "quote" on the two-page spread that begins the story; unfortunately, the purple prose isn't Brown's:

He had a very handy motto—"The first killing is the toughest." Blondes, brunettes, or red heads; any girl who made trouble for him, he'd just take out his little pistol and stop all that noise for good. (40)

Fun, yes; relevant, unfortunately not. Other than the title, the short version of *His Name Was Death* is valuable only as an example of how a novel was condensed to make a sale, and of the type of slick men's magazine that was taking over the field by the late 1950s, replacing the pulps.

His Name Was Death was also performed live on television, on the March 18, 1957 episode of *Robert Montgomery Presents*. The teleplay was written by Frank Telford and it starred Henry Jones, presumably as Darius Conn. Since the broadcast was live, it's uncertain whether a film exists of this adaption; I've never come across one, but such things do turn up.

Other than foreign editions, *His Name Was Death* lay forgotten until 1990, when it was once again published in paperback in the U.S.A. No such timely revival has yet occurred for Brown's next mystery novel, *The Wench is Dead*, and this is most unfortunate for it is among his best work.

To find the origins of *The Wench is Dead* one must go back to early 1953, before Brown cut *Madball* to make "The Pickled Punks," and before he wrote *His Name Was Death*. While still living in Venice, California, Brown received an offer of $1000 for a 10,000-word story, to be written specifically for *Manhunt* magazine. In reply, he wrote "The Wench is Dead," which the magazine's editors loved and published in the July 1953 issue (*Oh, for the Life* 233-34).

The novelette tells the story of Howard Perry, a young man from a good family in Chicago who has drifted onto skid row in Los Angeles and is living as a wino. It begins with a clever take on Gertrude Stein's famous line: "A fuzz is a fuzz is a fuzz when you awaken from a wino jag" (*The Water-Walker* 5). He has a job washing dishes and intends a return to normalcy:

In a few weeks I'd be back in Chicago, back at my desk in my father's investment company... (5)

He recalls his fall from grace:

It's funny, the way those things can happen. You've got a good family and a good education, and then suddenly, for no reason you can define, you start drifting. You lose interest in your family and your job, and one day you find yourself headed for the Coast. (6)

Perry has a girlfriend, Wilhelmina "Billie the Kid" Kidder, who calls him "Professor" due to his cultured speech and font of knowledge, and he lives among the lower class of whores and petty criminals that haunt the streets and cheap rooming houses of L.A. The plot begins when Howie visits Mame, an upstairs neighbor of Billie's, to borrow liquor and learns she had a visitor the night before named Jesus Gonzales who ran off suddenly when he heard a knock on the door. In his haste he dropped a fountain pen, which Howie finds and Mame lets him keep.

Mame is stabbed to death in chapter two while Howie is at work. Billie tells him to avoid the cops, since he was seen visiting Mame's apartment that morning. In this chapter, we also meet Ramon, the Spanish cook at the restaurant where Howie works. He's a heroin addict and often must run outside for a fix; this is the first example in Brown's writing of a character's being involved with heroin, and in this and several subsequent works the drug and its use are linked to a lower order of vice than alcoholism. In fact, in "The Wench is Dead," the hero is an alcoholic and the killer a drug addict—quite a picture of life in the sordid world of the Los Angeles underclass.

Billie continues to look out for Howie the next day, when he's so hung over that he can't remember getting drunk the night before. He's amused at the prospect of getting caught and imagines a headline: "Chicago Scion in Heroin Murder Case"(19), but Billie realizes the danger he's in and convinces him to alter his appearance and avoid his room. After cleaning himself up a bit Howie reads about Mame's murder in the paper and sees a story about the death of Jesus, Mame's guest. When Howie goes to work and sees that Ramon's face has "four long scratches, downward, about an inch apart" (29), he speaks the truth without thinking: " 'Mame had sharp fingernails, huh?' " (29).

Ramon attacks Howie with a cleaver but Howie manages to avoid it and push Ramon, who stumbles and falls, fatally hitting his head on "a sharp corner of the big stove" (30). Howie escapes unnoticed, meets Billie, and tells her the truth about his background in Chicago. He decides to return to his family and takes out the fountain pen Mame gave him to write down an address where he can contact Billie. Diamonds spill out of the hollow pen and Billie excitedly tells him they can go to Mexico together. She goes to sell the diamonds to a fence and Howie must decide: should he go "Back to Chicago, back to respectability, back to my right name—Howard Perry, B.A.S., not Howard Perry, bastard, wino ..." (31), or should he go to Mexico with Billie, "And stop drinking, straighten out?" (35).

Earlier in the story, Howie had asked himself why he felt uncomfortable about taking money from Billie:

> What kept me from taking it, then? A gal named Honor, I guess. Corny as it sounds, I said it lightly. "I could not love thee, dear, so much, loved I not Honor more." (11)

Billie the Kid (and some of Brown's critics) have read this to mean that Howie actually left behind a girl in Chicago named Honor. At the story's end, as Billie heads out to sell the diamonds, she turns to Howie and asks:

> Howie, were you kidding when you said you were in love with a girl named Honor in Chicago? I mean, is there a real girl named that, or did you just mean—?

Howie replies:

> I was just kidding Billie the Kid.

Howie then pours himself a drink after she leaves and thinks:

> Yes, I'd known a girl named Honor in Chicago, once, but—...*but that was in another country, and besides, the wench is dead.* (35)

Howie sits, immobile, until Billie returns—and there the story ends.

The question of Honor in "The Wench is Dead" is an important one. Howie's first literary quotation,

> I could not love thee, dear, so much, loved I not Honor more. (11)

is from a famous poem by English poet Richard Lovelace, written in 1648 and titled, "To Lucasta, On Going to the Wars." The speaker of the poem addresses his beloved, telling her that he is not being unfaithful in leaving her to serve another mistress—his country in wartime—but that, rather, his duty to uphold his honor is an essential part of his being that cannot be separated from his love for Lucasta.

To hear such a quotation come from the mouth of Howie Perry, wino, directed toward Billie the Kid, whom he admits will sleep with anyone, is highly ironic. Howie still believes in his own honor, however, and perhaps there is a kernel of truth in his offhand literary quotation.

At the story's end, then, when Howie again resorts to literary quotation to express his thoughts, he continues his discussion of honor:

> Yes, I'd known a girl named Honor in Chicago, once, but—...*but that was in another country, and besides, the wench is dead.* (35)

This quotation is from the play *The Jew of Malta*, written by Englishman Christopher Marlowe around 1590. The line is not of central importance in the play and is in fact a humorous throwaway: Barabas, the Jew, is being questioned by two friars who have come to accuse him of conspiracy leading to murder. Barabas will not let them finish their sentences, so intent is he on confessing old sins and explaining them away. Thus, the following exchange takes place:

Friar Barnardine. Thou hast committed—

Barabas. Fornication? But that was in another country, and besides the wench is dead. (iv. i. 40-43)

The implicit meaning is that the sin should be forgotten because it was committed long ago and far away, with one now dead.

In Fredric Brown's "The Wench is Dead," Howie Perry's use of these lines has great significance. Honor, of course, is not a real girl; it is the personification of the honorable life that Howie has drifted away from, the life with his wealthy family in Chicago where he was assured a secure and comfortable time. Up until the end of the story he fools himself into believing that he can and will voluntarily climb out of the pit into which he had fallen and return to his old life, but, as he awaits Billie's return with enough money to go to Mexico, he realizes his self-deceit and accepts his own ruin.

Brown's use of poetry in "The Wench is Dead" follows his similar use in *Madball* and recalls T.S. Eliot's technique in *The Waste Land*, where bits and pieces of cultural history are placed together like bags used to shore up a dam and prevent chaos from bursting through. The Los Angeles of "The Wench is Dead" is a waste land, too, but all the poetry in the world is not enough to save Howie Perry from sinking into darkness.

After Fredric Brown completed "The Wench is Dead" in early 1953, he worked on "The Pickled Punks" and wrote *His Name Was Death*. In January 1954, he began expanding "The Wench is Dead" to novel form. The Browns moved from El Segundo, California, to Tucson, Arizona, in about May 1954, and it was there that Brown completed *The Wench is Dead* in September 1954 (*Oh, for the Life* 233-71). The novel was published by Dutton in early May 1955 and is strikingly different from the novelette in a number of important ways.

The first and most surprising is found in the first paragraph; "A fuzz is a fuzz is a fuzz" is still there, but now, when Howie recalls blacking out in an alcoholic stupor the night before, he thinks: "that's when research stopped" (4). Research? The Howie of the novelette may have had a B.A. in sociology, but he never mentioned research. More details come slowly—he mentions "this down-and-out-on-skid-row summer you wanted to try and are trying" (11) and finally reveals that he's a high school sociology teacher from Chicago who has come to Los

Angeles to live on skid row as a wino in order to gather material for his thesis. Howie Perry in the novel is quite different from Howie Perry in the story; here, he has not drifted to Los Angeles and become a wino by chance, he has chosen this place and this life of his own volition, slumming among the lower orders of society in order to study them.

Perry, it seems, is a do-gooder who yearns for acceptance from those he aids. He did social work in Chicago but was always viewed as an outsider; he came to Los Angeles to get the inside story. He rode freight cars cross-country to get to Los Angeles, as Fredric Brown did in the Great Depression, yet his background and speech mark him as an outsider of sorts, earning him the ironic nickname of "professor" (he's not really a professor, of course, but he surely enjoys the flattering nickname just as he "professes" to be a wino). Perry makes an interesting observation on the surprisingly good grammar of the denizens of L.A.'s lower depths:

some of its denizens had been newspapermen once, some had written poetry; one I'd met was a defrocked priest who now made drinking his religion. (15)

The mystery plot of the novel unfolds along the same lines as that of the novelette; the long version includes scenes and characters that expand the insight into the milieu and expand Brown's investigation of sordidness and the life of an alcoholic. One such character is Ike Batchelor, a drunk and former ad copywriter who now hates advertising so much that he won't buy advertised goods or drink where there's a television or a radio. He tells Howie that a rule of the street is not to ask "why a man is what he is" (27) and calls society an "emulsion," where bums—like particles—sink to the bottom. Brown thus adds philosophical discussion to his plot to fill out the novel; happily, it also adds insight to the characters.

As the novel progresses, Howie occasionally thinks about the denizens of skid row:

These people I pass, these shadow faces on a shadow street, what are they and what makes them what they are? That Salvation Army girl going tavern to tavern with a tambourine to collect money from drunken bums to feed hungry bums—and a little Hell or Heaven thrown in with the food—is she one of the simple ones? Or is goodness more complicated than defeat?

Or are *any* people simple? And if once, all at once, all people were made simple would they stay that way because life would be and remain simple too? Or would it change them, within the space of a heartbeat, make them complicated again?

Nuts, I told myself. Sociology, that's your racket, not philosophy. If that *was* philosophy and not just the kind of fuzzy thinking that gets people talking to themselves. (65)

Howie's relationship with Billie is also expanded, and his background receives further revisions—he's 28 years old, and his parents died during his second year of college. His father was "a scholar...editor and reader for a publisher of textbooks" (74), and insurance money after his death paid for the rest of Howie's four years in college. Howie thinks he belongs in the "lost generation" of F. Scott Fitzgerald but laments that "that school had been dismissed long ago" (75).

Chapter six of the novel is haunting and new, as Howie gets drunk and walks through skid row. Brown uses images, bits of overheard conversation, pieces of songs, and briefly-glimpsed characters to paint an evocative portrait of despair. By the end of the chapter, both Howie and the reader are well familiar with the dissolution and disillusionment that inhabit the lower depths, and Howie suddenly steps on the head of a chalk figure marking the scene of a murder. Chapter seven is a relief: chapter six marked Howie's deepest involvement in the world of darkness and his next step would have been into madness. Chapter seven is the novel's turning point, or so we think—yet chapter eight then begins with Howie's waking up with a hangover, sharing an unfamiliar room with two strange men. Howie has had a blackout and, though he doesn't know it yet, is no longer fully in control of his own actions. He foolishly keeps trying, though, thinking "This is the day to change things, a lot of things. Let last night be an ending and a fitting climax" (98).

Howie suspects that the chalk outline he discovered may have marked the spot where the body of Mame's visitor, Jesus, was found, as the mystery moves on. The plot resembles that of the story, but it has undergone a sea change; the added characters and incidents do not seem tacked on and are integral to the novel's broader concerns. Another lost night occurs, where Howie recalls: "I don't remember getting back to my room" (142), and Howie becomes the object of an active police search. Howie decides to go back to Chicago, taking what he thinks will be his last look at Fifth St. and noting that "skid rows never change."

> The people on them come and go; Ike had gone and I was going, but from somewhere two other lost ones were already taking our places. There's always room at the bottom.
> Room at the top, too, but you have to fight for that. To reach the bottom all you have to do is let go of whatever you're holding onto. Try it sometime; there's nothing easier. *Anybody* can be a bum. (155)

As the novel comes to a close, Howie begins to realize he's an alcoholic when he sits without a drink for 20 minutes and thinks two hours have passed. In chapter 14, Howie confronts Ramon and Ramon dies. In most novels, this would be it: the murder solved, the killer dead, the masquerade about to end. But Brown's concerns in *The Wench is Dead* involve much more than plot, as the final chapter shows.

The final chapter, of course, includes the story's surprise ending. Howie prays to himself:

> Oh, Billie, Billie the kid, live up to your name, be dishonest, don't come back, keep it all, let me drink myself to sleep this one, this final time. And wake up to an empty room in which there is no choice, no decision to make, because I'm not strong enough to make it. Make it for me, Billie. Don't come back, don't come back. (189)

But Billie does come back, and then asks him the question about Honor. In the story, Howie only hears her footsteps; in the novel, she actually returns and begins to make drinks. In both cases it's clear that the Honor that is gone is Howie's, and that he has finally accepted his inability to escape the sordid life of the wino that he has chosen.

The Wench is Dead in both its forms is thus a worthy successor to *Madball*, for each examines an unforgiving world of darkness from which the characters find no escape. The decision to make Perry a slumming sociology teacher in the novel is clever and memorable, but it is the incisive writing, the deep characters, and the painstaking portrait of the "other side" that make both novels outstanding reading.

Unlike *Madball*, *The Wench is Dead* was published in hardcover and reviewed in a number of periodicals. Anthony Boucher wrote that

"The setting is so sharply observed that one almost believes Brown must have done the same [as Howie Perry]; and the gratifyingly unconventional story is told with conciseness and bite." *Kirkus Reviews* called the novel a "pro job," and Lenore Glen Offord remarked that "his Skid Row scene and characters are fine."

Sadly, after the usual Bantam paperback reprint in 1957, *The Wench is Dead* joined *Madball* in the ranks of forgotten novels. It hasn't been reprinted in the U.S. since 1957, and critics have largely ignored it. No French critic has discussed it except for Jean-Pierre Deloux, who compares Howie Perry to Bill Sweeney of *The Screaming Mimi*, writing that Sweeney "accepts himself as he is in the same manner as Howard Perry in *The Wench is Dead*" (10).[4] The penalty for Perry seems much greater, though, since *The Wench is Dead* is by far the bleaker of the two novels.

The novel seems to have stuck in the memory of American readers, though; witness Lawrence Block's comment that

> I wanted to follow in the footsteps of the hero of *The Wench is Dead*, a sociology professor spending his sabbatical incognito on Skid Row and ultimately seduced by life at the bottom. (7-8)

Block's memory is slightly off—Howie Perry is not a sociology professor on sabbatical, he's a high-school teacher spending his summer vacation in a rather perverse way. *The Wench is Dead* also earned an entry in *College Mystery Novels*, where its plot is well summarized and the editor concludes that "Textbooks in sociology often describe the virtues and shortcomings of 'participant-observation' as a research device. *The Wench is Dead* is better than any textbook in detailing the method's pitfalls" (Kramer 204).

The only critic to deal with *The Wench is Dead* in any depth is Newton Baird, who devotes almost two full pages of his *Armchair Detective* series to the book. Baird also mistakenly calls Howie a "sociology professor" ("Paradox and Plot" 157) and apparently seems to think that Honor is an actual former girlfriend. I differ from Baird's interpretation that Howie faces a moral choice between "self-sacrifice (staying) and self-interest (going). He soon realizes that either way leads to corruption" (158). In my opinion, it's clear at the end of the novel that Howie realizes the better choice is to return to his life of honor in

Chicago, yet he also realizes that he has grown too weak to make such a difficult choice and must continue along the downhill path that his decision to experience the life of a wino set in motion. Baird's conclusion, however, is interesting: "The lesson may be this: real value is in the choices each of us makes, and it is our values that make up our *real identity*" (159). For Howie Perry, the discovery of his real identity is an unpleasant one, and his seduction by the darker side of life marks the novel version of *The Wench is Dead*.

The Wench is Dead was completed in mid-September 1954. Brown then worked on expanding his novelette "Martians, Go Home!" to novel length, finishing in March 1955. His next novel, *The Lenient Beast*, was then written in five months, the last of which using a new electric typewriter that helped speed things up. The novel is preceded by the following epigraph, from which Brown plucked the title:

When I said that mercy stood
Within the borders of the wood,
I meant the lenient beast with claws
And bloody, swift-dispatching jaws.
—Lawrence P. Spingarn

Beth Brown remarked that her husband met the poet Spingarn in late 1953 or early 1954 while still living in El Segundo, California. Spingarn's book, *Roccoco Summer*, had been published by Dutton and Brown liked these lines from the poem "Definition." He got the poet's permission to use them in a book and filed them away until he sat down to write *The Lenient Beast* (*Oh, for the Life* 275-77).

Like its companion novel *His Name Was Death*, *The Lenient Beast* is written from the perspective of its various characters, but this time the narration is in the first person rather than the third. It is one of Brown's boldest narrative experiments and, like his other extreme experiment, *Here Comes A Candle*, the tricks fail to succeed in capturing the reader's imagination and deepening the novel's effect. Yet *The Lenient Beast* is not nearly as dull as the earlier novel; it features interesting characters and a fairly good plot.

Chapter one is told by John Medley, a religious fanatic who is both educated and gentle and who kills out of a belief that he's being merciful to his victims. Medley, like Fred Brown, was born in

Cincinnati; he's 56 years old (Brown was 49 at the time of writing), intellectual, and retired in Tucson, where Brown was also living. As the story opens, he discovers a dead body in his back yard under a Chinese elm and calls the police. He meets Frank Ramos, an investigating officer who shares his intellectual bent, and admits to the reader that he killed the man and placed his body in the yard. He prays to God, thinking:

He asks much, but someday He will take away from me the mark of the beast and I shall be free. Someday He shall extend His mercy even unto me. (23)

Chapter two is told by Ramos's partner, Fern "Red" Cahan (guess the hair color), who is young and uncomplicated. He and Ramos begin their investigation and learn that the dead man was Kurt Stiffler, whose family was killed not long before when their car crashed on the way back from a wedding in the border town of Nogales, Arizona. Ramos himself narrates the third chapter, and details of the continuing investigation are mixed with details of his personal life: his wife, Alice, is a troublesome drinker, whom he has to track down in taverns and bring home. Ramos is a parallel character to Medley; both are erudite and both are troubled.

Medley narrates chapter four, dreaming of his late wife and praying to God to let him stop killing. His dream recalls that of Darius Conn in *His Name Was Death*:

How many times will You let him make me kill Dierdre again, and in how many ways?

This time it is the pistol and I hold it to the back of her head as she looks unsuspectingly from the window, and then I pull the trigger. The gun explodes deafeningly in the room and I see the tiny mark where it entered. But she does not fall.

She turns back toward me and *her face is gone*. It is a red, bloody oval out of which one eye stares at me and from which the other eye dangles horribly. Her lipless mouth is open and she screams, she *screams*. (50-51)

Although Medley's tortured nightmare about the wife he killed is not as wildly inventive as Conn's, it does serve to convey the chaos inside his head.

After a chapter narrated by police Captain Walter Pettijohn, the story is again taken over by Frank Ramos, and chapter six continues to show the varieties of intolerance and misunderstanding that often occur when those of different religious beliefs live and work together. A central theme of *The Lenient Beast* is that of prejudice, be it religious or racial. John Medley constantly prays to God and is obsessed with his mission to kill those in pain. Frank Ramos is a Mexican-American intellectual whose religious beliefs are not the strongest. Walter Pettijohn is a Presbyterian elder who is subtly prejudiced against Ramos; he doesn't like educated Mexicans who display their education and he doesn't like Ramos's flippant view on suicide. Even Rhoda Stern, a secretary who worked with the late Kurt Stiffler, didn't like Stiffler because she thought he was a Jew; ironically, Stiffler was Lutheran. The world of *The Lenient Beast* is an unpleasant one, where marriages crumble and murders are committed in the name of the Lord.

After some more investigation in chapter seven, which is narrated by Red Cahan, Frank's wife Alice takes over in chapter eight, a chapter that is almost solely concerned with painting a portrait of a marriage in trouble, as in *The Far Cry*. Alice is frustrated, unhappy, and no longer in love with Frank. She hates the desert and longs to flee Tucson with her "exciting" boyfriend, a salesman named Clyde. She lost her first baby and can't have another, and she no longer enjoys sex. She's also an alcoholic. She once "believed in a heaven and a hell, an afterlife of some kind, until Frank showed me how silly it was to believe in something like that" (112). Brown the agnostic thus makes a very subtle point here: while Frank may have lost his faith due to his reading and intellectual interests, the end result was that he extinguished what may have been his wife's last means of self-respect, in the form of her religion, and in doing so put out the flame of her love for him.

Yet Ramos is not wholly against the idea of God. In chapter nine, which he narrates, he listens to the Latin mass at Stiffler's funeral and it makes him "almost feel for the moment that there really *is* a God, a merciful God who cares about us and what we do..." (116).

Some comic relief appears in chapter ten, told by Red Cahan: he and Ramos interview Harvey Klinger, an out-of-towner who must come to Tucson every six months to get drunk because his wife runs the Women's Christian Temperance Union in his hometown of Benson, Arizona! By the end of this chapter, Ramos is certain that Medley killed

Stiffler out of mercy—his thoughts have been leading toward this conclusion throughout the investigation.

Medley returns as narrator of chapter 11, revealing that he decided to kill Stiffler after he overheard a young couple discussing the man while he sat in the park reading *Revelations*. He then relates the details of the killing and its preparations.

Ironically, Medley is invited to visit a kindly neighbor, Mrs. Armstrong, whose daughter Caroline has just become engaged to Red Cahan. Medley's casual mention of the play *Life With Father* causes him to recall the night eight years before when he and his wife saw the play and she was horribly injured in a car accident on the ride home. Medley ended her screams and suffering with a rock.

Chapter 11 is an outstanding chapter that delves deeply into John Medley's mind. His every thought concerns God and he quotes the passage about the beast from *Revelations*: to him, "the beast of the Apocalypse is Mercy" (132) and Medley is God's instrument. After killing his wife Medley found God in the wilderness when God told him to kill an injured doe. "And until God takes it away, the mark of the beast is upon me, and the beast is Mercy" (144). He prays to God to show him the same mercy he shows others. In a way, Medley is like Cain, who slays Abel and is cast out by the Lord:

> And now art thou cursed from the earth...a fugitive and a vagabond shalt thou be in the earth...And the Lord set a mark upon Cain, lest any finding him should kill him. (*Genesis* 4.11-15)

Yet Medley doesn't believe he's been separated by God; he is perhaps more like Job in this way, accepting his great punishment with the attitude that "God knows best"; finally, he may even be compared to Jesus Christ in a strange way (he'd probably approve the comparison), when Christ begins the Passion and prays, "Father, if thou be willing, remove this cup from me: nevertheless not my will, but thine, be done" (*Luke* 22.42). Medley is more confused than anything else; his grief was so great that it threw him into a religious fervor that almost defies explanation.

Chapter 12 deals with Frank Ramos, who tells of a holdup in which he's shot in the arm. Just prior to the holdup Frank calls Alice to ask if she'll join him in celebrating Red and Caroline's engagement; his fear that she'll be too dissolute to accompany him turns to shock when she answers the phone, "Clyde?" Alice narrates chapter 13, deciding to leave Frank and run off with Clyde. On the way out of town she passes the site of the holdup just as Frank is shot; she hesitates then continues on her way, unaware that her stopping might have altered hers and Frank's destiny if she saw him in distress. Frank's physical and emotional wounds are thus connected in time and place and, when he learns of his wife's treachery, he is little better emotionally than Medley must have been when he killed his own wife.

This blasted state allows Ramos to take a surprising step, that of visiting Medley at his home and airing his suspicions about the identity of Kurt Stiffler's murderer. Ramos comes close to the mark when he asks Medley,

did you ever kill anyone not out of mercy, not on an order from God? Perhaps someone you loved very much? (187)

Medley's narration in this chapter reveals his thoughts, portraying his dawning revelation that he has been found out. As the chapter ends he prepares to kill himself.

The novel's final chapter, narrated by Chief Pettijohn, explains that Frank Ramos took a long vacation deep in Mexico and returned to find Medley dead and Red Cahan on his honeymoon. By writing this chapter from Pettijohn's perspective Brown deprives the reader of Ramos's reaction to his wife's actions and to Medley's death; by the time he returns from Mexico, Ramos appears fine and not very upset, at least to Pettijohn. However, the fact that he vacationed in a Spanish town in Mexico suggests that he made a healing return to his roots.

Frank Ramos is a good man and a good cop, doing the honorable thing at all times. His reward? He's shot, his wife leaves him, and he's never certain whether his suspicions about John Medley's guilt are accurate. The moral points in *The Lenient Beast* are tricky, and they are left unresolved. The method of telling the story through the various characters' points of view is also tricky, and it is frustrating because Brown never provides much in the way of resolutions to the inner conflicts he sets up. In the end, *The Lenient Beast* is a novel that's more interesting to write about than to read; the mix of police procedural and

religious or moral essay is an uneasy one, made even less sure by the
extreme narrative experiment.

The reviews at the time the novel appeared were generally positive.
Anthony Boucher, who rarely had a bad word for a Brown book, wrote
in the New York *Times* that the book represents an extraordinarily

successful fusion of "Dragnet"-like police routine with the novel of
psychological suspense...the complex characters come alive as successfully as
does the desert-bounded city of Tucson, Ariz.

Kirkus Reviews was neutral, calling it a "Straight line confession type,"
while Lenore Glen Offord called it "a powerful human novel, still with
plenty of suspense." Only James Sandoe, of The New York *Herald
Tribune*, was definitely negative, stating that

narrative fidget, domestic cares, romance and a final irrelevant burst of gunnery
can't distract one from a slim plot worked with effort rather than skill.

The novel was not again mentioned until it popped up in 1971's *A
Catalogue of Crime* as one of the four Brown novels listed with
comments. The authors write: "This race and class problem (early
example) is complicated by marital and other pressures to form a
moving and entertaining story, just short of notable" (Barzun 78).

More detailed analysis had to wait until Newton Baird's landmark
series of articles in *The Armchair Detective*, where Baird devotes a page
and a half of praise to *The Lenient Beast*, calling it one of Brown's "four
or five best detective/mystery novels" ("Paradox and Plot" 249) while
still noting its flaws.

The novel was published in France in 1967, as *La bête de
miséricorde*, but Francis Lacassin missed listing it in his 1974
bibliography and thus did not discuss it. As with so much of Brown's
writing, the main critical work was done by Jean-Pierre Deloux; in
"Mouvement brownien" he writes that Brown makes "a curious
reflection on the good, pity, the rationalization of madness, fanaticism
and justice" (10).[5]

The Lenient Beast was reprinted in France in 1980 and in the
United States in 1989, making it one of the more easily obtainable of
Brown's mystery novels. It is his most extensive use of the Tucson,

Arizona location (where he lived at the time) and, while not wholly successful, it is worth reading.

After completing the novel in mid-1955, Brown wrote *Rogue in Space*, which his wife claimed he did not enjoy doing. He then began work in earnest on his masterpiece, a novel he had been writing on and off for 15 years: *The Office*.

Chapter Twelve
The Office

On March 5, 1958, E.P. Dutton published *The Office*, Fredric Brown's novel loosely based on his own experiences as an office boy at a Cincinnati machine-tool jobber from about 1922 to 1924. The novel is perhaps his most accomplished work and is in many ways the culmination of his career as a writer; of the six novels he wrote in the years that followed, all but one were well below the quality his work had been reaching steadily since the early 1940s.

In her autobiography, Beth Brown discusses the genesis of *The Office*:

He would like to write serious novels, but a serious novel usually takes much longer to write, and then there is no guarantee that it will sell. He could not afford to take that gamble. Several years ago he got about a ten thousand-word start on one, but he had to put it aside in the hope of getting far enough some day that he could take that gamble. He had to stick to his mysteries and science fiction, which took less time to write and which he knew would sell.

(Oh, for the Life 80)

A look back at Brown's early logbook is illuminating. On May 20 or 21, 1945, he mailed "2 chapters of The Office" to Harry Altshuler, comprising about 21,000 words. This means that, after finishing *The Fabulous Clipjoint* in November 1944, Brown wrote some columns for *The American Printer*, may have begun revising "Murder Can Be Fun," and wrote this early fragment of *The Office*. A later note shows that the manuscript was returned unsold to Brown on November 1, 1945.

The novel apparently remained in Brown's mind, however, and Beth Brown wrote that, after finishing *Madball* in October 1952,

He wanted very badly to go back to work on *The Office*, the straight novel he had started years before but had had to put aside because he could not take the time to do them. But not knowing *when* his current book would sell, he did not feel he could now take the time to do something in a field new to him.

(*Oh, for the Life* 227)

Madball was the book Brown used to try to negotiate a new contact with Dutton; the process was long, and instead of *The Office* Brown wrote *The Lights in the Sky Are Stars*.

In late 1955, Brown completed *The Lenient Beast*, and,

with this accomplishment, Fred wanted very much to go back to *The Office*. But before he did, he wanted the *Beast* contract in hand. (*Oh, for the Life* 277)

Apparently, the themes of *The Lenient Beast* caused more contract delays, and Brown again passed on *The Office* to write *Rogue in Space*. That took eight months, and

With that burden off his chest, he pulled some good fresh air into his lungs, and decided that writing was a pretty good profession, after all.

And went to work on *The Office* with a determination to finish it.

For the first time in his career as a novelist he was doing a rough draft of a book. But also, for the first time in his career as a novelist he was doing a serious novel, and he wanted it to be a good job.

He worked happily and enthusiastically, for at least he was doing what he had wanted for so long to do. Though he did only a few pages some days, there were many days when he wrote eight or nine pages, and some days ten or eleven. Which, for Fred, is akin to a miracle.

So, after more than ten years, Brown finally took a break from his mysteries and science fiction and took the time he felt was necessary to write a "serious" novel. He must have completed the final draft in 1957; the first edition was published on March 5, 1958. It has never been reprinted, although Brown's first draft was published in a limited edition in July 1987.

The Office is Brown's longest novel, divided into four sections and running nearly 250 pages. Section one, entitled "The Beginning," is made up of 11 short chapters that set the scene beautifully. Chapter one begins á la John Steinbeck by establishing the place and time of the story in detail before introducing characters. The story begins on Thursday, June 29, 1922, as the Roaring Twenties get underway. The office is that of Conger and Way, a jobber that acts as a middleman, buying and selling machine tool parts. It is located on Commerce Street in Cincinnati, Ohio, near the suspension bridge that "leads across the wide, muddy Ohio River to Covington, Kentucky" (9), a few blocks from Fountain Square, "the heart of town" (9). Cincinnati is, of course, the city of Brown's birth and young manhood, and the exposition of *The Office* resonates with remembered detail.

Chapter two takes the setting further back, all the way to the long-ago time when the spot was occupied by a thorn tree, in which lived a butcherbird on the spot of the inkwell on bookkeeper Marty Raines's desk. The butcherbird/thorn tree symbolism foreshadows Marty's later role as both killer and Christ figure in the novel's most shocking sequence. Marty's story begins in chapter three, as he gazes at file clerk Stella Klosterman, wondering how he can get a date and finally proposing the idea in a dry business letter he slips into her filing pile.

Marty is a warped young man of 21, whose mother had been "a whore in a Baltimore crib" (14) in the late 1890s, saved by a Presbyterian businessman who married her and died three years later. Converted, she latched onto religion as a life raft, growing ever more fanatical and raising her boy to believe in God and the Sacredness of Womanhood. The narrator calls Marty "a loaded gun with a hair trigger" (15).

The third member of the office is introduced in chapter three: he is Geoffrey Willoughby, about 36 years old and light years wiser than Marty. He loves puns and wordplay (like Brown, the author) and substitutes a poetic love letter for Marty's dry letter to Stella without the boy's knowledge. Ironically, Willoughby quotes the biblical *Song of Songs*, whose erotic content is wholly inappropriate for the repressed Marty, but of whose biblical origin he would surely approve.

As chapter four ends, young Fred Brown arrives from the Queen City Employment Agency to apply for a job as an office boy. In chapter five he describes the layout of the shabby but functional office and recalls that reading at his desk was his favorite pastime; he read like an alcoholic drinks...Library books,of course...my entire earnings would not have bought a fraction of the reading material I devoured. (24)

Brown interrupts the story of his hiring to introduce another character in chapter six: she is Mary, the secretary, age 22, who is a devout Catholic in love with Eddie, a young Communist who can't keep a job because he alienates his employers.

Brown is interviewed and hired in chapter seven, mentioning that this was his eighth job interview in the two weeks since he graduated from Hughes High. He gives more autobiographical details: he had an uncle in Oxford, Ohio, and finished high school living with a friend's family in Northside before moving into a room downtown on Race Street. In reality, Brown was only 16 years old on the date given, but makes himself 18 in the novel. He remarks on his parents' death and on his favorite writers, noting that he sees the persons of the office

Across the mists of thirty-five years, half a lifetime...You'll never gather them all in one office again...I myself haven't been back [to Cincinnati] for over twenty years and write this two thousand miles away [in Tucson]. (34)

The other men of the office are introduced: Ed Conger, the boss, whom Brown thinks of as "the grand panjandrum himself, with the little round button on top" (30); Brian Danner, the young, ambitious salesman; and George Sperling, the slightly older and less successful salesman. Each of them has his own problems and concerns, and each is followed in both his office life and his outside life. By the end of the first section all of the employees of the office have been introduced and all of the novel's major conflicts set up. Structurally, it's masterful; Brown's skill at characterization is most evident here, while the rest of the novel will testify to his ability to weave plots and subplots together to make a whole that is greater than the sum of its parts.

Section two has 12 chapters and is aptly titled "The End of the Beginning." It begins with a chapter of the straight narration that really holds the novel together; Brown ironically recalls thinking, as an aspiring young writer, that the men and women of the office were dull, and that he was (at the time) much more interested in the characters of the many books he read. Brown then begins this section by examining the home life of Willoughby, because "I like him best" (46). Willoughby is kind, gentle, and generous to a stray cat he brings in from the rain and names Cat—as did the narrator in Brown's 1949 story, "Mouse." Subsequent chapters depict the home lives of George Sperling (who has an understanding wife), Stella Klosterman (who dates Marty and wonders why he doesn't kiss her), and Marty Raines (who lives with his religious-fanatic mother and is deeply disturbed about women and sex). In chapter six, Brown tells of a day he visited Willoughby at home and met Max, the prior office boy, who was sick in bed. The visit is a lesson for young Fred; he enjoys Max's company but is later told by Willoughby that the boy is dying.

The home lives of the rest of the characters fill the next three chapters: Mary goes out with Eddie, who has landed a job as a delivery boy for Jake, a bootlegger; Brian Danner lives the life of a handsome, young, single man in the Roaring Twenties (ironically, he reads *Babbitt* on loan from Willoughby and finds Babbitt "a good salesman, a good mixer, and a successful man" (95), completely missing the point); and old man Conger bears the many burdens of a company boss and family patriarch.

The office story picks up in chapter ten, during which, in late May 1923, Stella breaks a date with Marty to see an old boyfriend. In chapter eleven, the news arrives that Max has died, and Brown remarks that office workers are never happy: they're there "to keep the wolf from the door, and it's dull, dull" (117). The last chapter of section two finds George Sperling at home in bed, thinking and dreaming. He realizes he's not a success, but is proud that he never gave up and went on Skid Row; in a passage recalling *The Wench is Dead*, he thinks:

There's security on Skid Row. You can't lose a job when you haven't one and aren't looking for one. You can't fall off the bottom. (132)

George also has a recurring dream, which follows the text of Brown's 1950 story, "The Last Train"; he sees a fire in the sky and hurries to see a train departing, which he is told is "the last train." The train agent turns, and "George saw his head against the fiery crimson sky. But not his face, for he had no face" (132). What does this dream mean? Lost opportunity? A vision of the end of the world? Brown withholds an answer until the novel's end.

Section two brings the story through almost a year of young Fred Brown's term at the office and follows each of his co-workers through representative scenes of their lives. Yet the characters are probably not even very close to those Brown actually worked with in the early twenties; they are too representative of various types and issues of the times. *The Office* is really more a meditation on the times in which it is set, and the author uses the setting of the office as a central point where the intersecting lives of his various characters meet. Newton Baird has correctly placed the novel in the Sinclair Lewis tradition, and Brown's characters are not so much characters as they are types. Their lives are set up in the first two sections; section three deals with their various fates. Titled "The Beginning of the End," it includes 14 chapters and develops each of the several subplots to their conclusions.

Chapter one opens beautifully, with the narrator recalling a time in his childhood when Cincinnati was in an uproar over a man's prophecy of the end of the world. Based on *Revelations*, it was to happen one July day. His parents, "intelligent people," scoffed, yet he recalled that biblical prophets had also been the objects of scorn. He only recalls one bit of prophecy: at the end of the world, "The first sign was to be the appearance in the sky of a cloud no larger than a man's hand." He recalls the day and the cloud, which dissipated without a "last trump, no sudden influx of angels with swords" (133-34).

This symbolic opening is reflected in reality when Ed Conger gets a letter from Beamis-Hodgson, Conger and Way's biggest supplier, stating that they're opening a Cincinnati branch office and no longer need his services. The letter is "smaller than a man's hand"—yet "big enough to cast a shadow from which the office never completely emerged" (134). It is the cloud of the prophecy, and it signals the end of Conger and Way.

The rest of section three plays out the fates of the members of the office, alternating chapters in order to build tension and contrast the various temptations, crimes, and heroic gestures that surround the office's decline.

First comes Brian Danner. A young, ambitious salesman, he takes the advice of his stockbroker and arranges an interview with a Beamis-Hodgson representative regarding the position of manager of their new Cincinnati office. Danner realizes he is betraying Conger but goes through with his meeting, which occurs in chapter six. Brian meets the company rep, Mr. Corey, at the Sinton Hotel and accepts the position as manager until Corey insists that he rifle through Conger's desk and steal information on all of his customers. Danner balks at this and storms out, shunning the man's dishonesty. The description of the meeting with Corey is marvelous; Corey is bad and colorful, providing whiskey and whores to celebrate Danner's giving in to temptation. He is the epitome of the powerful, amoral businessman—the dark side of the Roaring Twenties. He is also the traditional Satan who tries to get Danner to sell his soul for wealth and power: when Danner balks at spying on Conger, Corey asks with astonishment and ridicule if he's a "Christer or something" (123). Thus, Brian Danner proves himself worthy by resisting temptation and following the path of honesty. The mantle of leadership will be his reward, if only briefly.

The second character whose story concludes in section three is the pretty file clerk, Stella Klosterman. In chapter one, Conger and Willoughby discuss ways to cut costs after losing the Beamis-Hodgson account; they decide to fire Stella, whom Willoughby sees as "a human sacrifice" (141). She solves the moral dilemma in chapter three by resigning in order to marry Herman Reuter, her old boyfriend. Chapter seven celebrates her last day at the office, and she does not reappear until chapter 13 when, in March 1924, Willoughby meets her on the street. He invites her home and she tells him that she left Herman after he slept with another woman. She asks Willoughby (who has lusted after her in secret throughout the novel) to sleep with her to even the score; he declines, telling her to forgive Herman and go home.

On a smaller scale, then, Willoughby also resists temptation. Yet he wonders, "What would one night's ecstasy weigh against a clear conscience...and the almost certain knowledge that he could have had her this night?" (226). No firm answer is given.

The next character to be followed is Ed Conger, who exhausts himself traveling to drum up new business in chapter four. Conger's story is tied to that of the office, however, and does not end until the novel's fourth and final section.

Two more characters' stories are developed in this section: the secretary, Mary, and the bookkeeper, Marty Raines. Mary's fate begins to be set in the menacing chapter five, in which two bootleggers discuss "Jake's" intrusion into their territory and decide to have his errand boy beaten up as a lesson. That errand boy is, unfortunately, Mary's boyfriend Eddie.

This chapter is well done, portraying the types of men who became big businessmen with the advent of prohibition: they are wealthy and powerful, yet they speak as criminals. Their "business meeting" is on the same day as Danner's meeting with Corey and Conger's return from drumming up business; Brown carefully interweaves his stories here to enhance the portrait of the times.

The consequences of this meeting are shown in chapter nine, when Mary excitedly tries on her daring new red bathing suit in anticipation of vacationing with Eddie, only to receive a letter telling her that Eddie has been killed by a rival gang during a delivery. The letter also includes a note from Eddie, who suspected he might die and wrote Mary to say it's for the best—he would never have converted to Catholicism (as she wanted him to) and would have left her to avoid hurting her any more. The chapter is poignant, demonstrating the effects of bootlegging on the innocent and the way a "business action" can have immense human consequences.

The final subplot to be played out in this chapter is that dealing with Marty Raines, and his story is the highlight of the novel. It has been foreshadowed since the novel's very start (recall the thorn three and the shrike's nest), and Stella's decision to marry Herman—and thus stop dating Marty forever—is its immediate catalyst. We know that Marty's mother is an ex-whore and a religious fanatic, and that Marty has odd ideas about the "sanctity of woman" (he never even tried to kiss Stella), but the way Brown portrays Marty's last temptation is brilliant and shocking.

The trouble begins in chapter eight, which is set in Marty's apartment. His mother asks him why he's glum at dinner, and he thinks sadly of Stella. He suggests going into the ministry, and his mother tells him he should begin by teaching Sunday school. He later reads *Revelations* and has trouble going to sleep. Clearly, Marty's ideas about becoming a minister stem from a desire to escape the office and his thoughts of Stella; he reads about the Whore of Babylon in the Bible and is terribly shaken; he reads the start of *Genesis* and equates the "void" with the current state of his mind; he thinks of Stella's wedding night and sex as *"horrible, unthinkable"* (182) and mentally equates her with the Whore of Babylon.

In chapter 11, it is January 1924, and Marty comes home to find the apartment freezing cold and his mother sleeping deeply. His mother's doctor warns of possible pneumonia and tells Marty that she is a secret alcoholic—the bottles of vinegar in the kitchen cupboard contain gin. Marty, ever the diligent son, stays home from work to care for her. One night she grows delirious and reverts to her old personality as a whore—she speaks in vulgar language and offers sex to Marty, imagining him a pimp or a john. His mind snaps, and he strangles her to death.

This is certainly the most surprising part of the novel, and Brown handles the suspense beautifully. He toys with the reader: will Mrs. Raines die? does she have pneumonia? will she discover that Marty has learned of her alcoholism? Her sudden reversion to crudity and her past life is a surprise, yet it fits in with the already-established extremes of her behavior. Throughout the novel, Brown makes Marty more and more obsessive about hating and fearing women's sensuality; he holds his mother up as an icon, divorced from sensual nature. When she becomes (almost literally) the Whore of Babylon and tempts him he slays her, at once a religious and a psychological response recalling yet again the end of *Here Comes a Candle*, where the right psychological trigger causes Joe Bailey to kill his fiance.

Perhaps, with the story of Marty Raines, Brown contrasts the life of religion with the life of the flesh, showing the tension that ignorance of sensual reality can cause. In any case, Marty's actions are tragic yet thrilling, adding a note of horror and suspense to an otherwise rather straightforward novel.

The next morning, Willoughby arrives at the office with the news that Marty killed his mother and was found catatonic by police. He is taken to "the state asylum up at Columbus..." (222), and his final end is related in the novel's last section.

Section four of *The Office* is the shortest, titled, of course, "The End" and consisting of a mere four chapters. Ed Conger suffers a heart attack and Brian Danner considers buying the business; his dream ends when he discovers that his stockbroker has disappeared with all of his money. In his despair he is saved by Mary, who is now free of Eddie and able to love Danner. The office closes, the bills are paid, and the employees disperse. Willoughby asks young Fred Brown if he'll ever write a book about his experiences there, and Fred thinks not:

Books, I knew then, had to be written about exciting things if they were light books or about significant things if they were serious books. (239)

The novel's final chapter outlines the subsequent lives and careers of the characters: Ed Conger dies in less than a year; Marty dies in 1937, still in the asylum; Stella goes back to her husband; Brian and Mary wed; Willoughby retires to edit a local newspaper; George Sperling buys a tobacco shop after the death of his wife.

This chapter concludes *The Office* on a lyrical note, summing up everything beautifully, from the fate of the building where the office stood to the lives of each person in it. Brown concludes by returning to George Sperling's dream of the "last train"; it came true in 1943, but it was only a train line that was losing money and went out of business.

> So you see it wasn't the end of the world, nor even the end of the world for George Sperling.
> Dreams mean nothing. There is no pattern, there is no significance in a dream. Not even in this dream of an office that lived, for me, two years and then died, for all of us, half a lifetime ago and half a continent away. (246)

Thus ends *The Office*, a lovely blend of naturalism and romanticism, reality and dream, memory and speculation.

Contemporary reviews were rather good. *Booklist* called the novel "an unpretentious, convincing story," while *The New Yorker* remarked that it was "a simple story, human and plain and believable, if a little monotonous." *Kirkus Reviews* wrote that "the virtuoso ingenuity of his science fiction and mystery stories gives way to the flat reality of ordinary lives and the shabby sphere of their existence which the general reader will be disciplined to share." Lenore Glen Offord, writing in the San Francisco *Chronicle*, was filled with praise:

> What he has told of the lives of "those dull people" illustrates once more the precept that drama is made of ordinary human beings' emotions, and that melodrama can appear in the most unexpected places. What he has made of his remembered knowledge is a fine story, homely in its basic quality and filled with sympathetic perceptions.

She concludes her review by writing that:

> The straight novel is a new direction for Brown. It will not surprise anyone who knows his great ability in story-telling that he has made such a rich

human document of "The Office." Its easy-going narration almost conceals its underlying strength, and long after you have finished reading you remember it with pleasure.

These sentiments were echoed by P. Schuyler Miller, reviewing for the science fiction magazine *Astounding Science Fiction*, who wrote that "With 'The Office' he has proved that there are other kinds of books in him as well."

The Office has never been reprinted, and was for the most part forgotten (except for a brief quotation by William F. Nolan in a 1972 article following Brown's death [191]) until 1976, when *The Best of Fredric Brown* was published with an introduction by Robert Bloch. Bloch unfairly faulted the novel for being

humdrum and pedestrian in the telling. Minus murder and mayhem, *sans* piled-up plot complications, and lacking rapid-fire repartee, this day-by-day account of real people in an ordinary office setting seemed dull to readers who expected a typical Fredric Brown entertainment.

He never repeated the venture. (6)

Bloch's criticism surely did not help the reputation of *The Office* which, by dint of never having been reprinted, was surely little remembered by readers nearly 20 years later.

The only critic to deal with *The Office* at length has been Newton Baird, in his "Paradox and Plot" series and in "A Key to Fredric Brown's Wonderland."

The Office did resurface in July 1987, when Dennis McMillan published the first draft of the novel with an introduction by Philip Jose Farmer. Farmer concludes by writing that:

What Brown has done herein is what only a very good writer could do. He has taken the essentially mundane, the banal, the boring, if you will, and, through his splendid sense of story and his skills or craft, has metamorphosed these unpromising elements into a tale that keeps you reading and keeps you caring for the people. (8)

A careful comparison of the two versions of *The Office* is enlightening in the way it demonstrates Brown's ability as a *reviser*. At the novel's start, Brown originally took the history of the building in which the office was located back to the cosmic gases and forward to an H-bomb explosion. He wisely cut this in the second draft—it's too self-conscious and overdone.

The second draft is also much more carefully organized and written—ungrammatical or fragmentary sentences are corrected and overly long paragraphs broken up. The first draft also omits chapter breaks, thus losing the carefully-orchestrated structure of the final version. The version published by Dutton in 1958 is, in fact, considerably rewritten, with some important changes.

One portion of the first draft that Brown excised is the haunting and lyrical section from page 73 to page 75, which tells of a drunken, homeless, nameless man who staggers along the nighttime street and sleeps in front of the office door, leaving before morning. He dreams of lust, of falling between moving train cars, and of "the thing behind the night" (75); the narrator asks if this incident is relevant, and answers: "It happened; that is all, but perhaps it is enough." The incident is referred to again at the very end of the novel, when the narrator concludes that "Dreams mean nothing," but is left out of the final draft entirely.

Another dream that recurs at the end of the first draft is Ed Conger's dream of Harry Way ascending a golden staircase. Critic Newton Baird interprets this as a carefully-worked-out metaphor of Conger's yearning to return to the early success he and his partner enjoyed. Yet a brief remark in the first draft sheds an entirely different light on the relationship between Conger and Way: Conger, says the narrator, is "an ill and aging fairy who had never known that he was one and never would know..."! (100). Brown's decision to omit this direct remark about Conger's repressed homosexual desires in his final draft was entirely correct; without it, the reader is allowed to draw the same conclusions Mr. Baird did: that Conger's dreams were of success and youth rather than homosexual longing.

The first draft of *The Office* does not include the marvelous prophecy of the end of the world that opens section three; Brown must have come up with this as he revised, and it is certainly a marvelous segue into the decline of the office. The final draft also includes more erotic description of the whores Danner turns down at his meeting with Corey; this suggests that Brown was not revising solely to delete seemingly "obscene" portions of the novel, such as the sequence where

Marty's mother reverts to being a whore: in draft one, she curses a bit more, but in draft two, she actually approaches her son.

Another surprising change between drafts occurs when Stella proposes sleeping with Willoughby—in the first draft, he sleeps with her! The revision wisely keeps Willoughby true to his character, and he resists the considerable temptation that Stella offers.

The last real difference between drafts concerns Augie "Red" Plunkett, who replaced Fred Brown as office boy after Marty was committed and Fred promoted to bookkeeper. In the final draft, the narrator mentions that Red had a brief career in jazz; in the first draft, one paragraph about his career is expanded to a page and a half. The excision is no loss.

In short, a careful reading of both versions of *The Office* demonstrates that Brown did, in fact, rewrite the novel entirely. The second draft concentrates more on characters, omitting needless details about place and time. It is also more smoothly written, probably due to Brown's taking a second look. The plotting is tighter as well, with chapters rearranged to juxtapose important events. The final draft also places more emphasis on Marty's story and moves inexorably toward it from the very beginning.

The fact that Brown was able to make such changes in the novel without compromising its integrity brings into question its value as autobiography. Beth Brown commented twice on this point: "It is autobiographical, or at least partly so. That part of his life—he was about sixteen—seems to have been very important to him, and he felt he had to write about it" ("Fredric Brown, My Husband" 22), and "The incidents may have been factual, but I'm sure he would have arranged them to suit his purpose. The names were not factual" (Baird, "Paradox and Plot" 287). Of course, Mrs. Brown wasn't there and would only know what Fred had told her. The nature of her comments suggests that he didn't tell her much, at least not much that she remembered.

We are thus left with internal evidence alone on which to base our judgments. Happily, there are two versions of the novel, and the changes between them suggest possible points of invention.

Brown grew up in Cincinnati, so the details about the city and its alcoves are probably as accurate as memory allowed. The first three chapters occur before young Fred Brown applied for work at the office, so they are almost surely made up. The location of the building is different in the two versions of the story (120 East Oak Street in the first draft; Commerce Street in the second) and the office is on different floors, so it's tough to tell where the truth lies. The name of the office is almost certainly fictitious, as well, since Mrs. Brown wrote that the names of the characters were invented. Details of how Fred finished high school are probably true, through he was 16 in 1922, not 18, the age he makes himself in the novel. Consequently, he either finished high school at age 16 or changed the dates he worked in the office.

I don't believe for a moment that the stories of the other characters in the office have any basis in fact—they are too exemplary of their time and fit together too well to create an overall picture. Even the date of the letter from Beamis-Hodgson changes: in the first draft, it's a Thursday in September 1924; in the second, it's late July 1924.

In effect, almost none of *The Office* can be relied on as factual autobiography. Brown's recollection of things he actually observed takes up a very small portion of the novel, and even those observations are questionable. In *The Office*, Brown succeeds in writing what is commonly referred to as a "first novel"—partly based on his young life but expanded cleverly into a wide and rich portrait of the persons, places, and events that contributed to the *zeitgeist* of Cincinnati or Midwestern America in the early 1920s.

As such, it holds a special place in Brown's oeuvre. His other work is overwhelmingly in the sub-genres of crime fiction or science fiction; his early short stories cast around a bit, looking for a comfortable method of expression, but by the early 1940s he was set. This novel was a pet project of his, one he worked on (on and off) for over ten years and probably contemplated for even longer.

And it is great success. He did the unthinkable and wrote out a complete draft, then rewrote the entire novel, improving it considerably. The result is a "straight" novel that may well be his best work; certainly, *The Office* stands with the finest things he ever did.

Chapter Thirteen
A Short Subject

Though he wrote hundreds of short stories and more than 20 novels, a large portion of Fredric Brown's reputation today rests on a series of "short-short" stories written throughout the 1950s. Bill Pronzini called him "a master of the mordant short-short" ("Introduction: Dreamer in Paradox" viii) Douglas J. McReynolds called him "a master of the so-called short-short story" (1956), and French writer Robert Louit remarked that Brown became famous for his "short-shorts" (30).[1] Algis Budrys went so far as to write, regarding other writers who used the form, that "none...are masters of this form in a field which has only one Fredric Brown" (279), and Jack Sullivan, writing in *The Penguin Encyclopedia of Horror and the Supernatural*, called Brown "the undisputed master of the form" (60).

Just what is a short-short? According to Brown, in his introduction to his collection, *Angels and Spaceships*, they are "vignettes, the stories of three or four hundred words each..." (11). Brown's short-shorts tended toward the humorous, often including puns and almost invariably ending with a twist. His earliest work in this form was also some of his earliest published writing—short, humorous stories written for various trade papers in the mid- to late-1930s. In his introduction to the posthumous collection, *Thirty Corpses Every Thursday*, William Campbell Gault recalled

We were all new to the trade with a few five dollar sales to newspaper syndicates who published short-short stories. (5)

There was the "Willie Skid" series of short-shorts, published in various issues of the *Ford Dealer Service Bulletin* in 1937 and 1938 and featuring jokes and puns on an automobile service theme. There was of course the Colonel Kluck series, out of which Brown got a lot of mileage with columns in *The Michigan Well Driller* and *The Inventor*; these were fictional question and answer pages filled with one pun after another. Brown also published a series of "Barnyard Bill Says..." short-shorts in *Feedstuffs* in 1937; they were puns in a farm setting. Also in *Feedstuffs* was the "Feedum and Weep" series, which showed how feed dealer helper Ernie Scofield solved brief rural mysteries and helped business in the process. Finally, there were the "V.O.N. Munchdriller" short-shorts, which popped up in various late 1930s issues of *The Michigan Well Driller* and related the adventures of the ambitious, eponymous driller.

All of these series of short-shorts were clearly written quickly to supplement Brown's meager income during the Great Depression. Some were regular features for a brief time; others, like "Barnyard Bill" and "Willie Skid," were written to fill holes on magazine pages. As such, these short pieces were always in demand by harried copy editors. Brown also wrote a few children's games and crossword puzzles, though it's uncertain where they saw publication.

By the early 1940s, Brown had quit nearly all of his writing for trade papers in favor of writing and selling mystery and science fiction stories to the pulps. By necessity these were longer, since the rate of pay was often a penny a word at best and a 500-word story (minus the agent's ten percent and postage) might net only a few dollars. Consequently, the number of short-shorts Brown wrote and published in the 1940s was small. Beth Brown called "Town Wanted" (*Detective Fiction Weekly* September 7, 1940) "a short-short about racketeers" (*Oh, for the Life* 134), and as such it succeeds in packing social commentary into a couple of well-crafted pages. "Starvation" (*Astounding Science Fiction* September 1942) is more of a history lesson than a story, telling of the last days of Tyrannosaurus Rex. Richard Lupoff calls the story "a *tour de force*, a hopelessly silly tear-jerker" that "manages to succeed in spite of itself" ("Introduction" xxii). "Boner" (*Popular Detective* October 1942) is a corny Nazi story about Carl Heofener, a German-American who is being pressured by a Nazi agent to let him into the munitions plant where he works. FBI agents arrest the Nazi and take him away before Heofener reveals to the reader that his cousin in Germany—whom the Nazi agent had threatened to harm if his wishes were denied—is actually Himmler, head of the Gestapo! "Boner" has all the depth of a comic book story, as Max Allan

Collins noted when he compared it to "the similarly constructed short-shorts [Mickey Spillane] did as fillers for Timely Comics in the 1940s" (8).

Other than these three brief stories, Brown did not write short-shorts in the 1940s. He was probably more concerned with making money, and at a penny a word a pulp writer wouldn't make much of a living writing two- or three-page stories.

With the end of the 1940s, Brown's interest in writing short-shorts grew, as they were convenient ways to earn a few dollars between novels. The boom in science-fiction publishing meant that there were suddenly a lot of magazines hungry for stories, and Brown's story output in 1950 reflects this market. In the midst of all of his science fiction stories he found the time to write a handful of short-shorts as well. The first was "The Last Train" (*Weird Tales* January 1950), in which a man's missing the last train becomes a metaphor for his inability to succeed in life and for mankind's inability to avoid total destruction. Newton Baird has called "The Last Train" one of Brown's "best fantasy stories" ("Paradox and Plot" 155).

Next came "Vengeance Unlimited" (*Super Science Stories* July 1950), in which Earth develops a super-fast fleet of ships to travel into deep space and destroy the alien race or planet that sent a similar fleet toward Earth. The ending is ironic—the first fleet is revealed to have been the Earth fleet which, flying faster than the speed of light, returned ten years before it left and destroyed Venus by mistake!

"Vengeance Unlimited" is Brown's first short-short to deal with the paradox of time and space travel, and he concludes that the emotional reaction of men pales in comparison with the power of science and mathematics to create paradox.

Brown's next short-short, "The Weapon" (*Astounding Science Fiction* April 1951), has been called "a wise, moving parable" (Lupoff, "Introduction" xxii). In it, Dr. James Graham is working on the ultimate weapon in the name of science. A visitor by the name of Niemand argues with Graham, asking "is humanity *ready* for an ultimate weapon?" (*And the Gods Laughed* 235) but Graham refuses to discuss the matter further. Niemand gives a gift to Graham's retarded son Harry as he leaves, and Graham later takes the gift—a revolver—away from the boy, thinking "only a madman would give a loaded revolver to an idiot" (236).

"The Weapon" is careful, concise, and sure, a powerful statement about the dangers of nuclear weapons written at the height of the Cold War. Its message is subtle, though—no conclusions are drawn directly, and the argument hits home with the reader at the same moment it does with Dr. Graham: man cannot handle the ultimate weapon. The story is neither mystery nor science fiction; it is an example of Brown's ability to tell a "straight" story and it is very powerful.

Brown's next short-short appeared two and a half years later: "Hall of Mirrors" (*Galaxy Science Fiction* December 1953). It is another story about time travel and, as in "The Weapon," Brown and his protagonist conclude that man is not ready for a powerful device—here, a time machine. The inventor thus returns to a point before his own birth in order to delay the time when he must reveal his invention to the world. "Hall of Mirrors" is an unusual time travel story in that the object *inside* the time machine changes, rather than the world around it. The inventor gives himself immortality at a cost: he loses his memory every time he goes back in time.

Brown published a pair of short-shorts in *Galaxy Science Fiction*'s February 1954 issue: "Experiment" and "Sentry." "Experiment" is another version of the time-travel paradox; this time, the universe disappears. "Sentry" features an infantryman on a distant planet who kills an alien; the twist ending reveals the "horrible" alien to be a man. These short-shorts demonstrate the successful formula Brown was to use in dozens of vignettes: a few characters, a quick set-up of a situation, and an ironic (or twist) ending.

"Keep Out" (*Amazing Stories* March 1954) is a more complex version of the central irony of "Sentry"—here, a colony of mutated humans begun on Mars has developed to the point where the mutants hate humans and plan to murder them all. Racial prejudice and hate may grow in even the strangest places, Brown tells us, even when one race is hardly different from another.

A pair of supernatural short-shorts followed, in the September 1954 issue of *Beyond Fantasy Fiction*. "Naturally" concerns Henry Blodgett, a student who summons a demon to help with his geometry exam but becomes a victim when he draws the wrong geometric figure in the course of his incantation! "Voodoo" tells of a turnabout when a wife tries to use Haitian magic to kill her husband. These two short-shorts follow Brown's earlier story of witchcraft, "The

Geezenstacks," in their emphasis on themes of magic and ironic revenge.

Brown also published *Angels and Spaceships* in 1954. It is a collection of short stories with short-shorts in between, and Brown wrote that

> The nine vignettes, the stories of three or four hundred words each which alternate with the longer stories, are previously unpublished, and were written especially for this book. (4)

Beth Brown explained the genesis of these vignettes in her autobiography:

> Fred had recently taken an interest in a new, for him, kind of writing—the vignette. He had so thoroughly enjoyed writing the first, *Solipsist*, that he had written more of them. This is a particularly difficult field to write in because an idea must be developed in so few words. But Fred seemed to have the knack for it.
>
> He hadn't been sure what he would do with them, whether offer them individually or in groups, or whether he would hold them until he had enough of them for a collection.
>
> Bantam's request [for a new collection] helped him to decide. He selected eight of his short stories for the collection, but a collection ordinarily contains one or two *new* stories. Instead of new stories he decided to include nine vignettes, spacing them between the stories. But he had only five. After he had finished his editing, and while I typed, he wrote four more. (235)

The nine short-shorts written for *Angels and Spaceships* are "Pattern," "Answer," "Preposterous," "Politeness," "Search," "Reconciliation," "Daisies," "Sentence" and "Solipsist." All of the short-shorts Brown published in 1954 have one-word titles, and all are full of the pithy irony that became the hallmark of Brown's vignettes.

"Pattern" deals with huge aliens who view humans as insects and spray insecticide on two unknowing women who do the same to the tiny pests in their garden. "Answer," one of Brown's most famous short-shorts, tells of the final hookup of all of the monster computing machines of all the populated planets in the universe into a giant "cybernetic machine that would combine all the knowledge of all the galaxies." The switch is thrown and the question is asked: "Is there a

God?" The machine replies, "Yes, *now* there is a God," and a "bolt of lightning from the cloudless sky" prevents the user from disengaging the switch. Brown's atheistic beliefs are subtly set forth here by the implication that there was no God before the hookup. Brian W. Aldis called "Answer" "One of the most brilliant and pithy answers" (234) to questions about the role of computers in man's future.

"Preposterous" features a husband and wife living in a futuristic world and complaining that the science fiction magazine their son reads is filled with "inane and utterly preposterous tripe."

"Politeness" foreshadows the erotic humor that would mark Brown's later short-shorts; in it, a human makes the first friendship with a Venusian by telling him to "— yourself." This is an acceptable greeting among Venusians, and begins dialogue and understanding between the races. The twist is clever in that a chance variance in the interpretation of language opens the doors to communication.

In "Search," Peter goes to Heaven and searches till he finds God. The trick is one of perception: Peter is a dog, and his God is a man who in turn falls to his knees before a "shining light." The religious theme is different than that in "Answer"; here, there is a God, yet who he is depends on who does the searching.

"Reconciliation" is a nicely written short-short about a husband and wife whose bitter fighting ends when they feel an atomic explosion. It's last line is moving:

Outside in what had been the quiet night a red flower grew and yearned toward the canceled sky. (91)

"Daisies" tells of an invention that allows humans to communicate with flowers; unfortunately for the inventor, the old adage that "daisies do tell" is proven when his wife learns of his infidelity from the flower and shoots him and his female assistant. "Sentence" shows that a condemned man's last night isn't so bad when the nights on Antares II last 93 Earth years, and "Solipsist" features Walter B. Jehovah, who believes he's the only thing that exists and wills everything else out of existence. He then recreates everything from scratch: "It took him seven days."

The short-shorts in *Angels and Spaceships* are all excellent and, taken in concert, they represent a variety of ways to deal with the central theme of the differences in perception between humans and aliens and the often unexpected results. "Answer," "Search," and "Solipsist" question the nature of God, and Walter B. Jehovah is not terribly different from Fredric Brown, the author of the collection: Brown creates the universe of his book just as Jehovah re-creates the greater universe.

The nine short-shorts serve also to comment on the longer stories that surround them. In this way, *Angels and Spaceships* is comparable to Ernest Hemingway's *In Our Time*, in which the author collected previously published short stories and revised short-shorts to be placed between them. Both collections benefit from the juxtaposition and collection of stories on a general theme; each is far greater than the sum of its parts. *Angels and Spaceships* is one of Brown's best science fiction books; in its varied treatment of several interrelated themes it achieves a complexity and depth his science fiction novels often lack.

In 1955, Brown went back to placing his short-shorts in magazines. "Blood" (*The Magazine of Fantasy and Science Fiction* February 1955) is a fast and funny tale about two vampires escaping from the 22nd century in a time machine and finding blood scarce in a surprising future. "Millenium" (*The Magazine of Fantasy and Science Fiction* March 1955) features Satan entertaining visitors and hearing an unexpected wish. "Imagine" (*The Magazine of Fantasy and Science Fiction* May 1955) is a lovely little poem in which the author asks the reader first to imagine a series of old legends and beliefs, then the future, and then the miracle of man, the universe, and Earth. Richard Lupoff has called "Imagine" "a paean to science fiction, to science fiction's vision, to life itself" ("Introduction" xviii).

These three "fantastic" short-shorts (which were probably sold in a bunch and then spaced out over three issues by the editor) were followed by a pair published in *Ellery Queen's Mystery Magazine*: "The Perfect Crime" (June 1955) and "The Letter" (July 1955). The first is an ironic tale of a man who robs his uncle to cover up a planned murder. The second tells of a perfect crime in which a man kills another man with a surprising method. Both of these short-shorts concern "the perfect crime" and are devoid of the fantastic elements that mark most of Brown's short-shorts up to this point, signalling a turn in his interests away from science fiction themes in his vignettes.

Yet another variation on time travel pops up in "The First Time Machine" (*Ellery Queen's Mystery Magazine* September 1955); here, a man finds out what would happen if he killed his grandfather before the man met his grandmother. This was followed by the delightful "Too Far" (*The Magazine of Fantasy and Science Fiction* September 1955), a hilarious "story" that is really an excuse for one pun after another. The premise is that of a "werebuck" who loves puns; Brown's humor and skill with wordplay has led French translators of this short-short to admit the impossibility of conveying all of the puns in another language, titling their version "Intractable" (or "Untranslatable").

At this point, Brown was writing his short-shorts "between books, before his mind has latched onto a new plot." He had also, according to his wife, begun "to be called the 'Master of the Vignette' " (*Oh, for the Life* 235). He returned to a science fiction theme in his next-published short-short, "Expedition" (*The Magazine of Fantasy and Science Fiction* February 1957), in which a history professor tells his class about the first colony on Mars, begun by 29 women and one man—who clearly earned the nickname, "Mighty Maxon"! The sexual innuendo is funny, and Brown was beginning to rely on it more and more often as censorship eased up in popular magazines.

The Magazine of Fantasy and Science Fiction published Brown's two 1958 short-shorts in the October issue. "Jaycee" tells of the first parthenogenic baby who, as a 20-year-old, has an alarming habit of turning water into gin at parties and water-skiing without skis! It's a light but horrifying look at a religious theme in the year 2000—funny and shocking at the same time. "Unfortunately" turns on spelling: an astronaut asks in writing for "steak" and is burned at the "stake" by aliens who happen to be poor spellers.

Brown's last two short-shorts published in the 1950s appeared in men's magazines: "Nasty" (*Playboy* April 1959) and "Rope Trick" (*Adam* May 1959). "Nasty" involves a demon who gives an aging lecher a pair of swim trunks that impart virility, and "Rope Trick" tells of a frustrated wife on her second honeymoon who buys a fakir's flute, hoping that it will affect her husband as it did the snake! Both stories turn on sexual innuendo, yet both feature the same formula that Brown, by this time, had developed for writing successful short-shorts.

A trio of short-shorts appeared in the March 1960 issue of *Dude*, another men's magazine. "Abominable" tells of the capture of a starlet by an abominable snowman. "Bear Possibility" features a man who awaits the birth of his wife's baby with trepidation after an accident at the zoo. "Recessional" portrays a battle that turns out to be a chess game. None of the three stories is particularly memorable.

"The Power" (*Galaxy* April 1960) is more interesting; in it, small-time crook Larry Snell finds he has the power to make people do whatever he says but meets his end when he gloatingly yells "drop dead" to the world from the top of echo hill. The irony is clever: a loser gains absolute power but kills himself accidentally by using it once too often.

The June 1960 issue of *Alfred Hitchcock's Mystery Magazine* featured "Granny's Birthday," which Newton Baird has called "a satiric study of evil." It is a short tale of extreme family unity and terror set at the birthday party of a matriarchal grandmother.

"Earthmen Bearing Gifts" (*Galaxy* June 1960) was Brown's first short-short set in space in three years, and it tells the ironic tale of an Earth spaceship that accidentally wipes out the last of Martian society in its attempt to illuminate Mars for study. This ironic short-short recalls cautionary tales of the 1950s like "Vengeance Unlimited" and "Keep Out."

"The House" (*Fantastic* August 1960) is almost incomprehensible, tending more toward poetry in its symbolism. Amelia A. Rutledge has called it "deeply absurdist":

a man roams through a house which, with its inescapable, reserved rooms, is reminiscent of the grave. The reader is never sure whether the man has died; the horror of the story comes from its subtle imagery of being buried alive. (83)

A trio of interrelated short-shorts followed, in the February 1961 issue of another men's magazine, *Gent*, under the overall title, "Great Lost Discoveries." "Invisibility" is set in 1909, when an Englishman turns himself invisible and invades an Ottoman harem with tragic results. "Invulnerability" takes place in 1952, as a U.S. Navy officer uses a force field to protect himself from an H-bomb blast but is thrown into space, where he dies when his force field runs out of air. "Immortality" occurs in 1978 Moscow, as a chemist discovers a pill that will let him live forever but is cursed when he falls into a permanent coma. These three short-shorts show the usual irony and are related by their depiction of inventions that were known to no one but their creators not because they failed, but because they worked only too well.

Another set of related short-shorts appeared three months later in *Dude* under the title, "Five Nightmares." They ranged from "Nightmare in

Blue," in which a father allows his son to drown because the man can't swim, to "Nightmare in Grey," which is a heartfelt meditation on old age and forgetfulness. "Nightmare in Red" is silly, like "Recessional"; here, the protagonist is bounced about mysteriously until we learn he's a pinball. "Nightmare in Time" has also been published as "The End," and features a clever gimmick: Professor Jones flips a switch to reverse time, and the words of the story are then repeated in reverse. "Nightmare in Yellow" has a terrific surprise ending—a lawyer kills his wife on the porch of their home and opens the front door only to hear a cheer of "surprise" from the guests assembled for a birthday party she had planned.

Clearly, short-shorts had renewed interest for Fredric Brown by 1961, at which time he was writing little else. After publishing 25 between 1950 and 1955 and only five from 1956 to 1959, he published thirty in 1960 and 1961 together, culminating in the collection *Nightmares and Geezenstacks*, in which a good number of his short-shorts were brought together with a few new ones added.

But first there was "Hobbyist" (*Playboy* May 1961), a twist on the old tale of a druggist who will sell an undetectable poison cheaply and an antidote for a very dear price. And then came another trio of related stories in *Ellery Queen's Mystery Magazine* for June 1961, "Of Time and Eustace Weaver," in which Mr. Weaver invents a time machine and tries to use it to get rich. Of course, since this is a Fredric Brown short-short, his plan backfires on him when the Time Police arrive from the future to punish him for his illegal use of his instrument.

The idea of collecting so many short-shorts in one volume was a novel one when Brown published *Nightmares and Geezenstacks* in the summer of 1961. The book mixed ten stories of average length with 25 previously published short-shorts and ten new short-shorts. Anthony Boucher, reviewing the collection (which was originally published in paperback and which had gone through 11 U.S. editions at last count) in the New York *Times*, remarked that "there's more fun in this small volume than in a half-dozen collections by less miraculously concise writers." Another positive review appeared in *Analog: Science Fact and Fiction*, where the reviewer wrote that "this outrageous potpourri shouldn't be missed."

The book's contents are listed at the back of this volume, and it is successful by virtue of the sheer number of stories it contains: not all succeed, but enough are memorable that they carry the rest. Among the new short-shorts are two more "Nightmare" stories: in "Nightmare in

Green," a man who plans to leave his wife is surprised when she says *she's* leaving *him* for another woman; "Nightmare in White" is a shocking tale about mismatched lovers in the dark. "Cat Burglar" is as close to obscene as Brown ever got—it's basically a long dirty joke punning on the word "pussy." "Second Chance" is a listless tale about a baseball game of the future, after humans have been replaced by androids, and "The Ring of Hans Carvel" is a modern twist on Rabelais where Hans is given a ring by the devil in order to guarantee his wife's fidelity.

"Bright Beard" is a new variation on the Bluebeard legend, adding a dollop of technology and a Venusian spy to bring the story into the science fiction era. "Horse Race" is a shaggy dog (or shaggy horse) tale whose sole purpose is to work out a pun on "Horse's asteroid." "Death on the Mountain" is an unusual, almost poetic short-short filled with obscure religious images. It recalls "The House" in its oddity; its point is hard to guess, though it seems to suggest that the natural world is unaffected by the actions of men.

"Fish Story" is better—here, a man's wish to become a merman and consummate his love for a mermaid is finally granted, to his ultimate dismay. Finally, "Three Little Owls" (subtitled "A Fable") is a cute little story about predators and prey that recalls Aesop.

The newly-written short-shorts in *Nightmares and Geezenstacks* are of uneven quality, and perhaps by the time he finished the book Brown was tiring of this difficult form. In any case, he only wrote a few more in his lifetime.

The September 1962 issue of *Dude* featured "Aelurophobe," which puns on the word "cat" much in the same way "Too Far" punned on the word "buck." A total of 16 "Instant Novellas" then appeared in four consecutive issues of *Rogue* in 1963 (April through July); these were billed as "an entire story in four lines or less" and take the idea of a short-short to perhaps its farthest extreme. One of them, from the April issue, will suffice as an example:

Padriac jumped from a skyscraper, was not surprised to be caught by his heels by an Angel—until, singing sweetly to him that suicide is sinful, she bashed out his brains against a ledge. (41)

The "Instant Novellas" mix irony, humor, and contemporary references, but are of little value. The editor says they are written to follow "an old

French art form," and if this is true Brown is to be commended for his variety, but it's more likely that this is just a gimmick.

The last of the four "Instant Novellas" in the May 1963 issue has been reprinted as "Mistake," but in the original version none of them had titles. Frank McSherry wrote that these had "all the punch and off-beat way of looking at things that his longer stories do" (60), and that's true. But these were some of Brown's last published writing, and they are certainly a weak way to end a rich and varied career.

The last short-short Brown published in his lifetime was "Why, Benny, Why?" (*Ellery Queen's Mystery Magazine* November 1964). This little story is set in Santa Monica, California, and tells of a frightened college girl's walk home alone on a dark October night. She sees a moronic man and runs; he chases, catches, and kills her. When the police ask why he did it, he relies simply: "She ran." Benny, the moron of the story, recalls similar child-men of earlier Brown novels, especially Benny in *Knock Three-One-Two*. The story is ironic and chilling, a good end to Brown's catalog of vignettes.

Brown did write one more short-short; "Nightmare in Darkness" was found in his files many years after his death and first published in the 1990 volume of the same name. Like the other "Nightmare" stories, it is ironic and shocking: a blind man dies after living an evil life and opens his eyes only to find he's in Hell.

Fredric Brown wrote a tremendous number of short-shorts in his long career, from his early trade-magazine pieces to his last experiments in erotic humor and terror. The sheer number of them earned him a place as a leading practitioner of the form, and their regular excellence made them memorable and worth constant reprinting. In fact, it often seems that Brown is best remembered for his shortest work, even though it is hardly his most distinguished and he wrote it as a lark between novels. The greatest value of Brown's short-shorts—besides being very entertaining—is the variety they add to his *oeuvre*. In his career, Brown succeeded as a mystery novelist, a science fiction novelist, a writer of short stories in both sub-genres, and a writer of vignettes. He moved in and out of all of these forms for three decades, following changes in publishing and public taste but never losing sight of his individual skills. His short-shorts are perhaps a microcosm of his body of work as a whole, and they reward the casual and serious readers who seek them out.

Chapter Fourteen
A Mysterious Decline

Unfortunately, *Oh, for the Life of an Author's Wife*, Beth Brown's unpublished autobiography, ends as Fredric Brown is beginning to write *The Office* in 1956. The years that follow are undocumented by logbooks, notes, or written memories. We can say with certainty when Brown's remaining stories and novels were published and we have a general idea of where he lived and when, but background details are sadly absent during this final period of his writing career.

After *The Office*, his published work was—with the notable exception of *Knock Three-One-Two*—below the caliber of what he had done in years past. One may assume his health was getting progressively worse, there may have been implications of a growing problem with alcohol, and perhaps he was just getting tired.

From 1958 to 1963 (after *The Office*) Brown published seven novels, a handful of short stories, and a slew of short-shorts. Of the novels, two were in the Ed and Am Hunter series (*The Late Lamented* and *Mrs. Murphy's Underpants*) and one was the science fiction story, *The Mind Thing*. The remaining four were mysteries, and it is to them that this chapter is devoted.

One for the Road was published by E.P. Dutton & Co. in the summer of 1958, and thus almost certainly written in 1957. It is narrated by reporter Bob Spitzer, a 29-year old banker's son who left banking to work for a newspaper in the tiny town of Mayville, Arizona. As the novel opens, Spitzer accompanies Police Chief MacNulty to the LaFonda Motel to check on Amy Waggoner, a drunk who won't respond to knocks on her door. They find her naked and dead, stabbed through the heart on her bed.

In the course of the murder investigation, the relationships among the various townspeople are brought to light. Bob Spitzer loves Doris Jones, a telephone operator, but he once nearly made a pass at the late

Amy Waggoner and was saved when she fell asleep in a drunken stupor. Herbie Pembrook is a mentally retarded groundskeeper who bears an unexplained grudge against Spitzer and seems dangerous. And there is Cass Phillips, the friendly and intelligent owner of the "Bar Sinister," the best tavern in town, who sings opera and knows various languages.

Mixed in with the investigation of Amy Waggoner's murder are details of Bob's past, explaining how he came to Mayville. The past becomes important in Amy's case since her background is unknown to anyone in town and may provide a clue to the motive for her murder. There's a lot of talk and not much action; the characters are friendly and distinctive, but there's not much of a plot. Spitzer quotes poetry and has witty chats with Doris, and Cass Phillips is an unusual bartender, but the novel drags along without much reason. A drug angle provides both a red herring and an unintentionally humorous attempt to be hip, when Spitzer and his friend Willie Perkovich smoke marijuana and get high together. They begin talking in ridiculous "jive"; when Willie asks Bob if he likes it, Bob replies:

> "The most, man. Crazy." And wondered if reefers have a tendency to make people talk jive talk. Or was it just suggestion, because people who smoke reefers in books always talk that way? At any rate until just then I hadn't used any jive talk since I'd been in college, and not much of it then. But it seemed amusing to be using it now so I added, "Real cool."
>
> Willie laughed. I laughed with him, not because I knew what he was laughing at but because *everything* seemed funny. (96)

This is about as stupid a passage as Brown ever wrote. His characters in the late 1950s and early 1960s occasionally lapse into beatnik jargon, but it is rarely this gratuitous and clumsy.

Surprisingly, Spitzer finds that the marijuana has this effect:

> My mind was crystal clear, hitting on eight cylinders; it just didn't want to concentrate on something as irrelevant as a novel. It wanted to think big thoughts, accomplish big things. (97)

In this state he tries to work out a solution to the murder, and of course he comes up with the wrong one.

Finally, in chapter ten, Bob and the police begin to make some progress in their investigation when they track down John S. Waggoner, Amy's ex-husband. Bob stumbles across a wanted poster and asks Cass about it, only to learn that Cass is the wanted criminal and that he used to live with Amy when they had a singing act together. She learned of his criminal past and they split; he began a new life in Mayville. When she tracked him down and began blackmailing him he killed her. Unfortunately for the reader, all of these details are brought forth in a cliched scene where Cass explains himself while pointing a gun at Bob.

In the last chapter, Cass kills himself rather than face the police. Bob and Doris marry, and Bob plans to leave Mayville for a job with a friendlier editor. And Herbie is suddenly happy that Bob will no longer be working with Alicia Howell, the meek girl at the paper on whom he has a crush.

One for the Road is short on plot but long on talk, and its characters, while likeable enough, cannot carry the novel. It is one of Brown's weakest books, only slightly better than *We All Killed Grandma*.

The novel made another appearance as a novelette in the February 1958 issue of *The Saint Detective Magazine*, under the title, "The Amy Waggoner Murder Case." Although the magazine appeared months before the novel, it's quite possible that it features a cut-down version of the longer work. Main characters and plot are the same; missing are chapter divisions and peripheral characters like Herbie and Doris. The novelette is much more of a straightforward investigation into a murder; the novel expands its vista to become more of a study of various characters. Anything having to do with drugs is also omitted from the short version. It's hard to say for sure which version of the story came first; the novel has entire chapters and characters not found in the novelette. The point is rather moot, though, since neither one is terribly good.

After its hardcover publication in 1958, *One for the Road* was reprinted in paperback by Bantam in 1959, and has not been printed in the United States since. It was not translated into French until after 1979 (if at all) and no foreign editions seem to have been published after 1961.

Reviewers at the time of publication were surprisingly positive in their assessments. Sergeant Cuff, writing in the *Saturday Review of Literature*, wrote: "red-herring device cleverly employed; cast agreeably authentic throughout," while *Kirkus Reviews* called the novel "Not savory—but sound." James Sandoe found the book charming, and Lenore Glen Offord praised the "genuine feeling of its characters' day-to-day existence" and remarked, "There's plenty of excitement along with a sound plot handled with unobtrusive neatness." Only Anthony Boucher sounded a negative note: "As an old-line Fredric Brown fan, I'm disappointed in his first mystery in two years...the mystery is resolved in an unpardonably chancy manner."

Critics have been virtually silent on this novel; only Newton Baird, in "Paradox and Plot," even mentions it, and only then to say it's one of Brown's novels of lesser merit.

Brown's next published novel, *The Late Lamented*, appeared in February 1959 and is a return to the Ed and Am Hunter series he had abandoned seven years before. The novel is pleasant enough but not outstanding.

Happily, Brown's next novel was brilliant, one of his finest and most terrifying tales of suspense. *Knock Three-One-Two* was published by Dutton in August 1959 and demonstrates that, at this late date, Fredric Brown was still capable of stunning his readers.

The novel begins with a chilling opening line:

He had a name, but it doesn't matter; call him *the psycho*. (1)

The first chapter (and all subsequent chapters) is marked not "chapter one" but with the time of its occurrence, "5:00 P.M." Brown manages to tell a story in a very compressed time period, heightening the suspense by being so precise.

The first chapter jumps right into the action that sets the novel's events in motion: the psycho has killed two women in four months and, posing as a Western Union man, tries to kill again but runs when a woman opens her apartment door on a chain. The anonymity of the scene is terrifying, and the third-person narration gives us the sense of a godlike figure telling a story that will move inexorably toward its conclusion.

The second chapter is timed "5:02 P.M.," only two minutes after the psycho ran from the door. The location has changed, however; now we follow Ray Fleck, a gambler who is $500 in the hole and desperately in need of money. His wife Ruth, a waitress at a Greek restaurant, won't let him borrow against her insurance policy, so he tries Benny, a moron who sells papers from a corner stand. Benny confesses to the psycho murders, but Ray's thoughts reveal that he knows Benny is not the one.

In this chapter, the dark urban world of the novel begins to be portrayed: desperate men roam, surrounded by morons, psychos, and criminals. This is not the happily eccentric Mayville, Arizona, of *One for the Road*; instead, it is a return to the ominous world of *Madball* or *The Wench is Dead*, where innocence is a rare commodity indeed.

The third chapter is set in yet another place, at 5:20 P.M., at the restaurant of George Mikos where Ruth Fleck works. After some scene-setting, the chapter is concluded in the form of a letter from George to his friend Perry in which he reveals his love for Ruth and discusses the psycho. The method of telling a story through letters written by a character is old in literature but new for Brown; it acts in concert with the novel's other expository tricks (the timed chapters, for instance) to allow him to present a variety of interrelated characters, settings, and events in a short time and thus maximize pace and suspense.

At 6:15 P.M., Ray Fleck continues his attempts to borrow money to pay his gambling debts. From his thoughts we learn that he witnessed the psycho leaving the scene of his last kill two months before but never told the police; in this way, he implicates himself and demonstrates his capacity for evil.

An hour passes, and at 7:25 P.M. George Mikos makes a pass at Ruth Fleck, who responds by asking for advice with Ray's financial problems. Ruth is safe and good, shielded from the city outside by "the lights of the restaurant itself" (27). But outside where Ray Fleck and the psycho roam, well...

It was dark outside now, and the blackness pressed against the windowpanes of the restaurant. (27)

Ruth is an optimist, though, thinking it funny that outside seems so dark when "if you went outside through the door the sidewalk wasn't really dark at all" (27). Yet at the chapter's end she wonders about Ray, "what he was doing now, out there in the darkness..." (35). The darkness is clearly both physical and spiritual; interestingly, a character who seems caught between good and evil, Benny the moron, sees "as through a defective windowpane that lets in light but distorts the images that the light beams ...a twisted cosmos peopled by phantoms..." (59). In other words, through a glass darkly.

As the evening progresses, Ray keeps trying to raise money by taking money to place bets. He counts on his girlfriend Dolly to help him, recalling an old Guy de Maupassant story where a mistress helped her lover.

Dolly is the focus of the seventh chapter, in which she takes Ray's phone call and then jumps in bed with another lover, seedy private detective Mack Irby (recalling *Madball*'s carney thief, also named Mack Irby). Dolly is promiscuous and Mack hardly a hero, as the novel will reveal. This chapter also demonstrates how censorship was easing by 1959: Mack calls Dolly a "little bitch" (45) and her erect nipples are described in loving detail.

The eighth chapter, set at 8:24 P.M., seven minutes after Ray's phone call to Dolly, tells of another failed attempt by the psycho to kill a woman. He tries to pry a window open but the woman hears him and calls the police. Brown teases the reader with foreshadowing:

> For tonight, he thought, the Need would have to go unsatisfied. He'd have to settle for the poor consolation of a few drinks to calm his nerves, and then sleep.
> That's what he thought. But then, he had not yet met Ray Fleck. (48)

The noose around Ray Fleck's neck grows tighter at 8:26 P.M., in the ninth chapter, when a visit to his bookie turns sour as the man confronts Ray with the fact that Ray has been taking money to place bets and thus stealing his business. As punishment, Ray is given one day to raise all the money he owes.

Chapter ten, set at 8:47 P.M., is a fascinating departure from a rather straightforward suspense novel. The story of Benny, the idiot newsagent, is told, and it is harrowing, recalling the story of Marty Raines in *The Office*. After his mother died, Benny was raised by his father, a fiery Baptist minister who instilled in him a belief in a literal Heaven and Hell. Benny's schooling ended at age 14 when authorities decided he could not learn anything more.

But Benny's biggest problem was one of confessing to crimes he didn't commit. After his father died, Benny lived with a kind woman who managed his money for him, and 15 years went by before he confessed again, this time to murder. The second time he did so he was examined by a police psychiatrist, who called his confessions harmless attempts to expiate deep-seated guilt.

Brown's examination of the effects of strong religion on an unstable mind seem to say that, while religious beliefs and religious men are not inherently bad, they may warp impressionable young minds because the images are so powerful. Benny confuses his "father in Heaven and his Heavenly Father" (67), and mentally pictures his late father's face telling him to confess to avoid going to Hell.

The story proper picks up at 9:00 P.M., as Ray Fleck visits Dolly and steals her jewels when she laughs at his plea for money. Some of Ray's history is also given: he's a loser and a quitter who dropped out of high school, failed at many jobs, and was discharged from the Army because of an allergy. He eventually found a place as a liquor salesman but, as his actions in the novel show, is far from honorable.

Even his theft fails him. Dolly's boyfriend Mack Irby quickly tracks Ray down and blackmails him, forcing Ray to sink further into debt and despair! Ray has already learned that the jewels are virtually worthless by the time he confronts Mack, so when he learns that the psycho is on the loose tonight he has all the information he needs to betray his wife.

In the meantime, Benny goes to the police station to confess to the psycho's murders; he's locked up overnight to await a visit from the psychiatrist. Benny perceives as a child does: one of the motivations for his confession is to get a ride "in the squad car, with the siren going and the red light flashing" (91).

The 16th chapter, set at 11:16 P.M., is an even greater departure from the narrative than was the story of Benny. Here, the devil and his aide discuss Ray Fleck and agree that he's ripe for the picking. At that moment, Ray looks up from his drink and sees the man he knows to be the psycho.

This chapter shows how far Brown has come since *The Screaming Mimi* in 1949, when he wanted to include a fantasy sequence set in Heaven but settled for a straightforward conclusion. It also recalls Brown's early pulp fantasy, "The New One" (*Unknown Worlds* October 1942), in which fire elementals observe and influence the actions of a defense factory worker in World War Two. Chapter 16 begins:

This is the transcript of a conversation that might possibly have happened. If you believe in such things you'll come to see that it could have happened. If you do not believe, it doesn't matter. (107)

The chapter is but a page long, yet it serves to universalize the moment of Ray's fall and place his predicament as a whole in the context of sin and damnation.

The following chapter, set at 11:17 P.M., begins "Avaunt, ye demons, and away with imaginary conversation" (108). In it, Ray talks with the psycho, telling him that Ruth is home and revealing their secret knock: three raps, one rap, two raps—hence, the novel's title: *Knock Three-One-Two*. Ray betrays Ruth willingly, setting up her murder in a way that can never be traced to him.

The next chapter occurs soon after, at 11:34 P.M., as Ruth gets ready to go home. She receives a phone call and the caller hangs up; George Mikos is worried and takes her home, checking her apartment before leaving her. The suspense by this point is terrific, as the reader wonders whether the psycho will attack Ruth.

The last four chapters, taking place from 11:55 P.M. to 2:45 A.M., show the ends that each of the novel's main characters come to. Ray works very hard to get an alibi, going from a poker game to a bar and finally punching a cop to try to get locked up. He finally has to confess to the jewel robbery before they'll take him to jail. Nothing goes right for Ray throughout the novel, though, and he soon gets his just desserts.

The next chapter is brief but suspenseful—Ruth sits alone in her apartment and decides to give Ray the money he needs. Just then there's a knock on the door—the secret knock that Ruth thinks only Ray knows. Ironically, just minutes after Ray has been taken to jail and moments before his murderous plan will be enacted, she makes the decision that would have solved all his problems.

The knock at the door is a tried and true technique of suspense, especially for Brown; he wrote his famous science fiction story "Knock" (*Thrilling Wonder Stories* December 1948) around it, and a character in *His Name Was Death* is killed after a similar knock.

The next to last chapter is set at 1:05 A.M. (the knock was at 1:01) and tells of the final irony to befall Ray Fleck. Benny Knox awakens from a dream where he was in Hell, with the devil laughing at him. He sees Ray, who shares his cell, and recognizes him as the devil from his dream, then strangles Ray to death. Benny rattles the bars of his cell to summon the police, yelling:

"Policemen! Policemen! Come here and see. *Now* do you believe me? *Now* will you try to tell me I never killed nobody?" (153)

The narrator tells us, "This time they believed him." Ray's sin is punished by the misguided idiot Benny, a strange but somehow fitting agent of justice in the novel.

Knock Three-One-Two's final chapter is set at 2:45 A.M., and takes the form of another letter from George Mikos to his friend. In the letter George writes of how he waited outside Ruth's building until he saw Ray enter. He then realized it was the psycho, not Ray, broke down the door to Ruth's apartment, and broke the psycho's neck in a wrestling hold. Ruth was okay and the police called with news of Ray's death, so George confides to his friend that he's sure Ruth will marry him after a period of mourning.

The novel has a surprisingly happy ending, much different from the conclusions of Brown's dark quartet of novels in the mid-fifties that so evocatively portrayed the darkness of modern life. The narrative technique is brilliant, using a tightly-controlled time span to present a series of related events over the course of an evening. The novel begins at 5:00 P.M. and ends at 2:45 A.M., less than ten hours but a very long time in the life of Ray Fleck. Exposition occurs in two forms: the letters of George Mikos and the narratives of Benny's and Ray's past. Irony is high, as is suspense, and there is even a little fantasy thrown in to expand the novel's meaning. All of this occurs in 138 quick pages (in the paperback version), and it's an exciting and rewarding read.

Reviewers at the time *Knock Three-One-Two* was published were full of praise; perhaps the most telling comment was that of James Sandoe, who called the novel "an evocation bright through grime and one of the cleverest things Mr. Brown has done, sour and knowledgeable." At least three reviewers complained about the conclusion's reliance on coincidence (presumably referring to the placing of Ray Fleck and Benny Knox in the same jail cell), but this does not seem to dampen their enthusiasm for the novel as a whole, which is really based on a series of ironic coincidences and should not be faulted for any one.

Knock Three-One-Two was serialized in the June 1959 issue of *High Adventure* as "Night of the Psycho"; the magazine version thus appeared two or three months before the book. Unfortunately, after the 1960 Bantam paperback edition, the novel has not been reprinted in the United States. A French edition was published in 1963, and various other foreign editions have appeared over the years, but this chilling classic has not been available in English since 1960, other than in a 1983 British collection entitled *4 Novels*.

Critics have paid more attention to this than to almost any other Fredric Brown novel. In 1974, Francis Lacassin wrote about its timing, noting that:

> Character or reader hardly ever has the time to catch his breath, they are swept away and stunned by the succession of events: all is chaos, annulled or dislocated. (257)[1]

Lacassin's other remarks on the novel are equally interesting, and he makes apt comparisons between it and three other novels in which time is compressed: *The Screaming Mimi, Night of the Jabberwock,* and *His Name Was Death.*

Newton Baird devoted two full pages of his "Paradox and Plot" study to *Knock Three-One-Two,* rightfully praising Brown's adroit handling of multiple points of view and calling the novel "one of the author's most successful works...a masterwork of irony" (252).

British mystery writer H.R.F. Keating, in his introduction to the 1983 collection *4 Novels,* calls *Knock Three-One-Two* "well worth reading, especially for its excellent plot and the high last-pages tension it generates" (viii-ix). The last critic to write about the novel was Jean-Pierre Deloux who, in his 1984 article "Mouvement brownien" calls Brown's respect for temporal unity "remarkable," and writes that "Time, and its inexorable procession [put] a definitive limit on [Ray Fleck's] race against it" (6).[2]

Knock Three-One-Two has twice been adapted on film; once, as an hour-long episode of the American television series *Thriller* (aired December 13, 1960) and later, as the French film *L'Ibis Rouge,* released in 1975. The novel remains one of Brown's most memorable tales of suspense.

One for the Road was set in Arizona, where Fredric Brown had been living for several years. *The Late Lamented* was set in and about Chicago, the usual setting for Ed and Am Hunter stories. *Knock Three-One-Two* was set in an unnamed city, notable mostly for its darkness and cruelty. After *Knock Three-One-Two* was published in August 1959, Fredric Brown did not publish another novel until *The Mind Thing*, a science fiction paperback original, in January 1961. In the meantime he must have been working on short-shorts and an occasional story, since *Nightmares and Geezenstacks* was published in the summer of 1961.

According to Newton Baird's chronology in "Paradox and Plot," Brown began traveling back and forth to Los Angeles in 1960 to write for the television series *Alfred Hitchcock Presents* (though only one episode of the series, an adaption of "Human Interest Story," bears his name as writer of the teleplay), returning to the city he had lived near briefly in the early 1950s. He apparently moved to nearby Van Nuys, California, in 1961, to be closer to the center of the film and television industry, finally moving back to Tucson for good in 1963, probably because his lungs could no longer stand the L.A. smog.

This sojourn in Los Angeles was reflected in Brown's next mystery novel, *The Murderers*, published by Dutton in August 1961. Narrated by twenty-seven year old television actor Willy Griff, it tells the story of his affair with Doris Seaton and their plot to murder her husband, John "Seat Cover" Seaton, a man who makes automobile seat covers and is often seen selling his wares on television.

As the novel begins, Willy is confronted by Seaton, who has learned of the affair and convinced his wife to end it. Duplicitous Doris instead agrees with Willy that her husband must be disposed of and raises the money Willy tells her the killing requires.

Willy's world is that of the beatniks, the young, disaffected precursors of the hippies that Jack Kerouac wrote about so well. Willy and his friends are amoral, as demonstrated by Willy's reminiscence of the time he and Charlie Hayes disguised themselves and spent time with winos "for fun and games" (13)—they went to a mission and "confessed our sins and promised to straighten up and become good Christian teetotalers" (13). They have continuous parties at the Zoo, a rooming house where a number of beatniks live, and listen to jazz records and beat poetry—Brown has one of his characters recite his own verse,

"Pattern," which is both hilarious and totally accurate as an example of bad modern poetry.

After making tentative plans to kill Seaton, Willy happens to discuss the idea with his friend Charlie, who would like to kill producer Manny Radic, whom he feels is purposely interfering in his career. In a plot device borrowed from Patricia Highsmith's *Strangers on a Train* Willy and Charlie have the bright idea of exchanging murders so that neither will have a traceable motive. To test their theory that a motiveless murder will go undetected, they befriend and kill a pitiful old wino on Skid Row.

The scene with the wino is troubling, especially when recalling Brown's prior examination of the alcoholic's milieu in *The Wench is Dead*. Willy selects an old man, "a derelict, all right, pretty far gone" (69). He convinces himself that the man's condition is such that he'd be "better off dead than alive. Or was I rationalizing? All right, so I was rationalizing" (70). Willy pretends to be a young man the wino had helped years before, and the wino sheds tears of happiness—so Willy gives Charlie the signal and Charlie bludgeons the old man with a lead pipe.

Willy is not the murderer, but he is just as guilty. His character flaw is simply this: he is never what he pretends to be; he is an actor in real life as well as in his profession. He spends much of his time with beatniks, but says that while he and Charlie "used hip language for kicks" they both "completely rejected the philosophy" (67). And, at least with the old wino, Willy pretends to be a friend while actually leading him to his death.

Right after the old man's murder, Willy carries out the murder of Manny Radic, shooting him at his home and getting away clean. The stage is set and the pressure on for Charlie to murder Seat Cover Seaton, but this proves more complicated (morally as well as logistically) than Willy's murder of Radic, especially after Seaton hires Willy as a television announcer and gives his career a sizeable boost! Amoral Willy still wants Seaton dead, however, and Charlie goes ahead as planned. Unfortunately, the plans go awry, causing Charlie to kill Seaton in front of Willy and Doris in a San Diego hotel room. The trio simply sit and wait for the police as the novel ends, their general poor planning, stupidity, and amorality rewarded.

The Murderers is a fun novel to read because of Willy's brisk narration, the beat background, and the colorful characters. Brown uses his California setting to enhance the youth and vitality of his characters, especially Willy Griff, whose amorality leads him to a bad end.

Yet the novel is very short, only 119 pages in paperback, and seems insubstantial, as if Brown were too tired or too busy to write any more. It begins quickly and zips to the end without much of a break. The derivative plotline (Brown surely had some familiarity with *Strangers on a Train*, if not the novel then the Alfred Hitchcock film of the same name) is uncomfortable; the reader knows what Willy and Charlie will do, and also that they will fail.

Unlike Guy and Bruno in *Strangers on a Train*, however, both Willy and Charlie have every intention of going through with both murders. In the only review of note to appear after the publication of *The Murderers*, Anthony Boucher wrote that Brown used Highsmith's theme "so freshly and skillfully that I doubt if even Miss Highsmith could complain...his astutely devised plot of retribution is quite different from Highsmith's...and in some ways more satisfactory..." Though Boucher liked the novel, it has not been seen as worthy of critical mention in the ensuing years. Newton Baird lists it among Brown's novels of lesser merit (calling it "one of the weakest" [156]) in "Paradox and Plot," and no one else has bothered to discuss it. After a Bantam paperback in September 1963 (more than two years after the appearance of the hardcover), it has not been reprinted in America.

The Murderers has its merits and is far from Fredric Brown's worst novel. It is certainly better than *The Five-Day Nightmare*, published by Dutton in April 1962. The novel, narrated by Lloyd Johnson, starts promisingly as he finds a kidnaper's ransom note in his own typewriter telling him that he must raise $25,000 in five days if he wants to see his wife alive again. They had just had a terrible quarrel, and Lloyd's guilt adds to his despair. The kidnaper has struck twice before: Arthur Sears called the police and his wife died; Randolph Early kept quiet and his wife lived. Lloyd sets up a meeting with Early to discuss what to do.

The Five-Day Nightmare starts at a dead run, promising an exciting story in which exposition will be catch as catch can as the plot speeds along. It soon falters, however, as subsequent chapters describe Lloyd's slow investigation into the kidnaping. Like many of Brown's heroes Lloyd gets drunk in the face of difficult circumstances, yet instead of having an interesting dream all he does is moon over his lost spouse.

Lloyd spends several chapters raising the ransom money by appealing to friends, including Joe Sitwell, his business partner and Ellen's cousin. An interesting passage occurs in chapter nine that places Lloyd's problems in a larger context. Lloyd tells Joe he looked at the paper and there was "Nothing in it," referring, of course, to news about his kidnaped wife. Joe's reply:

> He grimaced a little. "A plane crash in Florida with forty-two killed, one new African revolution, atomic war with Russia one step closer, two new satellites put in orbit—Yeah, I know what you mean by nothing in the paper." (78)

In two sentences Brown places Lloyd's story in 1962, a hectic and tension-filled year in the world. To Lloyd, however, the events happening to him at that moment outweigh any major catastrophe. This passage serves to depict the importance of personal events to one man, yet it also points out a flaw in *The Five-Day Nightmare*—with all of these dramatic events going on in the world, the rather straightforward tale of a kidnapping is not terribly interesting.

Lloyd keeps trying in vain to *do something*, as the days pass with agonizing slowness for him and us. At last Wednesday night arrives, and while the five days leading up to it have occupied the first 15 chapters of the novel, the final events are raced through in chapter 16's 12 pages. Lloyd drops off the money in a culvert out of town then finds a note indicating that Ellen was not kidnapped at all—she just went to visit her sister to cool off after her argument with Lloyd! He deduces that his partner Joe set up the kidnap scheme to get money, and Lloyd elicits a confession at gunpoint and a promise to leave town. The story ends as he calls Ellen and awaits her return.

The solution to the mystery of *The Five-Day Nightmare* is a trick, one that happens too quickly to be satisfying. The novel is dull in many spots and lacking in action (much like *One for the Road*), and the kidnaper—about whom characters speculate for 150 pages—is forgotten entirely in the last chapter. Brown has taken a very thin plot and padded it as best he could, but the novel lacks almost everything that can be found in his better work, especially his sense of quirky imagination.

Surprisingly, reviewers gave the novel better notices than it deserved. Sergeant Cuff of the *Saturday Review of Literature* noted its "moderately surprising finish" and "Air of authenticity," while *Kirkus Reviews* called it "Taut." The San Francisco *Chronicle's* Lenore Glen Offord wrote that "There is a neat double turn to this apparently simple story, done in the expert Brown manner," while James Sandoe complained that the novel "may settle for a conclusion you guess and hope against but in the running it is lean, taut and very compelling." Only Anthony Boucher, in the New York *Times* Book Review, sounded a strongly negative note:

Even as brilliant a technician as Fredric Brown can encounter difficulties in stretching a short-story plot to 50,000 words; and I fear that THE FIVE-DAY NIGHTMARE (Dutton, $2.95) shows the strain. But there's still a fascination to this account of what is usually overlooked in fiction: the economics of kidnaping—how do you go about raising, under extreme pressure, the amount of cash needed to save your wife?

As a primer for the families of kidnap victims *The Five-Day Nightmare* may have some value, but as a mystery novel it is decidedly dull.

A book club edition was published simultaneously with the first edition, then no paperback until Tower Books issued one three years later, in 1965.

Critical attention has been scarce. *A Catalogue of Crime* devoted an entry to the novel, noting that, while

the story has suspense enough...one is ready to hurl the book into the passing garbage truck when one finds out what lies behind the threat and what its business consequences are for the frightened hero, who refuses to go to the police. Here F.B. forgoes his usual sex tricks and depicts only the nicest, weakest kind of people, barring the would-be kidnaper—another proof of 'scratch a tough guy to find a sentimentalist.' (Barzun 78)

Francois Guerif listed *The Five-Day Nightmare* in 1979 as one of Brown's lesser novels, as did Newton Baird in "Paradox and Plot." Jean-Pierre Deloux, in "Mouvement brownien," briefly mentions the novel's time element, yet even this is a failure—most of the story occurs in the first two days and the last five minutes, making most of *The Five-Day Nightmare* quite uneventful. The story is set in Phoenix, Arizona, but such little use is made of the setting that it could take place anywhere.

* * *

After *The Five-Day Nightmare*, Brown published *Mrs. Murphy's Underpants* in about November 1963, a couple of stories in 1964 and 1965, and then nothing more until his death in 1972. A few very short stories went unpublished for many years, as did the fragment of the novel *Brother Monster*, but, after 1965, Brown seems to have done almost no writing.

It is unfortunate that the last few years of Fredric Brown's career as a writer produced so little work of note, but it is not surprising. He had been writing steadily for three decades and was surely exhausted. Never prolific, he admitted that he loved to put off writing and took breaks whenever he could. His health deteriorated as he edged toward age 60, and even the little writing he had been able to do soon became too much.

But his legacy is a complex and rich one, full of novels and stories of terror and humor, sometimes affirming the sheer joy of life and sometimes wallowing brilliantly in its despair. He is beloved by readers of mystery and science fiction and he is seen as a master of short-shorts and short stories. His novels remain his most lasting work, however; unfortunately, some of the best ones have languished unreprinted for decades and become the province of collectors, who pay large sums for copies of even the weakest books by Fredric Brown. And deservedly so, for he was one of the most wide-ranging and talented of the popular American writers of the mid-twentieth century.

Notes

Chapter Five

[1]The actual copy of the poem that has survived is untitled; I assume the title from internal evidence.

[2]Once again, I assume the title.

[3]Another assumed title.

Chapter Seven

[1]The original reads, "la tapisserie de Pénelope reconstituée d'un seul coup."

[2]"un petit chef-d'oeuvre méconnu du roman policier, certainement le chef-d'oeuvre de Fredric Brown."

[3]"*La nuit du Jabberwock*, alliant le polar au fantastique, occupe une place totalement à part dans la littérature policière...son chef-d'oeuvre."

Chapter Eleven

[1]The original reads: "la densité de l'action, souvent contenue dans un laps de temps relativement court."

[2]"l'excès de vitesse commis par l'action..."

[3]"qui, par ses conséquences grotesques, transformera le récit en cauchemar éveillé."

[4]"il s'acceptera tel qu'il est de la même manière qu' Howard Perry dans *The Wench is Dead*."

[5]The original reads: "une curieuse réflexion sur le bien, la pitié, la rationalisation de la folie, le fanatisme et la justice."

Chapter Thirteen

[1]Louit calls them "la nouvelle ultra-court."

Chapter Fourteen

[1]"Personnage ou lecteur n'ont guère le temps de reprendre le souffle, emportés, étourdis par la succession des événements: tout se brouille, s'annule ou se disloque."

[2]"Et c'est encore le Temps, et son mortel cortège, qui mettra un terme définitif à sa course contre la montre."

A List of Writing by Fredric Brown

Part Two
Short Stories

1936

"Munchdriller's Vacuum Vengeance." *The Michigan Well Driller.* September 1936.

"Business is Booming." *Excavating Engineer.* November 1936.

1937

"We've Tried Everything." *Excavating Engineer.* February 1937.

"Willie Skid (Cub Serviceman) Says:" [One]. *Ford Dealer Service Bulletin.* February 1937.

"Let Colonel Cluck Answer Your Questions" [One]. *Independent Salesman.* February-March 1937.

"Dear Boss (Letters of a Traveling Salesman to His Wife)." *Independent Salesman.* March 1937.

"Willie Skid (Cub Serviceman) Says:" [Two]. *Ford Dealer Service Bulletin.* March 1937.

"But You Never Know." *Excavating Engineer.* April 1937.

"Let Colonel Cluck Answer Your Questions" [Two]. *Independent Salesman.* April 1937.

"Willie Skid (Cub Serviceman) Says:" [Three]. *Ford Dealer Service Bulletin.* April 1937.

"Willie Skid (Cub Serviceman) Says:" [Four]. *Ford Dealer Service Bulletin.* May 1937.

"Barnyard Bill Says" [One]. *Feedstuffs.* June 1937.

"Willie Skid (Cub Serviceman) Says:" [Five]. *Ford Dealer Service Bulletin.* June 1937.

"The Worst is Yet to Come." *Excavating Engineer.* June 1937.

"Ernie, Minister of Peace and Goodness, or the Case of the Multiplying Eggs." *Feedstuffs.* No date - written June 1937.

"Rio Bound." Unpublished - written June 1937 and lost.

"Willie Skid (Cub Serviceman) Says:" [Six]. *Ford Dealer Service Bulletin.* July 1937.

"Fairyland ABC Book." Unpublished - written July 1937 and lost.

"Old Judge Lynch." Unpublished - written July 1937 and lost.

"Something May Happen." *Excavating Engineer.* August 1937.

"Willie Skid (Cub Serviceman) Says:" [Seven]. *Ford Dealer Service Bulletin.* August 1937.

"Murder Wears Red." Unpublished - written August 1937 and lost.

"Barnyard Bill Says" [Two]. *Feedstuffs.* September 1937.

"Willie Skid (Cub Serviceman) Says:" [Eight]. *Ford Dealer Service Bulletin.* September 1937.

"Let Colonel Cluck Answer Your Questions" [Three]. *Independent Salesman.* October 1937.

"Wait and Pray." *Excavating Engineer.* October 1937.

"Willie Skid (Cub Serviceman) Says:" [Nine]. *Ford Dealer Service Bulletin.* October 1937.

"The Case of the Shrinking Stallion." *Feedstuffs.* No date - written November 1937.

"The Case of the Wandering Scarecrow." *Feedstuffs.* No date - written November 1937.

"This Will Surprise You." *Excavating Engineer.* December 1937.

"No Story." Unpublished - written December 1937 and lost.

1938

"Willie Skid (Cub Serviceman) Says:" [Ten]. *Ford Dealer Service Bulletin.* January 1938.

"The Case of the Apocryphal Ark." *Feedstuffs.* No date - written January 1938.

"The Case of the Bewildering Barn." *Feedstuffs.* No date - written January 1938.

"Lucky Valley." Unpublished - written by January 1938 and lost.

"Klepto Trouble." Unpublished - written January 1938 and lost.

"Bear With Us." *Excavating Engineer.* February 1938.

"The Case of the Conjurer's Cat." *Feedstuffs.* No date - written February 1938.

"The Case of the Rebellious Rooster." *Feedstuffs.* No date - written February 1938.

"Long Term Contract." Unpublished - written February 1938 and lost.

"The Moon for a Nickel." *Street & Smith Detective Story.* March 1938.

"You Can't Get Broadway's Goat, or the Case of the Kidnapped Kid." *Feedstuffs.* No date - written March 1938.

"The Adventures of Dink." Unpublished - written March 1938 and lost.

"Headstone for a Grave." Unpublished - written March 1938 and lost.

"Lion Likes the Noise." Unpublished - written March 1938 and lost.

"The Magic Lamp." Unpublished - written March 1938 and lost.

"Sing While You're Able." Unpublished - written March 1938 and lost.

"Sleeping Dogs." Unpublished - written March 1938 and lost.

"To Fill a Grave." Unpublished - written March 1938 and lost.

"Hot Air Rises." *Excavating Engineer.* April 1938.

"Ernie Stops Shivering, or the Case of the Trackless Tractor." *Feedstuffs.* No date - written April 1938.

"Money Doesn't Matter." *Excavating Engineer.* No date - written April 1938.

"Tit for Tat." *Feedstuffs*. No date - written April 1938.

"Death Comes Creeping." Unpublished - written April 1938 and lost.

"Habeus Ex Corpus." Unpublished - written April 1938 and lost.

Two Paydirt Pete stories. Unpublished - written April 1938 and lost.

"Greengood's Hideout." Unpublished - written May 1938 and lost.

"Willie Skid (Cub Serviceman) Says:" [Eleven]. *Ford Dealer Service Bulletin*. October 1938.

"The Eyes Have It." Unpublished - written December 1938 and lost.

1939

"The Cheese on Stilts." *Thrilling Detective*. January 1939.

"Willie Skid (Cub Serviceman) Says:" [Twelve]. *Ford Dealer Service Bulletin*. January 1939.

"Blood of the Dragon." *Variety Detective*. February 1939.

"There Are Bloodstains in the Alley." *Detective Yarns*. February 1939.

"Let Colonel Cluck Answer Your Questions" [Four]. *Independent Salesman*. May 1939.

"Murder at 10:15." *Clues*. May 1939.

1940

"Bloody Murder." *Detective Fiction Weekly*. January 10, 1940.

"Cause and Defect." *The Inventor*. March 1940.

"The Prehistoric Clue." *Ten Detective Aces*. March 1940.

"Questionable Answer Department." [One]. *The Inventor* March 1940.

"Questionable Answer Department" [Two]. *The Inventor* April 1940.

"The Case of the Bargain Butter." *Feedstuffs*. April 13, 1940.

"The Case of the Rattled Robber." *The Inventor*. May 1940.

"Hex Marks the Spot." *Excavating Engineer*. May 1940.

"Questionable Answer Department" [Three]. *The Inventor* May 1940.

"Spice of Life!" *The Coin Machine Review*. May 1940.

"Raw Magic." Unpublished - written May 1940 and lost.

"A Matter of Taste." *The Layman's Magazine*. June 1940.

"Movie Masquerade" [One]. *Hollywood Magazine*. July 1940.

"Trouble in a Teacup." *Detective Fiction Weekly*. July 13, 1940.

"Murder Draws a Crowd." *Detective Fiction Weekly*. July 27, 1940.

"The Phantom Fights Broadcast Terror" (synop.). Unpublished - written July 1940 and lost.

"The Thought Bomb " Unpublished - written July 1940 and lost.

"Movie Masquerade" [Two]. *Hollywood Magazine*. August 1940.

"The Clutch of Morpheus." Unpublished - written August 1940 and lost.

"The Phantom, Mortician" (synop.). Unpublished - written August 1940 and lost.

"Footprints on the Ceiling." *Ten Detective Aces.* September 1940.
"Movie Masquerade" [Three]. *Hollywood Magazine.* September 1940.
"Town Wanted." *Detective Fiction Weekly.* September 7, 1940.
"Breath of Beelzebub." Unpublished - written September 1940 and lost.
"The Phantom and the Flying Death" (synop.). Unpublished - written
     September 1940 and lost.
"The Little Green Men." *Masked Detective.* Fall 1940.
"Movie Masquerade" [Four]. *Hollywood Magazine.* October 1940.
"Herbie Rides His Hunch." *Detective Fiction Weekly.* October 19, 1940.
"Movie Masquerade" [Five]. *Hollywood Magazine.* November 1940.
"The Stranger from Trouble Valley." *Western Short Story.* November 1940.
"The Strange Sisters Strange." *Detective Fiction Weekly.* December 28, 1940.

1941

"Not Yet the End." *Captain Future.* Winter 1941.
"Number Bug." *Exciting Detective.* Winter 1941.
"Fugitive Impostor." *Ten Detective Aces.* January 1941.
"The King Comes Home." *Thrilling Detective.* January 1941.
"Miracle on Vine Street." *The Layman's Magazine.* January 1941.
"The Sematic Crocodile." *The Layman's Magazine.* February 1941.
"Big-Top Doom." *Ten Detective Aces.* March 1941.
"The Discontented Cows." *G-Men Detective.* March 1941.
"Life and Fire." *Detective Fiction Weekly.* March 22, 1941.
"Coming Georgia." Unpublished - written March 1941 and lost.
"Big-League Larceny." *Ten Detective Aces.* April 1941 (as Jack Hobart).
"Client Unknown." *Phantom Detective.* April 1941.
"Homicide Sanitarium." *Thrilling Detective.* May 1941.
"Angel Aware." Unpublished - written May 1941 and lost.
"Your Name in Gold." *Phantom Detective.* June 1941.
"The Lights." Unpublished - written June 1941 and lost.
"Here Comes the Hearse." *Ten-Story Detective.* July 1941 (as Allen Morse).
"Six-Gun Song." *Ten-Story Detective.* July 1941.
"Star-Spangled Night." *Coronet.* July 1941.
"Wheels Across the Night." *G-Men Detective.* July 1941.
"How Tagrid Got There." Written July 1941, published 1986.
"Armageddon." *Unknown Worlds.* August 1941.
"Little Boy Lost." *Detective Fiction Weekly.* August 2, 1941.
"House of Silence." Unpublished - written September 1941 and lost.
"Bullet for Bullet." *Western Short Story.* October 1941.
"The Ancient Art." Unpublished - written October 1941 and lost.
"Pentagram." Unpublished - written October 1941 and lost.

"Roman." Unpublished - written October 1941 and lost.
"Listen to the Mocking Bird." *G-Men Detective*. November 1941.
"You'll End Up Burning." *Ten Detective Aces*. November 1941.
"Selling Death Short." *Ten Detective Aces*. December 1941.
"Thirty Corpses Every Thursday." *Detective Tales*. December 1941.
"Trouble Comes Double." *Popular Detective*. December 1941.

1942

"Clue in Blue." *Thrilling Mystery*. January 1942.
"Death is a White Rabbit." *Strange Detective Mysteries*. January 1942.
"Twenty Gets You Plenty." *G-Men Detective*. January 1942.
"Etaoin Shrdlu." *Unknown Worlds*. February 1942.
"Little Apple Hard to Peel." *Detective Tales*. February 1942.
"Pardon My Ghoulish Laughter." *Strange Detective Mysteries*. February 1942.
"Audience." Unpublished - written February 1942 and lost.
Eight Dink Stories. Unpublished - written February 1942 and lost.
"Death in the Dark." *Dime Mystery*. March 1942.
"Everything is Ducky." *Excavating Engineer*. March 1942.
"Handbook for Homicide." *Detective Tales*. March 1942.
"The Incredible Bomber." *G-Men Detective*. March 1942.
"Twice-Killed Corpse." *Ten Detective Aces*. March 1942.
Six Start Your Engine stories. Unpublished - written March 1942 and lost.
"Mad Dog!" *Detective Book*. Spring 1942.
"Moon Over Murder." *Masked Detective*. Spring 1942.
"The Star Mouse." *Planet Stories*. Spring 1942.
"A Cat Walks." *Street & Smith Detective Story*. April 1942.
"Who Did I Murder?" *Detective Short Story*. April 1942.
"Callisto Deadline." Unpublished - written April 1942 and lost.
"Case of Joseph Clark." Unpublished - written April 1942 and lost.
"Dreamer." Unpublished - written April 1942 and lost.
"Murder in Furs." *Thrilling Detective*. May 1942.
"Haft." Unpublished - written May 1942 and lost.
"Suite for Flute and Tommy Gun." *Street & Smith Detective Story*. June 1942.
"Three Corpse Parlay." *Popular Detective*. June 1942.
"Acme." Unpublished - written June 1942 and lost.
"Dog Bites Man." Unpublished - written June 1942 and lost.
"Intercepted Pass." Unpublished - written June 1942 and lost.
"A Date to Die." *Strange Detective Mysteries*. July 1942.
"Red is the Hue of Hell." *Strange Detective Mysteries*. July 1942 (as Felix
　　Graham).
"Two Biers for Two." *Clues*. July 1942.

"You'll Die Before Dawn." *Street & Smith Mystery Magazine*. July 1942.

"The Sheriff Lays an Egg." Unpublished - written August 1942 and lost.

"Get Out of Town." *Thrilling Detective*. September 1942.

"A Little White Lye." *Ten Detective Aces*. September 1942.

"The Men Who Went Nowhere." *Dime Mystery*. September 1942.

"Nothing Sinister." *Street & Smith Mystery Magazine*. September 1942.

"The Numberless Shadows." *Street & Smith Detective Story*. September 1942.

"Satan's Search Warrant." *Ten-Story Detective*. September 1942.

"Starvation." *Astounding Science Fiction*. September 1942.

"Where There's Smoke." *Black Book Detective Magazine*. September 1942.

"On the Dotted Lion." Unpublished - written before September 1942 and lost.

"Boner." *Popular Detective*. October 1942.

"Legacy of Murder." *Exciting Mystery*. October 1942.

"The New One." *Unknown Worlds*. October 1942.

"The Santa Claus Murders." *Street & Smith Detective Story*. October 1942.

"Auf Wiedersehen, Mein Fuehrer." Unpublished - written October 1942 and lost.

"Double Murder." *Thrilling Detective*. November 1942 (as John S. Endicott).

"A Fine Night for Murder." *Detective Tales*. November 1942.

"Heil, Werewolf." *Dime Mystery*. November 1942 (as Felix Graham).

"I'll See You At Midnight." *Clues*. November 1942.

"The Monkey Angle." *Thrilling Detective*. November 1942.

"Satan One-and-a-Half." *Dime Mystery*. November 1942.

"The Printer and the Flag." Unpublished - written December 1942 and lost.

1943

"A Lock of Satan's Hair." *Dime Mystery*. January 1943.

"The Spherical Ghoul." *Thrilling Mystery*. January 1943.

"The Wicked Flea." *Ten Detective Aces*. January 1943.

"Mr. Toyama's Box." Unpublished - written January 1943 and lost.

"The Angelic Angleworm." *Unknown Worlds*. February 1943.

"Death is a Noise." *Popular Detective*. February 1943.

"The Hat Trick." *Unknown Worlds*. February 1943 (as Felix Graham).

"Hound of Hell." *Ten Detective Aces*. February 1943.

"The Sleuth from Mars." *Detective Tales*. February 1943.

"A Change for the Hearse." *New Detective*. March 1943.

"Encore for a Killer." *Street & Smith Mystery Magazine*. March 1943.

"Trial By Darkness." *Clues*. March 1943.

"Cadavers Don't Make a Fifth Column." *Detective Short Story*. April 1943.

"Murder, or Something." Unpublished - written April 1943 and lost.

"Death of a Vampire." *Strange Detective Mysteries*. May 1943.

"Death's Dark Angel." *Thrilling Detective*. May 1943.

"The Freak Show Murders." *Street & Smith Mystery Magazine*. May 1943.
"Market for Murder." *The Shadow*. May 1943.
"Day of the Ogre." Unpublished - written May 1943 and lost.
"This is the Forest Primeval." Unpublished - written June 1943 and lost.
"The Corpse and the Candle." *Dime Mystery*. July 1943.
"Madman's Holiday." *Street & Smith Detective Story*. July 1943.
"Blue Murder." *The Shadow*. September 1943.
"The Geezenstacks." *Weird Tales*. September 1943.
"Tell 'em, Pagliaccio!" *Street & Smith Detective Story*. September 1943.
"Whispering Death." *Dime Mystery*. September 1943.
"Daymare." *Thrilling Wonder Stories*. Fall 1943.
"Death Insurance Payment." *Ten Detective Aces*. October 1943.
"The Motive Goes Round and Round." *Thrilling Detective*. October 1943.
"Paradox Lost." *Astounding Science Fiction*. October 1943.

1944
"The Djinn Murder." *Ellery Queen's Mystery Magazine*. January 1944.
"Murder in Miniature." *Street & Smith Detective Story*. January 1944.
"The Ghost of Riley." *Detective Tales*. February 1944.
"The Devil's Woodwinds." *Dime Mystery*. March 1944.
"And the Gods Laughed." *Planet Stories*. Spring 1944.
"Nothing Sirius." *Captain Future*. Spring 1944.
"The Yehudi Principle." *Astounding Science Fiction*. May 1944.
"Arena." *Astounding Science Fiction*. June 1944.
"The Jabberwocky Murders." *Thrilling Mystery*. Summer 1944.
"The Ghost Breakers." *Thrilling Detective*. July 1944.
"The Gibbering Night." *Detective Tales*. July 1944.
"Murder While You Wait." *Ellery Queen's Mystery Magazine*. July 1944.
"The Bucket of Gems Case." *Street & Smith Detective Story*. August 1944.
"To Slay a Man About a Dog." *Detective Tales*. September 1944.
"A Matter of Death." *Thrilling Detective*. November 1944.

1945
"Pi in the Sky." *Thrilling Wonder Stories*. Winter 1945.
"The Night the World Ended." *Dime Mystery*. January 1945.
"The Waveries." *Astounding Science Fiction*. January 1945.
"No Sanctuary." *Dime Mystery*. March 1945.
"Compliments of a Fiend." *Thrilling Detective*. May 1945.
"Ten Tickets to Hades." *Ten Detective Aces*. May 1945.
"Murder-on-the-Hudson." *Thrilling Detective*. June 1945 (with Bob Woehlke and under his name).

1946

"Dead Man's Indemnity." *Mystery Book Magazine.* April 1946.
"Placet is a Crazy Place." *Astounding Science Fiction.* May 1946.
"Song of the Dead." *New Detective.* July 1946.
"Obit for Obie." *Mystery Book Magazine.* October 1946.
"Whistler's Murder." *Street & Smith Detective Story.* December 1946.

1947

"A Voice Behind Him." *Mystery Book Magazine.* January 1947.
"Light Fantastic." Unpublished - written April 1947 and lost.
"Don't Look Behind You." *Ellery Queen's Mystery Magazine.* May 1947.
"Miss Darkness." *Avon Detective Mysteries* #3 (1947).

1948

"I'll Cut Your Throat Again, Kathleen." *Mystery Book Magazine.* Winter 1948.
"The Dead Ringer." *Mystery Book Magazine.* Spring 1948.
"Four Letter Word." *Adventure.* April 1948.
"The Four Blind Men." *Adventure.* September 1948.
"What Mad Universe." *Startling Stories.* September 1948.
"The Laughing Butcher." *Mystery Book Magazine.* Fall 1948.
"If Looks Could Kill." *Detective Tales.* October 1948.
"Cry Silence." *Black Mask.* November 1948.
"Red-Hot and Hunted!" *Detective Tales.* November 1948.
"Knock." *Thrilling Wonder Stories.* December 1948.

1949

"This Way Out." *Dime Mystery.* February 1949.
"All Good Bems." *Thrilling Wonder Stories.* April 1949.
"Mouse." *Thrilling Wonder Stories.* June 1949.
"Murder and Matilda." *Mystery Book Magazine.* Summer 1949.
"Come and Go Mad." *Weird Tales.* July 1949.
"Last Curtain." *New Detective.* July 1949.
"Crisis, 1999." *Ellery Queen's Mystery Magazine.* August 1949.
"Each Night He Died." *Dime Mystery.* August 1949.
"Letter to a Phoenix." *Astounding Science Fiction.* August 1949.
"The Cat from Siam." *Popular Detective.* September 1949.
"The Sinister Mr. Dexter." *New Detective.* September 1949.
"Deadly Weekend." *Mystery Book Magazine.* Fall 1949.
"The Bloody Moonlight." *Two Detective Mystery Novels.* November 1949.
"Gateway to Darkness." *Super Science Stories.* November 1949.

1950

"The Last Train." *Weird Tales.* January 1950.
"Death and Nine Lives." *Black Book Detective.* Spring 1950.
"The Blind Lead." *Detective Tales.* June 1950.
"The Case of the Dancing Sandwiches." *Mystery Book Magazine.* Summer 1950.
"The Nose of Don Aristide." *Two Detective Mystery Novels.* Summer 1950.
"Vengeance Unlimited." *Super Science Stories.* July 1950.
"From These Ashes." *Amazing Stories.* August 1950.
"The Undying Ones." *Super Science Stories.* September 1950.
"Walk in the Shadows." *Giant Detective.* Fall 1950.
"The Frownzly Florgels." *Other Worlds Science Fiction.* October 1950.
"Gateway to Glory." *Amazing Stories.* October 1950.
"The Last Martian." *Galaxy Science Fiction.* October 1950.
"Honeymoon in Hell." *Galaxy Science Fiction.* November 1950.
"Mitkey Rides Again." *Planet Stories.* November 1950.
"Device of the Turtle." *Worlds Beyond.* December 1950 (with Mack Reynolds).

1951

"Dark Interlude." *Galaxy Science Fiction.* January 1951 (with Mack Reynolds).
"Man of Distinction." *Thrilling Wonder Stories.* February 1951.
"The Switcheroo." *Other Worlds Science Fiction.* March 1951 (with Mack Reynolds).
"The Weapon." *Astounding Science Fiction.* April 1951.
"Cartoonist." *Planet Stories.* May 1951 (with Mack Reynolds).
"Something Green." *Space On My Hands.* July 1951.
"The Dome." *Thrilling Wonder Stories.* August 1951.
"A Word from Our Sponsor." *Other Worlds Science Fiction.* September 1951.
"The Gamblers." *Startling Stories.* November 1951 (with Mack Reynolds).
"The Hatchetman." *Amazing Stories.* December 1951 (with Mack Reynolds).

1952

"Me and Flapjack and the Martians." *Astounding Science Fiction.* December 1952 (with Mack Reynolds).

1953

"Witness in the Dark." *New Detective.* June 1953.
"The Pickled Punks." *The Saint Detective Magazine.* June/July 1953.
"The Wench is Dead." *Manhunt.* July 1953.
"The Little Lamb." *Manhunt.* August 1953.
"Rustle of Wings." *The Magazine of Fantasy and Science Fiction.* August 1953.
"Hall of Mirrors." *Galaxy Science Fiction.* December 1953.

1954

"Experiment." *Galaxy Science Fiction*. February 1954.

"Sentry." *Galaxy Science Fiction*. February 1954.

"Keep Out." *Amazing Stories*. March 1954.

"Martians, Go Home." *Astounding Science Fiction*. September 1954.

"Naturally." *Beyond Fantasy Fiction*. September 1954.

"Voodoo." *Beyond Fantasy Fiction*. September 1954.

"Answer." *Angels and Spaceships*. 1954.

"Daisies." *Angels and Spaceships*. 1954.

"Pattern." *Angels and Spaceships*. 1954.

"Politeness." *Angels and Spaceships*. 1954.

"Preposterous." *Angels and Spaceships*. 1954.

"Reconciliation." *Angels and Spaceships*. 1954.

"Search." *Angels and Spaceships*. 1954.

"Sentence." *Angels and Spaceships*. 1954.

"Solipsist." *Angels and Spaceships*. 1954.

1955

"Blood." *The Magazine of Fantasy and Science Fiction*. February 1955.

"Millenium." *The Magazine of Fantasy and Science Fiction*. March 1955.

"Imagine." *The Magazine of Fantasy and Science Fiction*. May 1955.

"Premiere of Murder." *The Saint Detective Magazine*. May 1955.

"The Perfect Crime." *Ellery Queen's Mystery Magazine*. June 1955.

"The Letter." *Ellery Queen's Mystery Magazine*. July 1955.

"The First Time Machine." *Ellery Queen's Mystery Magazine*. September 1955.

"Too Far." *The Magazine of Fantasy and Science Fiction*. September 1955.

1956

"Line of Duty." *Manhunt*. April 1956.

1957

"Murder Set to Music." *The Saint Detective Magazine*. January 1957.

"Expedition." *The Magazine of Fantasy and Science Fiction*. February 1957.

"Happy Ending." *Fantastic Universe*. September 1957 (with Mack Reynolds).

1958

"The Amy Waggoner Murder Case." *The Saint Detective Magazine*. February 1958.

"Jaycee." *The Magazine of Fantasy and Science Fiction*. October 1958.

"Unfortunately." *The Magazine of Fantasy and Science Fiction*. October 1958.

"Who Was That Blonde I Saw You Kill Last Night?" *Swank*. December 1958.

1959

"The Late Lamented." *The Saint Detective Magazine*. February 1959.
"Nasty." *Playboy*. April 1959.
"Rope Trick." *Adam*. May 1959.
"Night of the Psycho." *High Adventure*. June 1959.

1960

"Abominable." *Dude*. March 1960.
"Bear Possibility." *Dude*. March 1960.
"The Mind Thing." *Fantastic Universe*. March 1960.
"Recessional." *Dude*. March 1960.
"The Power." *Galaxy Science Fiction*. April 1960.
"Earthmen Bearing Gifts." *Galaxy Science Fiction*. June 1960.
"Granny's Birthday." *Alfred Hitchcock's Mystery Magazine*. June 1960.
"The House." *Fantastic*. August 1960.

1961

"Great Lost Discoveries I - Invisibility." *Gent*. February 1961.
"Great Lost Discoveries II - Invulnerability." *Gent*. February 1961.
"Great Lost Discoveries III - Immortality." *Gent*. February 1961.
"The Hobbyist." *Playboy*. May 1961.
"Nightmare in Blue." *Dude*. May 1961.
"Nightmare in Gray." *Dude*. May 1961.
"Nightmare in Red." *Dude*. May 1961.
"Nightmare in Time." *Dude*. May 1961.
"Nightmare in Yellow." *Dude*. May 1961.
"Of Time and Eustace Weaver." *Ellery Queen's Mystery Magazine*. June 1961.
"Bright Beard." *Nightmares and Geezenstacks*. 1961.
"Cat Burglar." *Nightmares and Geezenstacks*. 1961.
"Death on the Mountain." *Nightmares and Geezenstacks*. 1961.
"Fish Story." *Nightmares and Geezenstacks*. 1961.
"Horse Race." *Nightmares and Geezenstacks*. 1961.
"Nightmare in Green." *Nightmares and Geezenstacks*. 1961.
"Nightmare in White." *Nightmares and Geezenstacks*. 1961.
"The Ring of Hans Carvel." *Nightmares and Geezenstacks*. 1961.
"Second Chance." *Nightmares and Geezenstacks*. 1961.
"Three Little Owls." *Nightmares and Geezenstacks*. 1961.
"Before She Kills." *Ed McBain's Mystery Book* #3 (1961).

1962

"Aelurophobe." *Dude*. September 1962.
"Puppet Show." *Playboy*. November 1962.

1963

"Double Standard." *Playboy*. April 1963.
"Instant Novellas" [One]. *Rogue*. April 1963.
"Instant Novellas" [Two]. *Rogue*. May 1963.
"Instant Novellas" [Three]. *Rogue*. June 1963.
"Instant Novellas" [Four]. *Rogue*. July 1963.
"It Didn't Happen." *Playboy*. October 1963.
"Tale of the Flesh Monger." *Gent*. October 1963.
"The Missing Actor." *The Saint Detective Magazine*. November 1963.

1964

"Why, Benny, Why?" *Ellery Queen's Mystery Magazine*. November 1964.

1965

"Eine Kleine Nachtmusik." *The Magazine of Fantasy and Science Fiction*. June
    1965 (with Carl Onspaugh).

Posthumously Published

"Mirror." *Nightmare in Darkness*. 1987.
"Nightmare in Darkness." *Nightmare in Darkness*. 1987.
"The Water-Walker." *The Water-Walker*. 1990.
"The Cat and the Riddle." *The Pickled Punks*. 1991.

Undated Stories
(Probably published from 1936-1940)

"Advice—By Colonel Kluck." *The Michigan Well Driller*. No date.
"An Anagram Game." No date.
"Animal Hunt." No date.
"At the Circus." No date.
"The Case of the Flying Cow, or How Did the Critter Get Into the Silo."
    Feedstuffs. No date.
"The Case of the Haunted Haystack." *Feedstuffs*. No date.
"The Case of the Languid Lamb." *Feedstuffs*. No date.
"The Case of the Rambling Rocks." *Feedstuffs*. No date.
"The Case of the Refrigerating Windmill." *Feedstuffs*. No date.
"The Case of the Stuttering Shoat." *Feedstuffs*. No date.

"The Case of the Uncountable Sheep." *Feedstuffs*. No date.

"Dear Boss - Letters of a Traveling Salesman to His Wife." 5 stories written 1936-1938.

"Ernie Catches Up With Wily Willie, or the Case of the Vanishing Duck." *Feedstuffs*. No date.

"Hunting Birds." No date.

"Key Word Puzzles." No date.

"Let Colonel Cluck Answer Your Questions." *Independent Salesman*. 14 undated columns.

"Nothing is Impossible." *Excavating Engineer*. No date.

"Paper, Stone and Scissors." Undated.

"Puzzle Party." Undated.

"Questionable Answer Department" [One]. *The Michigan Well Driller*. No date.

"Questionable Answer Department" [Two]. *The Michigan Well Driller*. No date.

"Questionable Answer Department" [Three]. *The Michigan Well Driller*. No date.

"Questionable Answer Department" [Four]. *The Michigan Well Driller*. No date.

"Questionable Answer Department" [Five]. *The Michigan Well Driller*. No date.

"Rainy Afternoon Shadows." Undated.

"Trickword Puzzle." 3 undated puzzles.

"Tummy Trouble." Undated.

"V.O.N. Munchdriller Does it the Otter Way." *The Michigan Well Driller*. No date.

"V.O.N. Munchdriller Drills a Portable Well." *The Michigan Well Driller*. No date.

"V.O.N. Munchdriller Fights Fire With Fizz." *The Michigan Well Driller*. No date.

"V.O.N. Munchdriller Finds a Cold Answer to a Hot Problem." *The Michigan Well Driller*. No date.

"V.O.N. Munchdriller Gets Water." *The Michigan Well Driller*. No date.

"V.O.N. Munchdriller Harnesses a Thunderbolt." *The Michigan Well Driller*. No date.

"V.O.N. Munchdriller Saves 'Ozzie' From Digging Clear to China." *The Michigan Well Driller*. No date.

"V.O.N. Munchdriller Sinks First Horizontal Well Known to History." *The Michigan Well Driller*. No date.

"V.O.N. Munchdriller Solves a Problem." *The Michigan Well Driller*. No date.

Part Three
Poetry

Fermented Ink: Ten Poems. Privately published, ca. 1932.
> Contents: "Ode to a Stuffed Owl." "Interlude." "Gifts." "Unheard Serenade." "Melodie Moderne." "Rhapsody." "Hauteur." "Romance." "Midnight Sonata." "Slow Awakening."

Shadow Suite: Fifteen Poems. Privately published, 1932.
> Contents: "Red Wine." "Harlem Lullaby." "Prelude to Oblivion." "Shadow Dance." "Reflections." "Unseemly Queries." "Epic." "The Idol." "Cargoes." "Immortality." "The Oyster and the Shark." "Hymn of Hatred." "The Battle of the Lamp Posts." "Kol Nidre." "Scene Macabre."

"Prelude to Tracy." *American Poetry Magazine*, vol. 35, no. 2. (1954).

"Hands." *American Poetry Magazine*, vol. 35, no. 3. (1954).

Miscellaneous poems:
> "After Armageddon"
> "All things are strange things, seen but dimly"
> "Finale"
> "I am a liar"
> "Mens sana"
> "Mighty King Mene-Ptah"
> "Scaramouche Sings of Love and Strums His Lute"
> "Sing unto me a song, o beloved, with your lips"
> "Solomon, Solomon"

Part Four
Non-Fiction

"Proofreader's Page." *The American Printer* monthly column from March 1937 to November 1946.

"Card System Enables Feed Dealer to Follow Up On Sales." *The Feed Bag.* May 1937.

"Boundaries of the Pressroom." *The American Printer.* No date.

"The Proofroom Reference Shelf." *The American Printer.* No date.

"After Superman, What?" Letter in *The Author & Journalist.* October 1940.

"Why I Selected—Nothing Sirius." *My Best Science Fiction Story.* New York: Merlin, 1949. 103.

Letter introducing "The Frownzly Florgels." *Other Worlds Science Fiction.* October 1950.

Introduction. *Space on My Hands.* New York: Shasta, 1951. 2 pp.

Letter, dated 14 June 1952. Published in *Happy Ending*, 1990.

Introduction and seven story prefaces. *Science-Fiction Carnival.* Chicago: Shasta, 1953. 9-11, 15, 49, 89, 163, 189, 211, 283.

"Where Do I Get My Plots?" *Report to Writers.* May 1953.
"Fredric Brown says:" Introduction. *Human?* Ed. Judith Merril. New York: Lion, 1954. N. pag., but two pages.
Introduction. *Angels and Spaceships.* New York: Dutton, 1954. 9-12.
Letter, dated 17 November 1963, pitching a script for *Burke's Law.* Unpublished.
"Toward a Definition of Science Fiction." *Fantasy and Science Fiction.* 1963.
"Concerning Pygmalion 2113." Letters, dated 12 March 1965, 13 May 1965, 16 June 1966 (only the first is by Brown), published in *Happy Ending*, 1990.
"It's Only Everything." *Goliard* 836. April 1965.
Letter, dated 22 June 1965, regarding a call from director Roger Vadim. Unpublished.
"Sex Life on the Planet Mars." Published in *Sex Life on the Planet Mars.* 1986.

Part Five
Teleplays

"Human Interest Story." Based on the short story, "The Last Martian." Aired as the 24 May 1959 episode of *Alfred Hitchcock Presents* and published in *The Pickled Punks*, 1991.
"Mirror." Unproduced script based on the short story, "Mirror." Unpublished.
"Report to Earth." Written June 1952. Unproduced, but published in *Happy Ending*, 1990.
"A Woman's a Two-Face." Unproduced, but published in *Happy Ending*, 1990.

Part Six
Short Story Collections

Space On My Hands. Chicago: Shasta, 1951.
　　Contents: Introduction by Fredric Brown. "Something Green." "Crisis, 1999." "Pi in the Sky." "Knock." "All Good Bems." "Daymare." "Nothing Sirius." "Star Mouse." "Come and Go Mad."
Mostly Murder: Eighteen Stories. New York: E.P. Dutton & Co., 1953.
　　Contents: "The Laughing Butcher." "The Four Blind Men." "The Night the World Ended." "The Motive Goes Round and Round." "Cry Silence." "The Nose of Don Aristide." "A Voice Behind Him." "Miss Darkness." "I'll Cut Your Throat Again, Kathleen." "Town Wanted." "The Greatest Poem Ever Written." "Little Apple Hard to Peel." "This Way Out." "A Little White Lye." "The Dangerous People." "Cain." "The Death of Riley." "Don't Look Behind You."

Science-Fiction Carnival. Chicago: Shasta, 1953. Edited by Brown and Mack Reynolds, and including "Paradox Lost."

Angels and Spaceships. New York: E.P. Dutton & Co., 1954.

> Contents: "Introduction." "Pattern." "Placet is a Crazy Place." "Answer." "Etaoin Shrdlu." "Preposterous." "Armageddon." "Politeness." "The Waveries." "Reconciliation." "The Hat Trick." "Search." "Letter to a Phoenix." "Daisies." "The Angelic Angleworm." "Sentence." "The Yehudi Principle." "Solipsist."

Honeymoon in Hell. New York: Bantam, 1958.

> Contents: "Honeymoon in Hell." "Too Far." "Man of Distinction." "Millenium." "The Dome." "Blood." "Hall of Mirrors." "Experiment." "The Last Martian." "Sentry." "Mouse." "Naturally." "Voodoo." "Arena." "Keep Out." "First Time Machine." "And the Gods Laughed." "The Weapon." "A Word From Our Sponsor." "Rustle of Wings." "Imagine."

Nightmares and Geezenstacks. New York: Bantam, 1961.

> Contents: "Nasty." "Abominable." "Rebound." "Nightmare in Gray." "Nightmare in Green." "Nightmare in White." "Nightmare in Blue." "Nightmare in Yellow." "Nightmare in Red." "Unfortunately." "Granny's Birthday." "Cat Burglar." "The House." "Second Chance." "Great Lost Discoveries I - Invisibility." "Great Lost Discoveries II - Invulnerability." "Great Lost Discoveries III - Immortality." "Dead Letter." "Recessional." "Hobbyist." "The Ring of Hans Carvel." "Vengeance Fleet." "Rope Trick." "Fatal Error." "The Short Happy Lives of Eustace Weaver I." "The Short Happy Lives of Eustace Weaver II." "The Short Happy Lives of Eustace Weaver III." "Expedition." "Bright Beard." "Jaycee." "Contact." "Horse Race." "Death on the Mountain." "Bear Possibility." "Not Yet the End." "Fish Story." "Three Little Owls." "Runaround." "Murder in Ten Easy Lessons." "Dark Interlude." "Entity Trap." "The Little Lamb." "Me and Flapjack and the Martians." "The Joke." "Cartoonist." "The Geezenstacks." "The End."

The Shaggy Dog and Other Murders. New York: E.P. Dutton & Co., 1963.

> Contents: "The Shaggy Dog Murders." "Life and Fire." "Teacup Trouble." "Good Night, Good Knight." "Beware of the Dog." "Little Boy Lost." "Whistler's Murder." "Satan One-and-a-Half." "Tell 'em, Pagliaccio!" "Nothing Sinister."

Daymares. New York: Lancer, 1968.

> Contents: "Gateway to Darkness." "Daymare." "Come and Go Mad." "The Angelic Angleworm." "The Star Mouse" (and "Mitkey Rides Again," though it's not in the table of contents). "Honeymoon in Hell." "Pi in the Sky."

Paradox Lost and Twelve Other Great Science Fiction Stories. New York: Random House, 1973.
   Contents: Introduction by Elizabeth Brown. "Paradox Lost." "Puppet Show." "The Last Train." "It Didn't Happen." "Knock." "Obedience." "Ten Percenter." "Aelurophobe." "Eine Kleine Nachtmusik." "Nothing Sirius." "The New One." "Double Standard." "Something Green."

The Best of Fredric Brown. Garden City: Nelson Doubleday, 1976.
   Contents: Introduction by Robert Bloch. "Arena." "Imagine." "It Didn't Happen." "Recessional." "Eine Kleine Nachtmusik." "Puppet Show." "Nightmare in Yellow." "Earthmen Bearing Gifts." "Jaycee." "Pi in the Sky." "Answer." "The Geezenstacks." "Hall of Mirrors." "Knock." "Rebound." "Star Mouse." "Abominable." "Letter to a Phoenix." "Not Yet the End." "Etaoin Shrdlu." "Armageddon." "Experiment." "The Short Happy Lives of Eustace Weaver (I, II, and III)." "Reconciliation." "Nothing Sirius." "Pattern." "The Yehudi Principle." "Come and Go Mad." "The End."

Homicide Sanitarium. Fredric Brown in the Detective Pulps, vol. 1. Belen: Dennis McMillan, 1984.
   Contents: Introduction by Bill Pronzini. "Red-Hot and Hunted." "The Spherical Ghoul." "Homicide Sanitarium." "The Moon for a Nickel." "Suite for Flute and Tommy-Gun." "The Cat from Siam." "Listen to the Mocking Bird."

Before She Kills. Fredric Brown in the Detective Pulps, vol. 2. Miami Beach: Dennis McMillan, 1984.
   Contents: "Introduction: Fredric Brown Remembered" by William F. Nolan. "A Date to Die." "Mad Dog!" "Handbook for Homicide." "Before She Kills." "A Cat Walks." "The Missing Actor."

Carnival of Crime: The Best Mystery Stories of Fredric Brown. Eds. Francis M. Nevins, Jr., and Martin H. Greenberg. Carbondale and Edwardsville: Southern Illinois UP, 1985.
   Contents: "Introduction: Dreamer in Paradox" by Bill Pronzini. "Town Wanted." "Little Apple Hard to Peel." "A Little White Lye." "Blue Murder." "The Djinn Murder." "Murder While You Wait." "Mr. Smith Kicks the Bucket." "The Dangerous People." "The Night the World Ended." "A Voice Behind Him." "Don't Look Behind You." "Miss Darkness." "I'll Cut Your Throat Again, Kathleen." "The Laughing Butcher." "The Joke." "Cry Silence." "Cain." "The Case of the Dancing Sandwiches." "Witness in the Dark." "Granny's Birthday." "Hobbyist." "Nightmare in Yellow." "Mistake." "A Checklist of the Fiction of Fredric Brown," by Francis M. Nevins, Jr.

Madman's Holiday. Fredric Brown in the Detective Pulps, vol. 3. Volcano: Dennis McMillan, 1985.

> Contents: Introduction by Newton Baird. "Madman's Holiday." "The Song of the Dead."

The Case of the Dancing Sandwiches. Fredric Brown in the Detective Pulps, vol. 4. Volcano: Dennis McMillan, 1985.

> Contents: Introduction by Lawrence Block. *The Case of the Dancing Sandwiches* (unfinished novel). *The Case of the Dancing Sandwiches* (novelette).

The Freak Show Murders. Fredric Brown in the Detective Pulps, vol. 5. Miami Beach: Dennis McMillan, 1985.

> Contents: "Nice Mysteries" by Richard A. Lupoff. "Double Murder." "Two Biers for Two." "See No Murder." "The Freak Show Murders." "Fugitive Impostor." "Client Unknown."

Thirty Corpses Every Thursday. Fredric Brown in the Detective Pulps, vol. 6. Miami Beach: Dennis McMillan, 1986.

> Contents: Introduction by William Campbell Gault. "Murder Draws a Crowd." "I'll See You at Midnight." "Death's Dark Angel." "Thirty Corpses Every Thursday." "A Matter of Death." "A Fine Night for Murder." "Satan's Search Warrant." "Death Insurance Payment."

Pardon My Ghoulish Laughter. Fredric Brown in the Detective Pulps, vol. 7. Miami Beach: Dennis McMillan, 1986.

> Contents: Introduction by Donald E. Westlake. "The Incredible Bomber." "Death is a White Rabbit." "Death of a Vampire." "Pardon My Ghoulish Laughter." "Twice-Killed Corpse." "A Lock of Satan's Hair." "The Ghost Breakers."

Red is the Hue of Hell. Fredric Brown in the Detective Pulps, vol. 8. Miami Beach: Dennis McMillan, 1986.

> Contents: "Requiem for a Craftsman" by Walt Sheldon. "Murder While You Wait." "Twenty Gets You Plenty." "Legacy of Murder." "You'll End Up Burning." "Murder in Miniature." "Death and Nine Lives." "Red is the Hue of Hell." "Where Do I Get My Plots?"

Brother Monster. Fredric Brown in the Detective Pulps, vol. 9. Miami Beach: Dennis McMillan, 1987.

> Contents: Introduction by Harry Altshuler. *Brother Monster. Fermented Ink: Ten Poems.* "You'll Die Before Dawn." "Murder at 10:15." "Moon Over Murder." "It's Only Everything."

Sex Life on the Planet Mars. Fredric Brown in the Detective Pulps, vol. 10. Miami Beach: Dennis McMillan, 1986.

> Contents: Introduction by Charles Willeford. "Walk in the Shadows." "Blind Lead." "A Change for the Hearse." "Murder in Furs." "Publisher's

note" by Dennis McMillan. "How Tagrid Got There." "Sex Life on the Planet Mars." "The Sleuth from Mars."

Nightmare in Darkness. Fredric Brown in the Detective Pulps, vol. 11. Miami Beach: Dennis McMillan, 1987.
   Contents: Introduction by Linn Brown. "Get Out of Town." "The Cheese on Stilts." "Footprints on the Ceiling." "The Monkey Angle." "Original ending for *The Screaming Mimi*." "Why, Benny, Why?" "The House of Fear." "Trouble Comes Double." "Mirror." "Nightmare in Darkness."

And the Gods Laughed. West Bloomfield: Phantasia, 1987.
   Contents: "Honeymoons and Geezenstacks and Fredric William Brown" by Richard A. Lupoff. "The Star-Mouse." "Mitkey Rides Again." "Six-Legged Svengali." "The Switcheroo." "The Gamblers." "Honeymoon in Hell." "Too Far." "Man of Distinction." "Millenium." "The Dome." "Blood." "Hall of Mirrors." "Experiment." "The Last Martian." "Sentry." "Mouse." "Naturally." "Voodoo." "Arena." "Keep Out." "First Time Machine." "And the Gods Laughed." "The Weapon." "A Word From Our Sponsor." "Rustle of Wings." "Imagine." "Nasty." "Abominable." "Rebound." "Nightmare in Gray." "Nightmare in Green." "Nightmare in White." "Nightmare in Blue." "Nightmare in Yellow." "Nightmare in Red." "Unfortunately." "Granny's Birthday." "Cat Burglar." "The House." "Second Chance." "Great Lost Discoveries I - Invisibility." "Great Lost Discoveries II - Invulnerability." "Great Lost Discoveries III - Immortality." "Dead Letter." "Recessional." "Hobbyist." "The Ring of Hans Carvel." "Vengeance Fleet." "Rope Trick." "Fatal Error." "The Short Happy Lives of Eustace Weaver I." "The Short Happy Lives of Eustace Weaver II." "The Short Happy Lives of Eustace Weaver III." "Expedition." "Bright Beard." "Jaycee." "Contact." "Horse Race." "Death on the Mountain." "Bear Possibility." "Not Yet the End." "Fish Story." "Three Little Owls." "Runaround." "Murder in Ten Easy Lessons." "Dark Interlude." "Entity Trap." "The Little Lamb." "Me and Flapjack and the Martians." "The Joke." "Cartoonist." "The Geezenstacks." "The End."

Who Was That Blonde I Saw You Kill Last Night? Fredric Brown in the Detective Pulps, vol. 12. Miami Beach: Dennis McMillan, 1988.
   Contents: "An Embarrassment of Riches" by Alan E. Nourse." "The Strange Sisters Strange." "The Numberless Shadows." "Death in the Dark." "Letter." "The Frownzly Florgels." "Clue in Blue." "Your Name in Gold." "Death is a Noise." "Bullet for Bullet." "The Stranger from Trouble Valley." "The Devil's Woodwinds."

Three-Corpse Parlay. Fredric Brown in the Detective Pulps, vol. 13. Missoula: Dennis McMillan, 1988.
   Contents: "Don't Look: An Introduction" by Max Allan Collins. "Six-

Gun Song." "Blood of the Dragon." "The Little Green Men." "Murder-on-the-Hudson." "Star-Spangled Night." "The Discontented Cows." "Boner." "Three-Corpse Parlay." "Here Comes the Hearse." "There Are Bloodstains in the Alley." "Murder and Matilda." "Heil, Werewolf!" "Big-League Larceny."

Selling Death Short. Fredric Brown in the Detective Pulps, vol. 14. Missoula: Dennis McMillan, 1988.

Contents: Introduction by Francis M. Nevins, Jr. "Selling Death Short." "Big-Top Doom." "The Prehistoric Clue." "The King Comes Home." "Cadavers Don't Make a Fifth Column." "Bloody Murder." "Premiere of Murder." "Who Did I Murder?" "Number Bug." "The Wicked Flea."

Whispering Death. Fredric Brown in the Detective Pulps, vol. 15. Missoula: Dennis McMillan, 1989.

Contents: "Murder Set to Music." "The Corpse and the Candle." "Wheels Across the Night." "Where There's Smoke." "Herbie Rides His Hunch." "Encore for a Killer." "Whispering Death." "Trial By Darkness." "Market for Murder."

Happy Ending. Fredric Brown in the Detective Pulps, vol. 16. Missoula: Dennis McMillan, 1990.

Contents: "Excerpt from *Oh, for the Life of an Author's Wife*" by Elizabeth Brown. "The Hatchetman." "A Woman's a Two-Face." "Concerning Pygmalion 2113." "Killers Three: (2) The Letter." "Letter." "Report to Earth." "Selected Poetry." "Happy Ending." "Finale."

The Water-Walker. Fredric Brown in the Detective Pulps, vol. 17. Missoula: Dennis McMillan, 1990.

Contents: "The Wench is Dead." "Miracle on Vine Street." "A Matter of Taste." "The 'Feedum and Weep' Stories." "Martians, Go Home!" "The Water-Walker."

The Gibbering Night. Fredric Brown in the Detective Pulps, vol. 18. Hilo: Dennis McMillan, 1991.

Contents: "Introduction" by Joe R. Lansdale. "The Gibbering Night." "After Superman, What?" "The V.O.N. Munchdriller Stories." "Cause and Defect." "The Case of the Rattled Robber." "The Sematic Crocodile." "The William Z. Williams Stories." "Dear Boss." "Spice of Life!" "Movie Masquerade." "The Proofreader's Page" (selections). "Double Standard."

The Pickled Punks. Fredric Brown in the Detective Pulps, vol. 19. Hilo: Dennis McMillan, 1991.

Contents: "The Pickled Punks." "The Men Who Went Nowhere." "The Cat and the Riddle." "Human Interest Story." "From the *Hughes High School Yearbook*." "Prelude to Tracy." "Hands." "Instant Novellas." "Barnyard Bill Says." "Willie Skid (cub serviceman) says."

"Questionable Answer Department." "The Case of the Bargain Butter." "What's Been Left Out and a Final Word" by Dennis McMillan.

Works Cited

Quotations in the text from works by Fredric Brown are from first editions or first magazine publications, except where noted below.

Adkins, Patrick H. "The Hugo Novel of: 1953." *The Fantastic Collector* 235-36 (Oct./Nov. 1991).

Aldis, Brian W. *Billion Year Spree: The True History of Science Fiction.* Garden City: Doubleday, 1973: 234, 289.

Algren, Nelson. "In Current Fiction." Rev. of *Here Comes a Candle*, by Fredric Brown. New York *Times* Book Review 13 Aug. 1950: 22.

Altshuler, Harry. "About Fredric Brown." *Unicorn Mystery Book Club News* 4.10 (1952): 4-5, 16.

_____. "The Early Career of Fredric Brown." *A Key to Fredric Brown's Wonderland*: 23-24.

_____. Introduction. *Brother Monster*. By Fredric Brown. Miami Beach: Dennis McMillan, 1987: 5-12.

_____. Letter to the author. 28 June 1988.

_____. Letter to the author. 24 Aug. 1988.

_____. Letter to the author. 13 Sept. 1988.

_____. Letter to the author. 13 Mar. 1989.

_____. Letter to the author. 10 Jan. 1990.

Anderson, Issac. "Criminals at Large." Rev. of *The Fabulous Clipjoint*, by Fredric Brown. New York *Times* Book Review 16 Mar. 1947: 43.

_____ "Criminals at Large." Rev. of *Murder Can Be Fun*, by Fredric Brown. New York *Times* Book Review 7 Nov. 1948: 40.

Arbur, Rosemarie. "Teleology of Human Nature *for* Mentality?" *The Intersection of Science Fiction and Philosophy: Critical Studies*. Ed. Robert E. Myers. Westport: Greenwood, 1983. 71-91.

Baird, Newton. "An Annotated Bibliographical Checklist of Fredric Brown's Writing." Baird, *A Key to Fredric Brown's Wonderland*. 27-51.

_____. "Chronology of Fredric Brown." Baird, *A Key to Fredric Brown's Wonderland*. 16-19.

_____. "Fredric Brown." *Twentieth Century Crime and Mystery Writers*. Ed. John M. Reilly. New York: St. Martin's, 1980. 206-08.

_____. *A Key to Fredric Brown's Wonderland*. Georgetown: Talisman, 1981.

_____. Letter. *The Armchair Detective* 20 (Spring 1987): 216.

_____. "Paradox and Plot: The Fiction of Fredric Brown." *The Armchair Detective* 10 (1977): 33-38, 85-87, 151-59, 249-60, 370-75; 11 (1978): 86-91, 102.

Barzun, Jacques, and Wendell Hertig Taylor. *A Catalogue of Crime*. New York: Harper & Row, 1971: 77-78, 466, 469, 702.

Bloch, Robert. "Introduction." *The Best of Fredric Brown*. Ed. Bloch. Garden City: Doubleday, 1976: 1-7.

Block, Lawrence. "Introduction." *The Case of the Dancing Sandwiches*. By Fredric Brown. Volcano: Dennis McMillan, 1985: 5-10.

"The Bloody Moonlight." *Unicorn Mystery Book Club News* 1.7 (1949): 6-7.

Blunden, Edmund, ed. *Selected Poems: John Keats*. 1955. London: Collins, 1972: 91.

Boucher, Anthony. "Criminals at Large." Rev. of *We All Killed Grandma*, by Fredric Brown. New York *Times* Book Review 25 May 1952: 37.

_____. "Criminals at Large." Rev. of *His Name Was Death*, by Fredric Brown. New York *Times* Book Review 20 June 1954: 13.

_____. "Criminals at Large." Review of *The Lenient Beast*, by Fredric Brown. New York *Times* Book Review 15 Apr. 1956: 20.

_____. "Criminals at Large." Rev. of *One for the Road*, by Fredric Brown. New York *Times* Book Review 17 Aug. 1958: 16.

_____. "Criminals at Large." Rev. of *The Late Lamented*, by Fredric Brown. New York *Times* Book Review 22 Feb. 1959: 31.

_____. "Criminals at Large." Rev. of *Nightmares and Geezenstacks*, by Fredric Brown. New York *Times* Book Review 20 Aug. 1961: 22.

_____. "Criminals at Large." Rev. of *The Murderers*, by Fredric Brown. New York *Times* Book Review 17 Sept. 1961: 50.

_____. "Criminals at Large. Rev. of *The Five-Day Nightmare*, by Fredric Brown. New York *Times* Book Review 12 May 1962: 20.

_____. "Murder, They Say." Rev. of *The Fabulous Clipjoint*, by Fredric Brown. San Francisco *Chronicle* 23 Mar. 1947: 14.

_____. "A Report on Criminals at Large." Rev. of *The Deep End*, by Fredric Brown. New York *Times* Book Review 28 Dec. 1952: 16.

_____. "Report on Criminals at Large." Rev. of *Madball*, by Fredric Brown. New York *Times* Book Review 4 Oct. 1953: 27.

_____. "Report on Criminals at Large." Rev. of *The Wench is Dead*, by Fredric Brown. New York *Times* Book Review 8 May 1955: 14.

_____. Rev. of *Rogue in Space*, by Fredric Brown. *The Magazine of Fantasy and Science Fiction* May 1957: 75.

Bourgeau, Art. *The Mystery Lover's Companion*. New York: Crown, 1986: 22.

Bretnor, Reginald, ed. *Modern Science Fiction: Its Meaning and Its Future*. New York: Coward-McCann, 1953: 89.

Brians, Paul. *Nuclear Holocausts: Atomic War in Fiction, 1895-1984.* Kent: Kent State UP, 1987: 13, 147.

"Briefly Noted: Fiction." Rev. of *The Office,* by Fredric Brown. *The New Yorker* 8 Mar. 1958: 144.

Brown, Elizabeth C. "Fredric Brown, My Husband." *A Key to Fredric Brown's Wonderland.* 19-22.

_____. Introduction. *Paradox Lost and Twelve Other Great Science Fiction Stories.* By Fredric Brown. 1973. New York: Berkley Medallion, 1974. vi-viii.

_____. Letter to Newton Baird. Quoted in Newton Baird. "Appendix: A Few Supplemental Matters." *A Key to Fredric Brown's Wonderland.* 52-53.

_____. *Oh, for the Life of an Author's Wife.* Unpublished autobiography, n.d.

Brown, Fredric. *And the Gods Laughed.* West Blomfield: Phantasia, 1987.

_____. *Angels and Spaceships.* New York: E.P. Dutton & Co., 1954. Book Club Edition.

_____. *The Best of Fredric Brown.* Garden City: Nelson Doubleday, 1976.

_____. *Carnival of Crime: The Best Mystery Stories of Fredric Brown.* Eds. Francis M. Nevins, Jr., and Martin H. Greenberg: Carbondale and Edwardsville: Southern Illinois UP, 1985.

_____. *The Case of the Dancing Sandwiches.* Volcano: Dennis McMillan, 1985.

_____. *Death Has Many Doors.* New York: E.P. Dutton, 1951.

_____. *The Deep End.* 1952. New York: Quill, 1984.

_____. *The Fabulous Clipjoint.* 1947. Boston: David R. Godine, 1986.

_____. *The Far Cry.* 1951. Berkeley: Black Lizard, 1987.

_____. *The Freak Show Murders.* Miami Beach: Dennis McMillan, 1985.

_____. *His Name Was Death.* 1954. Berkeley: Black Lizard, 1987.

_____. *Knock Three-One-Two.* 1959. New York: Bantam, 1960.

_____. *The Late Lamented.* New York: E.P. Dutton, 1959.

_____. *The Lenient Beast.* 1956. New York: Carroll & Graf, 1988.

_____. *The Lights in the Sky Are Stars.* New York: E.P. Dutton & Co., 1953. Book Club Edition.

_____. *Madball.* 1953. Greenwich: Fawcett, 1961.

_____. *Madman's Holiday.* Vol. 3. Volcano: Dennis McMillan, 1985.

_____. *Martians, Go Home.* New York: E.P. Dutton & Co., 1955. Book Club Edition.

_____. *The Mind Thing.* New York: Bantam, 1961.

_____. *Mostly Murder.* New York: E.P. Dutton, 1954.

_____. *Mrs. Murphy's Underpants.* New York: Dutton & Co., 1951.

_____. *Murder Can Be Fun.* 1948. New York: Carroll & Graf, 1989.

_____. *The Murderers.* 1961. New York: Bantam, 1963.

_____. *Night of the Jabberwock.* 1950. New York: Quill, 1984.

_____. *One for the Road.* New York: E.P. Dutton, 1958.

_____. *Rogue in Space.* 1957. New York: Bantam, 1971.

_____. *The Screaming Mimi.* New York: E.P. Dutton & Co., 1949. Book Club Edition.

_____. *The Shaggy Dog and Other Murders.* New York: E.P. Dutton & Co., 1963.

_____. *Space On My Hands.* 1951. New York: Bantam, 1980.

_____. *We All Killed Grandma.* New York: E.P. Dutton & Co., 1952.

_____. *The Wench Is Dead.* New York: E.P. Dutton & Co., 1955.

_____. *What Mad Universe.* 1949. Garden City: Nelson Doubleday, n.d.

_____. "Where Do I Get My Plots?" *Red is the Hue of Hell.* By Fredric Brown. Miami Beach: Dennis McMillan, 1986: 179-84.

_____. *Whispering Death.* Missoula: Dennis McMillan, 1989.

_____. *Who Was that Blonde I Saw You Kill Last Night?* Miami Beach: Dennis McMillan, 1988.

_____. "Why I Selected—Nothing Sirius." *My Best Science Fiction Story.* New York: Merlin, 1949.

Brown, Linn. Introduction. *Nightmare in Darkness.* Miami Beach: Dennis McMillan, 1987: 5-8.

_____. Letter to the author. 1 Jan. 1991.

_____. Letter to the author. 23 June 1991.

Budrys, Algis. *Benchmarks: Galaxy Bookshelf.* Carbondale and Edwardsville: Southern Illinois UP, 1985: 213, 277, 279.

Bullock, Elizabeth. "Criminals at Large." Rev. of *The Screaming Mimi,* by Fredric Brown. New York *Times* Book Review 27 Nov. 1949: 42.

Carruth, Hayden, ed. *The Voice That is Great Within Us: American Poetry of the Twentieth Century.* 1970. New York: Bantam, 1981: 164.

Clareson, Thomas. "Unknown Worlds." *Science Fiction, Fantasy, and Weird Fiction Magazines.* Eds. Marshall B. Tymn and Mike Ashley. Westport: Greenwood, 1985: 694-99.

Collins, Max Allan. "Don't Look: An Introduction." *Three-Corpse Parlay.* By Fredric Brown. Missoula: Dennis McMillan, 1988: 5-8.

Compère, Daniel. "Alice au pays des maléfices." *Europe* (Aug./Sept. 1984): 99-104.

Conklin, Groff. Rev. of *The Lights in the Sky Are Stars,* by Fredric Brown. *Galaxy* June 1954: 121.

Crane, Milton. Rev. of *Here Comes A Candle,* by Fredric Brown. *Saturday Review of Literature* 9 Sept. 1950: 36.

"The Criminal Record: The Saturday Review's Guide to Detective Fiction." Rev. of *The Fabulous Clipjoint,* by Fredric Brown. *The Saturday Review of Literature* 12 Apr. 1947: 68.

"The Criminal Record: The Saturday Review's Guide to Detective Fiction." Rev. of *The Dead Ringer*, by Fredric Brown. *The Saturday Review of Literature* 12 June 1948: 32.

"The Criminal Record: The Saturday Review's Guide to Detective Fiction." Rev. of *Murder Can Be Fun*, by Fredric Brown. *Saturday Review of Literature* 30 Oct. 1948: 36.

Cuff, Sergeant. "Criminal Record." Rev. of *One for the Road*, by Fredric Brown. *Saturday Review of Literature* 23 Aug. 1958: 31.

_____. "Criminal Record." Rev. of *The Late Lamented*, by Fredric Brown. *Saturday Review of Literature* 29 Aug.1959: 16.

_____. "Criminal Record." Rev. of *The Five-Day Nightmare*, by Fredric Brown. *Saturday Review of Literature* 26 May 1962: 36.

Cuppy, Will. "Mystery and Adventure." Rev. of *The Fabulous Clipjoint*, by Fredric Brown. New York *Herald Tribune* Weekly Book Review 6 Apr. 1947: 19.

Dedmon, Emmett. Rev. of *The Dead Ringer*, by Fredric Brown. Chicago *Sun* 2 Apr. 1948.

Deloux, Jean-Pierre. "Mouvement brownien." *Polar* 23 (1985): 5-14.

Doyle, Edward Dermot. "Murder, They Say." Rev. of *The Dead Ringer*, by Fredric Brown. San Francisco *Chronicle* 11 Apr. 1948: 22.

_____. Rev. of *Here Comes a Candle*, by Fredric Brown. San Francisco *Chronicle* 17 Sept. 1950: 22.

Dreiser, Theodore. *An American Tragedy*. 1925. New York: Dell, 1962: 19.

DuBois, William. "Books of the Times." Rev. of *Here Comes a Candle*, by Fredric Brown. New York *Times* 26 Aug. 1950: 11.

Farmer, Philip Jose. Foreword. *The Office* [First draft]. Miami Beach: Dennis McMillan, 1987: 5-8.

Gault, William Campbell. Introduction. *Thirty Corpses Every Thursday*. By Fredric Brown. Miami Beach: Dennis McMillan, 1986: 5-8.

Gerson, Villiers. Rev. of *Rogue in Space*, by Fredric Brown. "Spaceman's Realm." New York *Times* Book Review 17 Mar. 1957: 22.

Goulart, Ron. Introduction. *The Fabulous Clipjoint*. 1947. Boston: Gregg, 1979: v-vii.

Holmes, H.H. "Science and Fantasy." Rev. of *Martians, Go Home*, by Fredric Brown. New York *Herald Tribune* Weekly Book Review 26 Feb. 1956: 10.

Joyce, James. *Dubliners*. 1916. New York: Penguin, 1984: 223.

Keating, H.R.F. Introduction. *4 Novels*. By Fredric Brown. London: Zomba, 1983: v-ix.

Klass, Philip [William Tenn]. Introduction. *What Mad Universe*. By Fredric Brown. 1949. New York: Bantam, 1978: vii-xviii.

Knight, Damon. Rev. of *Martians, Go Home*, by Fredric Brown. Science *Fiction Quarterly* Aug. 1956: 75.

Kramer, John E. Jr., and John E. Kramer III. *College Mystery Novels: An Annotated Bibliography Including a Guide to Professional Series-Character Sleuths*. New York: Garland, 1983: 204.

Lacassin, Francis. "Fredric Brown ou Alice de ce côté du miroir." *Mythologie du roman policier* 2. By Lacassin. Paris: Union générale d'éditions, 1974: 255-67.

Lansdale, Joe R. Introduction. *The Gibbering Night*. By Fredric Brown. Hilo: Dennis McMillan, 1991: 5-8.

Louit, Robert. "Les 15 Grands de la science-fiction." *Magazine litteraire* Aug. 1969: 29-30.

Lundwall, Sam J. *Science Fiction: An Illustrated History*. New York: Grosset & Dunlap, 1977: 185.

Lupoff, R[ichard] A. "Introduction: Honeymoons and Geezenstacks and Fredric William Brown." *And the Gods Laughed*. By Fredric Brown. West Bloomfield: Phantasia, 1987: ix-xxii.

_____. Rev. of *Martians, Go Home*, by Fredric Brown. *Algol* (Spring 1977): 53.

Lyles, William H., comp. *Dell Paperbacks, 1942 to Mid-1962*. Westport: Greenwood, 1983: 62, 136, 203.

_____. *Putting Dell on the Map: A History of the Dell Paperbacks*. Westport: Greenwood, 1983. 41.

McComas, J. Francis. "Spaceman's Realm." Rev. of *Martians, Go Home*, by Fredric Brown. New York *Times* 4 Dec. 1955: 52.

McMillan, Dennis. Letter to the author. 10 Jan. 1988.

McReynolds, Douglas J. "The Short Fiction of Fredric Brown." *Survey of Science Fiction Literature*. Ed. Frank N. Magill. Englewood Cliffs: Salem, 1979: 1954-57.

McSherry, Frank D. Jr. Letter. *The Armchair Detective* 6.1 (1972/73): 60-61.

Miller, P. [Schuyler]. "The Reference Library." Rev. of *The Office*, by Fredric Brown. *Astounding Science Fiction* Sept. 1958: 147-48.

_____. Rev. of *The Lights in the Sky Are Stars*, by Fredric Brown. *Astounding Science Fiction* June 1954: 145.

_____. Rev. of *Martians, Go Home*, by Fredric Brown. *Astounding Science Fiction* July 1956: 156.

_____. Rev. of *Rogue in Space*, by Fredric Brown. *Astounding Science Fiction* Nov. 1957: 147.

_____. Rev. of *The Mind Thing*. *Analog: Science Fact and Fiction* Oct. 1961: 169.

_____. Rev. of *Nightmares and Geezenstacks*. *Analog: Science Fact and Fiction* Nov. 1961: 168.

Moskowitz, Sam. *Strange Horizons: The Spectrum of Science Fiction.* New York: Scribner's, 1976: 120-21, 157.

"Murder Can Be Fun!" *Unicorn Mystery Book Club News* 1.3 (1949): 6-7.

"Mystery and Adventure." Rev. of *The Screaming Mimi,* by Fredric Brown. New York *Herald Tribune* Book Review 4 Dec. 1949: 42.

Nolan, William F. "Thoughts on Fredric Brown." *The Armchair Detective* 5 (1972): 191-93.

Offord, Lenore Glen. "The Gory Road." Rev. of *Death Has Many Doors,* by Fredric Brown. San Francisco *Chronicle* 29 Apr. 1951: 26.

_____. "The Gory Road." Rev. of *The Wench is Dead,* by Fredric Brown. San Francisco *Chronicle* 5 June 1955: 19.

_____. "The Gory Road." Rev. of *The Lenient Beast,* by Fredric Brown. San Francisco *Chronicle* 13 May 1956: 20.

_____. "The Gory Road." Rev. of *One for the Road,* by Fredric Brown. San Francisco *Chronicle* 24 Aug. 1958: 30.

_____. "The Gory Road." Rev. of *The Five-Day Nightmare,* by Fredric Brown. San Francisco *Chronicle* 13 May 1962: 39.

_____. "A Straight Novel By Fredric Brown." Rev. of *The Office,* by Fredric Brown. San Francisco *Chronicle* 24 Apr. 1958: 33.

Pronzini, Bill. "Introduction: Dreamer in Paradox." *Carnival of Crime: The Best Mystery Stories of Fredric Brown.* Eds. Francis M. Nevins, Jr., and Martin H. Greenberg. Carbondale and Edwardsville: Southern Illinois UP, 1985: vii-xv.

Pronzini, Bill, and Marcia Muller. *1001 Midnights: The Aficionado's Guide to Mystery and Detective Fiction.* New York: Arbor House, 1986: 92-95.

Reginald, R. *Science Fiction and Fantasy Literature: A Checklist: 1700-1974.* Detroit: Gale Research, 1979: 1.72-73; 2.832.

Rev. of *Murder Can Be Fun,* by Fredric Brown. *Kirkus Reviews* 15 Aug. 1948: 416.

Rev. of *Murder Can Be Fun,* by Fredric Brown. *The New Yorker* 30 Oct. 1948: 111.

Rev. of *The Screaming Mimi,* by Fredric Brown. *Kirkus Reviews* 1 Oct. 1949: 564.

Rev. of *The Screaming Mimi,* by Fredric Brown. *The New Yorker* 17 Dec. 1949: 31.

Rev. of *Compliments of a Fiend,* by Fredric Brown. *Kirkus Reviews* 1 Feb. 1950: 78.

Rev. of *Here Comes a Candle,* by Fredric Brown. *Kirkus Reviews* 1 June 1950: 314-15.

Rev. of *The Deep End,* by Fredric Brown. *The New Yorker* 17 Jan. 1953: 100.

Rev. of *The Wench is Dead*, by Fredric Brown. *Kirkus Reviews* 1 Mar. 1955: 191.

Rev. of *The Lenient Beast*, by Fredric Brown. *Kirkus Reviews* 1 Feb.1956: 103.

Rev. of *The Office*, by Fredric Brown. *Booklist* 1 July 1958: 610.

Rev. of *The Office*, by Fredric Brown. *Kirkus Reviews* 1 Jan. 1958: 11.

Rev. of *One for the Road*, by Fredric Brown. *Kirkus Reviews* 1 June 1958: 395.

Rev. of *The Five-Day Nightmare*, by Fredric Brown. *Kirkus Reviews* 15 Feb. 1962: 202.

Rutledge, Amelia A. "Fredric Brown." *Twentieth Century American Science Fiction Writers. Dictionary of Literary Biography* 8.1 (A-L). Eds. David Cowart and Thomas L. Wymer. Detroit: Gale Research, 1981: 80-83.

Sandoe, James. "Mystery and Suspense." Rev. of *His Name Was Death*, by Fredric Brown. New York *Herald Tribune* Book Review 6 June 1954: 12.

_____. "Mystery and Suspense." Rev. of *One for the Road*, by Fredric Brown. New York *Herald Tribune* Book Review 17 Aug. 1958: 9.

_____. "Mystery and Suspense." Rev. of *Knock Three-One-Two*, by Fredric Brown. New York *Herald Tribune* Book Review 9 Aug. 1959: 11.

_____. "Mystery and Suspense." Rev. of *The Five-Day Nightmare*, by Fredric Brown. New York *Herald Tribune* Book Review 22 Apr. 1962: 11.

_____. Rev. of *The Lenient Beast*, by Fredric Brown. New York *Herald Tribune* Weekly Book Review 22 Apr. 1956: 11.

Sheldon, Walt. Letter to the author. 7 Jan. 1991.

Steele, Timothy. "The Structure of the Detective Story: Classical or Modern?" *Modern Fiction Studies* 27 (1981/82): 555-70.

Sullivan, Jack, ed. *The Penguin Encyclopedia of Horror and the Supernatural.* New York: Viking-Penguin, 1986: 60.

Thiessen, J. Grant. "Fredric Brown: An Appreciation." *The Science-Fiction Collector* 2 (1976): 26-33.

Westlake, Donald F. Introduction. *Pardon My Ghoulish Laughter.* By Fredric Brown. Miami Beach: Dennis McMillan, 1986: 5-7.

Wingrove, David, ed. *The Science Fiction Source Book.* New York: Van Nostrand Reinhold, 1984: 18, 110.

Wolfe, Gary K. "The Known and the Unknown: Structure and Image in Science Fiction." *Many Futures, Many Worlds: Theme and Form in Science Fiction.* Ed. Thomas D. Clareson. n.p.: Kent State UP, 1977: 94-116.

_____. *The Known and the Unknown: The Iconography of Science Fiction.* n.p.: Kent State UP, 1979: 32, 35-38, 151, 153.

Index

295

310 Martians and Misplaced Clues

CPSIA information can be obtained
at www.ICGtesting.com
Printed in the USA
FFOW03n1846070217
32088FF